POLITICO'S GUIDE TO

POLITICAL LOBBYING

POLITICO'S GUIDE TO

POLITICAL LOBBYING

Charles Miller

First published in Great Britain 2000

Published by Politico's Publishing

8 Artillery Row

Westminster

London

SW1P 1RZ

Tel 020 7931 0090

Fax 020 7828 8111

Email publishing@politicos.co.uk

Website http://www.politicos.co.uk/publishing

A catalogue record of this book is available from the British Library.
ISBN 1902301250

Printed and bound in Great Britain by St. Edmundsbury Press.
Cover Design by Advantage

ACKNOWLEDGEMENTS

I am grateful to Ross Laird and Thierry Lebeaux for providing information and checking parts of the text; to those organisations who permitted their case histories to be featured; to Tim Boyce for checking and correcting the section on procurement; to Richard Gibson and Paul Duke for assistance with formatting; and to the DTI for allowing us to reproduce its organisation chart.

CONTENTS

INTRODUCTION

- *How can we find out what is going on?*
- *How can we make our voice heard?*
- *How can we make sure that policy doesn't conflict with our corporate strategy?*
- *How can we make them stop criticising us and start promoting us?*

Familiar questions, no doubt.

Government, both centrally and locally and through a large number of agencies and other public bodies in the UK and in Brussels, makes thousands of decisions every day on policy, legislation and regulation. It is the largest purchaser of goods and services in Europe and it dispenses billions in grants and aid.

While politicians and officials talk of open government and of consultation, legislators and Civil Servants often forget that we put them there, we pay their salaries, and that they govern - at Westminster, in Scotland, Wales, Northern Ireland, and regional and local level and in Brussels - on our behalf. It is our right to know what is happening in the corridors of power, but the system is often reluctant to tell us what is going on; and if you do not make your case to Government, your competitors will - or decisions will be made within ivory towers.

Reluctant though it may be to open itself to scrutiny, Government depends on a constant flow of information and views from those who may be affected by its actions; and they also need, and have a right, to know what is going on inside the system. Organisations need to deal with the system either because they have a specific concern - a need to make representations on a policy, bill or commercial decision - or because they want to inform legislators and officials before the need to lobby may arise. Lobbying is an essential part of this process.

"WE'LL START LOBBYING WHEN THERE IS NO MORE ROOM FOR NEGOTIATION"

Several years ago, Lloyds of London sought to amend Government proposals that would have prejudiced a form of cover known as Reinsurance To Close. The Chief Executive, a former Civil Servant, was under pressure from his well-connected members to encourage all his Names to write to the Chancellor. His head was cooler: "we will not start to lobby until there is no more room for negotiation." He won, of course, not by shouting but by proving Lloyds' case.

A lobbying firm submitted an impressive application for an industry award for its work for an organisation seeking the right to sell certain television rights controlled by Government to satellite broadcasters. The firm cited the effectiveness of its MP briefings, organised debates, and media coverage but the judges felt they should check with the Department concerned. A very different story then emerged. "What decided it was the credibility of the Chief Executive and his ability to persuade during a critical meeting that mass market access would not be prejudiced", according to the lead official. "In any event, it was our feeling that the rights in question were not critical."

"As to all the political lobbying, it rather passed us and our Ministers by."

LESSON: do not confuse action with effectiveness.

An insurance company was concerned that Regulations due to be made under the 1999 Health Act would prevent it from providing professional indemnity cover to medical practitioners because it feared that a rival, which sold a different type of policy, had lobbied Government to require that only that type of cover would be acceptable. It assumed that the only course open to it was to target Ministers and persuade them to change their mind.

In fact, the solution was simple. Ministers were not particularly bothered about malpractice insurance, but a middle-ranking Department of Health official in charge of that area was. He had been briefed by the rival about the deficiencies of the company's cover and had no other information to set against the rival's representations. When this was discovered, it only needed the company to balance the file by meeting the official and providing him with a balanced rebuttal of the rival's (inaccurate) contentions for the threat to be averted.

LESSON: don't make a drama out of a crisis.

This guide seeks to show commercial organisations, public, and voluntary bodies, how the system works, how to monitor its work, and how to make it work for you. It tries to do so in a matter of fact way, assuming a degree of familiarity with at least the names of the institutions and the job titles of those who work within them, ignoring issues that are only of interest to students and seeking to strip away some of the mystique about the way decisions are made in order to show you how it is possible to lobby without unnecessary fuss or expenditure. At regular intervals in the text, we illustrate the narrative with examples drawn from real cases and cover the questions we have most often been asked about the fundamentals, fine detail, and ethics of effective lobbying.

Not everyone will agree with the principles we set out. Some may not be happy with the distinction we make between lobbying and PR techniques (good practitioners understand how to combine them); others may be surprised to find that in their dealings with Whitehall, regulatory bodies, and the European Commission, they are actually involved in an activity they may themselves have pilloried through misunderstanding of its rationale, scope and ethics. We apologise to them and to others who may demur at some of the advice we give. In lobbying there are often several different ways of achieving objectives and you may achieve success without following the "correct" route, but this manual attempts to give you guidance with which the system at least will concur - and that is the key need.

In this book, we have had to race across a vast and often crowded landscape. We have not sought to be exhaustive: some issues, such as competition lobbying and procurement negotiations, deserve a book to themselves if their complexities are to be fully explained. Instead, our aim is to give readers an idea of how Government operates and, in dealing with it, of what will and will not work - hopefully demystifying the process and correcting some misconceptions along the way. We are also conscious that the book has been written while the House of Lords is being reformed, new government structures for Scotland, Wales and Northern Ireland are being introduced (in most cases, the use in the book of "MPs" should be taken to include members of the other national assemblies, in the same way as male and female attributions should be read as interchangeable), the way in which local authorities contract for services is being changed, new European Commissioners have been introduced and the European

Union is about to admit members from Eastern Europe.

The effects of all this on the way the system works and its implications for those who need to deal with Government are - at least in late 1999 - to some extent unknown. And it is always easier to explain the visible mechanics of a process than the intangible alchemy that can make the difference between success and failure in working with institutions thick with rules and conventions but run by people. We apologise if in squeezing several quarts into a pint pot important points have been omitted; but we nonetheless hope that the pages that follow will help you to deal professionally with a system that is meant to operate in your interests. You must make sure that it does.

What is Lobbying?

Lobbying, quite simply, is any action designed to influence the actions of the institutions of government. That means it covers all parts of central and local government and other public bodies, both in the UK and internationally. Its scope includes legislation, regulatory and policy decisions, and negotiations on public sector contracts or grants. And although non-specific contact building or information programmes aimed at the system are often part of an organisation's public relations activities, many include them within the ambit of lobbying even though, as will become clear, lobbying techniques are often quite distinct from those of PR. In this book, we cover the methods of political PR, as it might be called, insofar as they relate to influencing policy, legislation and regulation.

Misconceptions about lobbying endure. They have not been helped by the lack of a consistent definition for the practice of lobbying. Some refer to it as "parliamentary lobbying", yet much of the work of the lobbyist may have little to do with Parliament. Some call it "public affairs". I confess that I have never understood what this means, nor have I seen a definition, but it is used by many to refer to a broad amalgam between lobbying and public relations activity. The title of this book refers to "political lobbying", although a large part of the text covers dealings on issues that do not necessarily involve political decisions. More often than not, officials are instrumental in the issues concerning organisations. Even where politicians are involved, they may only set the broadest parameters for action ("The Midland Main Line is a disgrace. What can we do about it?") and leave the rest of the work to those who have control of the files.

Some claim that lobbying is only about the addition of pressure to the making of representations (all campaigns, according to the media, are "intensive"). Wrong: some lobbying has to be high profile – when has nurses' pay ever been settled without a public row? – but most dealings with the system are settled by quiet negotiation and effectiveness is usually in inverse proportion to the amount of noise generated.

LOBBYING?

•Seeking to influence legislative proposals	✔
•Seeking to influence regulatory decisions	✔
•Negotiations on Government contracts (with a policy element)	✔
•Negotiations on Government contracts (no policy element)	✘
•Invite MP to open factory	✘
•Lunch programme to expand contacts with politicians	✘
•Lunch programme to brief politicians on Bill amendments	✔
•Send brief on your organisation to officials	✘
•Send policy proposals to officials	✔
•Launch new product in House of Commons	✘
•Hold briefing meeting in Commons on issue of concern to MPs	✔

These distinctions may look like hair-splitting but they can be fundamental: lobbying techniques may differ significantly from those used in PR or legal practice.

Many organisations may find that the association between lobbying and set piece campaigns deters them from getting the most out of their dealings with Government. Their most important requirement is the Need to Know. That need can be satisfied at two levels: by passive monitoring – making sure they know of everything that has happened; or through early warning – making sure they know in advance of likely policy planning or actions that could affect their interests.

DEALING WITH GOVERNMENT –
TECHNIQUES SHOULD MATCH NEEDS

POLITICAL PR: PR techniques directed at influencing Government/political perception of an organisation - reputation management (eg CFC manufacturers who need to correct political misconceptions about their operations). However, much politically directed PR (for example, getting a Minister to speak at a dinner or open a factory) has no connection with lobbying.

REGULATORY LOBBYING: dealing with OFT/DGIV, pharmaceutical or food additive clearances, Oftel etc.

LEGISLATIVE OR POLICY CAMPAIGNING: a mixture of advocacy, negotiation and, where needed, economic and PR support techniques to influence the formulation or passage of policy or Bills/Directives.

NEGOTIATION: on contracts, aid and trade, grants etc.

Of these, by far the most common - and the most successful - lobbying technique is that of negotiation. Although it is easy to be misled by the media's emphasis on the significance of high politics and by the system's reluctance to explain its processes, the critical factor in settling most issues between outsiders and Government is not pressure or heightened external awareness but a well-conducted negotiation in which the winner understands the other side's sensitivities and limits of action.

At the next stage of work with Government comes the Need to Inform – to know and be known by those officials and politicians who could formulate, consider, scrutinise, amend and endorse policies or commercial decisions that concern organisations; and to establish a relationship of trust that makes the system willing to use individuals, firms or trade associations as a source of the information it needs in order to produce representative policies, whether public or commercial. This need is frequently misunderstood by organisations, who often construct contact programmes without a clear understanding of their cost/benefits.

Higher still is the Need to Negotiate - to make representations to the components of the power structure where there is a need to change policy or where Government is a trading partner. The bulk of government-related issues are resolved through negotiation backed by well-assembled submissions. It may, however, be necessary to ally outside influences - the media and public or associated groups' opinion - for your view to get across. It is only at this level that the lobbyist actually starts to lobby.

LOBBYING DOES NOT AUTOMATICALLY MEAN PRESSURE. THE SUCCESSFUL PLAYERS

- *do their market research: understand their targets' needs, concerns and sensitivities and assemble their arguments accordingly - indeed, the simplest approach to productive dealings with Government is to regard them as no different from the development and marketing of a product;*
- *understand the route map of the system: how it works and who really makes the decisions;*
- *swim with the tide, wherever possible;*
- *work early: while policy is still malleable. Last minute firefighting costs a fortune and will take a lot of your time; and*
- *understand the need for constituency of interest.*

It is rarely dependent on

- *having friends in high places;*
- *developing support in peacetime (despite all apparent evidence to the contrary);*
- *using "communication" aids (lunches, brochures, videos etc) as a substitute for inadequate research.*

Why has lobbying attracted a bittersweet image? Firstly, despite all that talk about "Open Government", officials and politicians still prefer to operate behind the green baize door, and that creates the appearance of deals being struck in secret; the reality is that fear of being caught in the media's searchlight rules out favours. Second, many feel that the big battalions can buy influence. This is harder to rebut because governments around the world have always given great weight to the views of bodies claiming to represent large blocks of interest, whether those are employees or consumers. On a more controversial note, a wide variety of organisations have paid or sponsored legislators. I personally disagree with this practice; and the ultimate influence these MPs or MEPs have exercised has invariably been apparent rather than real. This guide will show how you can access the system without having to pay for the privilege.

Lastly, some crass or naïve lobbying exercises - exacerbated by the indiscreet marketing claims about effectiveness and influence made by consultancy firms - have encouraged suggestions of arm-twisting or distortion of the democratic process; but most lobbying is carried out ethically and without the need for procedural tricks.

It is your right to lobby. Use it well.

THE SYSTEM

The System - and how to work it

Although the media may suggest that the business of Government is essentially political, the process of decision taking and attitude formation is more complex than that. Journalists are rarely allowed to walk the corridors and their coverage of the system has to be geared to its front of house performers – MPs, MEPs, Commissioners, Councillors and Ministers. Politics, however, is really the system's surface tension: it holds everything together but the substance often lies below. This section explains the role of each institution in the work of Government, assessing the balance of power in the UK and in Brussels institutions as at July 1999.

The Route Map

Think of Government as a series of interlocking spheres of influence (see page 11).

For most of those lobbying a UK Government with a large majority, Whitehall – meaning Ministers and those who advise on and administer policy – should be the centre of their attention. Governments need to push through their programmes, and large majorities enable them to do so without fear of Parliament forcing either amendment or delay. Where votes are tight, as under the last years of the 1979-97 Conservative administration, it is possible to orchestrate effective parliamentary pressure but for the foreseeable future that possibility can be dismissed in most cases. However, the Westminster Parliament and the new Parliament and Assemblies in Scotland, Wales and Northern Ireland can, through their committee systems, force public institutions to account for themselves. They also have important PR power: they can influence media and public perception of your organisation. They should not be ignored.

Nor, for any modern lobbyist, can the principal European institutions - the Commission, Council and Parliament - which in many instances must be an organisation's primary focus if it is to influence policy and legislation affecting it. Although Brussels is generally more accessible than Whitehall, where the Green Baize Door philosophy is still widespread, European policy-making culture can be difficult to assimilate by those used to the UK system. Nonetheless, if you only try to monitor and deal with EU issues through our Civil Service you may find that you are disadvantaged alongside those who work direct with Brussels and understand the importance of developing support or limiting opposition within other Member States.

Organisations operating in Scotland, Wales or Northern Ireland have always had to deal with dedicated institutions administering policy decided upon in London. Those bodies, critically augmented by a much larger group of Ministers and elected chambers, now have the power to initiate and pass legislation in most of the policy areas of concern to organisations; and, as mentioned above, they have the ability to put the spotlight on their own national and local issues far more effectively than their forerunners, the Commons Select and Grand Committees.

Power in the UK, at least as far as economic development is concerned, has also been extended to the English regions. Since April 1999, Regional Development Agencies have been given the task of devising regional economic policy and coordinating the work of local authorities and other agencies at regional level. Their representative counterparts, called Regional Chambers, are slowly emerging, although at present they are unelected and comprised entirely of local councillors.

Apart from their obvious planning role, local authorities are also major contractors for building, educational, IT and other services and have significant trading standards and environmental regulatory role. Their representative body, the Local Government Association, has considerable influence over a wide range of policy areas. Their

The System

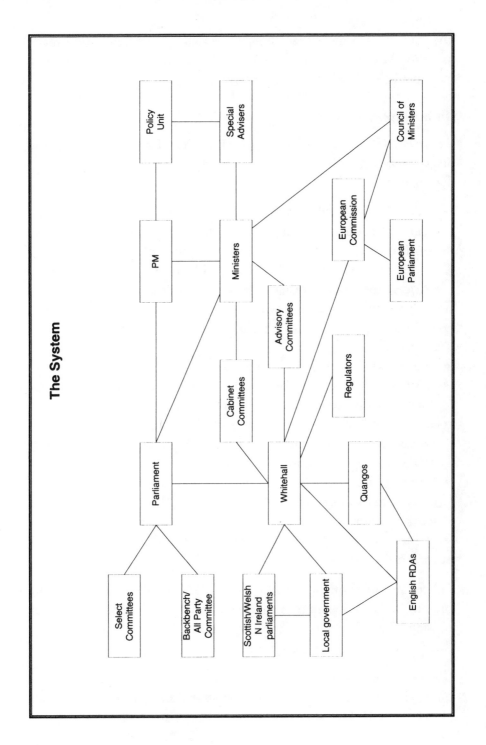

mechanics are simpler than those of central Government and organisations should bear them in mind where they are faced with a national issue that has a local dimension.

Prime Minister

Functions: Chairman of the Board and Chief Executive – leads the majority party, chairs Cabinet, reconciles policy differences between Departments. Serviced by

- a Chief of Staff, who coordinates the Private Office (comprising a Principal Private Secretary, two Assistant Private Secretaries, a personal assistant who handles visits and other planning issues, seconded officials who handle liaison with the Treasury and Foreign Office and with other Departments on home affairs, a Parliamentary Secretary who processes parliamentary questions, material for debates and other parliamentary business, and a Diary Secretary.
- the No 10 Policy Unit (see below).
- a Strategic Communications Unit, which drafts articles and coordinates media activity across Departments.
- a Political Secretary who advises the PM in his capacity as Party Leader (political speeches, election planning) and who will often be involved in policy advice.
- a press office which briefs Lobby Correspondents daily and coordinates, in conjunction with the Minister Without Portfolio, the work of information officers across Whitehall; and
- a Parliamentary Private Secretary (see below), the PM's eyes and ears in the House.

(There are other officials at No 10 but these are the most important ones for outsiders. Within this group at the time of writing, the Chief of Staff, Press Secretary and Foreign Affairs Private Secretary enjoy the greatest amount of "face time" with the PM).

Significance: intervention in issues is normally decisive, but the PM will only be involved on major policy matters, international (eg trade) negotiations or where important media opportunities exist. Will visit sites if a lead story (eg massive investment) or a photo opportunity in a key seat is involved. The Chief of Staff, Political Secretary and PPS can be useful conduits. The Strategic Communications Unit can be sent copies of press releases and articles on major policy issues – it has been known to circulate these around Whitehall for use in departmental press material.

HOW DO WE GET TO THE PM?

The Prime Minister will generally only consider invitations, requests for meetings or individual/collective campaign representations

- *where the approach is made by or through a major body such as the CBI or TUC*
- *where significant inward investment or closure is involved*
- *where a visit involves one or more of his party's "key seats" (winnable or vulnerable)*
- *where the policy issue has produced conflicts between departments or where it is a fundamental plank of the Government's programme*

Most approaches to the Prime Minister will be sent by No 10 to the relevant Department for advice. They may also be copied to the appropriate member of the Policy Unit. Unless you are one of the favoured few within the PM's circle, even if there is space in a diary where demand swamps supply (or in order to displace another commitment), you will need the support of these players.

No 10 Policy Unit

Functions: essentially the Prime Minister's own Civil Service, with a small number of advisers covering all the main departmental areas. Liaises with Whitehall officials and Ministers; briefs PM; can act as negotiators and progress chasers on the PM's behalf. Also plays a significant role in drafting election manifestos.

Significance: important not just as a conduit to the PM but also to reinforce your lobbying of Departments. Policy Unit members network closely with departmental Special Advisers. They can be rebuffed by Ministers but in the main are regarded as working with the authority of their boss.

Cabinet

Functions: main board of Government. As with most companies, decisions are usually taken at lower levels (either Cabinet Committees, comprising all the Ministers relevant to an issue and usually preceded by a meeting of their officials; or less formal inter-ministerial discussions). Only the biggest and most political issues, or those where agreement has not been reached in committee, are discussed in Cabinet. The Cabinet Office is Whitehall's coordination Department, servicing Cabinet Committees and ensuring that cross-departmental issues (such as Queen's Speech planning) are properly managed. It is divided into a series of secretariats covering areas such as Europe, defence, and economic and domestic affairs, and it also has recently-created units handling social exclusion and performance and innovation in the UK economy.

THE NO 10 POLICY UNIT *(March 2000)*

David Miliband	Director of policy.
Derek Scott	Economic policy
Geoff Mulgan	Social exclusion, Welfare to Work
Carey Oppenheim	Social security, housing
Geoffrey Norris	Trade and industry, employment
Robert Hill	Health, local governmernt
Liz Lloyd	Agriculture, home affairs
Jim Gallagher	Constitution, local government
James Purnell	Heritage, media, IT, training
Roger Liddle	Europe, defence
Peter Hyman	Links to the media
Andrew Adonis	Education, Freedom of Information
Brian Hackland	Environment and transport
Ed Richards	Long term policy planning

Significance: limited unless you feel you are going to lose at lower levels - for example an application for a large subsidy where the Treasury is implacably opposed to other Departments in Cabinet Committee. However, watch the work of the Performance and Innovation Unit and report relevant achievements to the Social Exclusion Unit.

Ministers

Functions: departmental front men (and women). Constitutionally, they take all decisions, although in fact most are heavily influenced by

---

A SELECTION OF CABINET COMMITTEES (March 2000)

Home & Social Affairs
Sub-Committee on health strategy
Sub-Committee on drug misuse
Crime reduction and youth justice
Constitutional Reform
Sub-Committee on freedom of information
Sub-Committee on Lords reform
Joint Consultative Committee with the LibDems
Europe
Defence and Overseas Policy
Northern Ireland
Intelligence Services
European aerospace/defence restructuring
Environment
Local Government
Sub-Committee on London
Public Expenditure
Economic Affairs
Sub-Committee on Welfare to Work
Sub-Committee on energy policy
Sub-Committee on productivity/competitiveness
Public services/public expenditure
Utility regulation
Biotechnology/genetic modification
Better Government
Queen's Speech/Future Legislation
Legislation
Modernising Government
Sub-Committee on European Issues
Sub-Committee on Women's Issues
Food Safety
Sub-Committee on Public Service Agreements

---

their advisers. They act as the ultimate departmental forum for representations. Accountable to Parliament. There are three grades:

A DAY IN THE LIFE OF A SECRETARY OF STATE

8.30-8.55am Daily meeting with ministerial team, PPS and Special Adviser
8.55am Private telephone call to another Minister
9.00-10.15am Meeting with Local Government Association, local government Minister and officials (five minute briefing by officials from 9.00-9.05)
10.15-11.00am Meeting with transport Minister of State and financial advisers on National Air Traffic Services flotation
11.00-11.45am Meeting with constituency secretary to discuss correspondence from constituents
11.45-12.15pm Meeting with officials, the Transport Minister, one of the Parliamentary Under-Secretaries and the Franchising Director to discuss a rail issue
12.15-1.00pm Briefing to journalists
1.00pm Lunch with a group of MPs (organised by his PPS)
2.45-3.15pm Meeting with the Environment Minister and English Nature
3.15-3.45pm Meeting with the Environment Minister and officials about air quality targets
3.45-5.00pm Deputation from the Coalfields Communities Campaign with the Minister of State, DTI
5.00-5.30pm Meeting with a train operating company
5.30-6.15 Meeting with officials and the Transport Minister on London Underground public-private partnership contracting
8.00pm Host dinner for Prime Minister of Trinidad and Tobago. That night there was a three-line running Whip in the House that meant he had to leave the dinner to vote in three Divisions.
12.00 Home. Read through three Red Boxes.

- Secretary of State (Cabinet level; overall responsibility for all departmental policy)
- Minister of State (line responsibility for broad sectors)
- Parliamentary Under-Secretary (understudies Ministers of State and may take responsibility for individual projects).

A certain number of Ministers are drawn from the Lords, with several other peers acting as spokesmen for the Government during debates or question times. Since they are few in number these days, they frequently have to cover the work of an entire Department and can often do little more than read out a brief on an unfamiliar issue.

DTI MINISTERIAL RESPONSIBILITIES (January 2000)

- **President of the Board of Trade** *(Stephen Byers)*
  Overall responsibility for DTI and Export Credits Guarantee Department. Special responsibility for competitiveness and science & technology
- **Minister of State for Energy and Competitiveness in Europe** *(Helen Liddell)*
  Energy, European Single Market, economic reform and enlargement, business preparation for the Euro
- **Minister for Trade** *(Richard Caborn - Minister of State)*
  Trade policy; ECGD, export promotion and control, regional policy and inward investment
- **Minister of State for Small Business and E-Commerce** *(Patricia Hewitt)*
  Small firms, e-commerce and the information society, industry, environment, Radiocommunications Agency
- **Parliamentary Under Secretary of State for Consumers and Corporate Affairs** *(Kim Howells)*
  Competition, consumer affairs, company law, company investigations, Insolvency Service, Patent Office, Companies House, Export Licensing.
- **Parliamentary Under-Secretary of State for Competitiveness** *(Alan Johnson)*
  Employment relations, Post Office, supports Patricia Hewitt on Industry.
- **Parliamentary Under-Secretary of State for Science** *(Lord Sainsbury of Turville)*
  Science, Research Councils, innovation, design and space

All Ministers have a Private Office, comprising a Principal Private Secretary, two or more Assistant Private Secretaries and a Diary Secretary. The P/Ss, as they are known, are Civil Servants who process all communication between their Minister and the system or outsiders (including preparation of the "Red Boxes" of papers for consideration by Ministers outside their office) and accompany him to most engagements.

Significance: critical player where issues have a political element, although they rarely make decisions on their own - they are usually only as good as the advice they get. They may second-guess but rarely go behind the backs of their officials. Their ability to generate media coverage can help – or damage – your cause. Most representations to Ministers are never seen by them: the Private Office will send letters and submissions to officials for response or advice on whether invitations should be accepted.

GO TO MINISTERS

- *where political misconceptions are driving officials' actions*
- *where officials refuse to listen (but take care - see main text below)*
- *where an interdepartmental or intergovernmental problem is unlikely to be resolved without intervention at senior level - and after you have done everything you can to condition the view Ministers will take, either through their official and political advisers or through the other influences on ministerial thinking: the media, constituency or party conduits and heavyweight supporters.*
- *if you seek to impress Government.*

Special Advisers

Functions: between one and three political appointees per Department who give advice to Secretaries of State – and occasionally to junior Ministers – on presentation or who may be heavyweight policy advisers in their own right. They may also write speeches and act as their Ministers' personal media managers – often being described as "sources close to X" when leaks take place.

Significance: more important now than under the Conservatives, with a number of advisers being closely involved in policy decisions, not just as ministerial bag carriers. Many of the Special Advisers appointed by the first tranche of Ministers in 1997 had worked for their Ministers while in Opposition and had developed a close bond with them; although this group will be eroded by reshuffles, they and some of the newer arrivals may be looked to for advice in preference to officials. Useful as a conduit to Ministers, although they do not have the access to their masters' diaries that they may have enjoyed as Opposition researchers, and as a means of taking soundings on ministerial views. Do not treat them identically: Special Advisers who major on media management are usually not interested in policy arguments.

Whips

Functions: ensure that their MPs and Peers follow the Party line by voting as directed, not making disloyal speeches etc. Considerable patronage powers (recommendations for foreign trips or for promotion). The Chief Whip sits in Cabinet; his deputies each have responsibilities for MPs within a geographical area (eg the North West) and one or more Departments (eg Home Affairs, Defence). They are always present at debates, Standing Committees and question times (see below) on their subjects and also at meetings of all backbench and some All-Party Groups. There are similar Whips in the Lords, although their tasks are largely restricted to votes in the Chamber.

Significance: limited, except on the few issues where parliamentary opinion may influence Ministers. In those cases, Whips will seek to corroborate rumours of backbench concern and report to Ministers. It is impossible to call their bluff: the 1994-5 campaign against Post Office privatisation succeeded because the Union of Communication Workers was able to secure firm support from 15 Conservative MPs prepared to vote against the Government. Had it simply made unsupportable claims in the media, the campaign would have been ignored.

Parliamentary Private Secretaries

Functions: a traditional first promotion, they are appointed by Secretaries of State and some Ministers of State from among their own backbenchers to act as the day-to-day liaison with them. Ministers can only spend limited time in the House and rely on PPSs to keep them informed about MPs' policy concerns and likely reactions to developments; to plant questions and find supportive speakers for debates; and to supplement the Whips in securing votes. They sit on Standing Committees with their Minister but in return cannot ask questions or speak on subjects covered by him. They must also give up their place on Select Committees and cannot sign Early Day Motions (see below).

Significance: can be a means of accessing or feeding views to Ministers. Where officials are being obstructive, PPSs are one means of raising a problem in confidence with Ministers – but if you take this route you must ensure that the Department really has slipped up, either in its handling of an issue or in its advice to Ministers, who would regard it as highly exceptional to question the facts presented to them by their advisers. Assume, in addition, that taking such a course will sour your future dealings with the Department(s) concerned, possibly for good.

> *"I was persuaded to take a problem to my Minister by the | | industry, which was concerned about subsidised Greek imports. When I showed him the industry's letter to me, he told me that I had only been given the favourable part of their argument and that he had been given a brief with all the facts, showing that the industry had itself been operating a cartel for years. I resolved to be much more careful about helping outsiders to circumvent officials in future."*
>
> *Labour PPS*

Departments

Functions: produce and administer policy, legislation and some regulation. Civil Servants advise Ministers, execute their decisions and manage ongoing policy commitments.

Although numbers have fallen sharply over the past 20 years, there are still over 460,000 Civil Servants, with three quarters concentrated in just six of the 50 Whitehall departments. Officials work in a pyramidal command structure. Job and working unit titles were once standard across Departments, but the old stratification is slowly disappearing: descriptions of grades now differ widely (for example, the Department of Trade and Industry now calls Deputy Secretaries

Directors General and some other Departments substitute Team Leader for the old Grades 5 or 7) and the breadth of responsibility handled by a G5 in the Department of Environment, Transport and the Regions might be assumed by a G7 in the Treasury. The main tiers, with their traditional titles, are as follows:

- Permanent Secretary (Grade 1) – all Departments have one; some (Treasury, Cabinet Office) have two or three. They are a Department's chief executive, the most senior official reporting to the board of Ministers and with daily access to them. Responsible for internal management and for policy advice on the most significant issues. Even though some Special Advisers now wield considerable influence over policy, Perm. Secs, as they are known, see themselves as Ministers' chief policy advisers. Typical age 50+.

- Deputy Secretary (Grade 2) – Departments will typically have between four and eight, each in change of broad areas such as trade or schools. They are generally involved when issues cross boundaries between the subjects under their command. Typical age 45+.

- Under–Secretary (Grade 3) – around three reporting to each Grade 2. The most senior of the middle management grades, handling more specific but still large portfolios such as school funding. Typical age: 40+ .

- Assistant Secretary (Grade 5) – three to five reporting to each Grade 3. At this grade, officials start to be responsible for fine detail such as drafting policy papers and approving drafts of ministerial correspondence and parliamentary answers on, for example, school places. Generally speaking, the lowest grade likely to advise Ministers personally. Typical age 35+.

- Principal (Grade 7) – three to five under each Grade 5. The first of the middle management grades, with detailed knowledge of a very specific subject such as rationalisation of surplus school place capacity. Control the flow of information up the pyramid. Typical age 28+.

• Higher Executive Officer – around three reporting to each Grade 7. The most junior grade at which any real responsibility is exercised; work may differ little from that of a G7.

Similarly, the use of the term "sponsorship" of a sector by officials, meaning no more than responsibility for representation of that sector's interests within Whitehall (or Cardiff, Edinburgh, and Belfast) is declining. But although the terminology may come and go, the function, work and outlook of the Civil Service has changed very little over the past decade or more.

WHITEHALL DEPARTMENTS (with abbreviations)

Ministry of Agriculture, Fisheries and Food (MAFF)
Cabinet Office/Office of Public Service (CO/OPS)
Culture, Media and Sport (DCMS)
Customs & Excise (C&E)
Ministry of Defence (MoD)
Education and Employment (DfEE)
Environment, Transport and the Regions (DETR)
Foreign and Commonwealth Office (FCO)
Inland Revenue (IR)
International Development (DFID)
Health (DoH)
Home Office (HO)
Lord Chancellor's Department (LCD)
Northern Ireland Office (NIO)
Scotland Office (ScO)
Social Security (DSS)
Trade and Industry (DTI)
Treasury (HMT)
Wales Office (WO)

Regardless of grade, Departments are an amalgam of officials who handle policy, supported by technical specialists such as economists, lawyers, scientists and parliamentary draftsmen.

All Departments have a large number of standing advisory bodies, each comprising either experts (eg Committee on Carcinogenicity) or representatives of interest groups (eg British Overseas Trade Board) who cover a specific issue such as policy on food regulation or renewable energy. In some cases, there is a statutory duty to consult them and their views may counter those received by Whitehall during public consultation. Their influence depends on who is on them and how stubborn or politically driven the Minister may be. When Labour took power in 1997 it also established a series of ad hoc Task Forces on issues such as the minimum wage and pension education. Both of these types of body are very useful to Ministers since someone else can be blamed if something goes wrong.

Significance: on most central Government lobbying issues it will be essential to contact Departments first; the vast majority of cases will be decided here – representations made via MPs may only take a longer route to a response from officials. Engine room grades (5-7) have considerable power because they vet all of the submissions and most of the arguments put to Ministers and to higher level officials; they are usually in command of their subject but are only as good as the information they receive. The Treasury is in a class of its own. It plays a decisive role in other Departments' formulation of policies involving public expenditure and its sectoral divisions vet Whitehall work programmes for their impact on the economy. It should not be ignored as a pressure point.

Quasi Departments

Functions: cover hundreds of bodies in five categories:

- Within (or attached to) Departments – units administering largely self-contained areas of technical or other specialist work and with some autonomy, although their overall policy is set by their Ministry. Some may have their own Ministers. Examples are the Export Credits Guarantee Department (DTI) and the Inland Revenue and Customs and Excise (Treasury)
- Regulatory bodies – exist to monitor and control commercial activity in sectors defined by legislation: Office of Fair Trading and Monopolies and Mergers Commission (competition and consumer

affairs); utility regulators (electricity, gas, water, telecoms, railways); Equal Opportunities Commission; Civil Aviation Authority; Medicines Control Agency (pharmaceuticals clearances)

- Agencies – undertake commercial activities of a public nature (eg Driver and Vehicle Licensing Agency)
- Non-Departmental Public Bodies ("NDPBs") – take work from Whitehall where an issue needs to be depoliticised or where a funding body is needed independent of day-to-day departmental control (eg Health Education Authority, Social Science Research Council, Countryside Commission, Intervention Board for Agricultural Produce).
- Quasi-Judicial bodies – whose work falls between departmental/ regulator and court control of activities (Advisory Conciliation and Arbitration Service, Local Government Commission, Parliamentary Commissioner for Administration).

Significance: can be considerable – in distributing Government funding; contracting; or in shaping and implementing departmental policy.

Parliament

Parliament is an institution at the centre of power. It has not for many years been the power centre. Its actual functions and importance diverge somewhat from constitutional fiction since a Government with a large majority can make either House do whatever it wants. Organisations should therefore look at Parliament in this light:

- It may have little influence on legislation for the foreseeable future, but it is the one institution of central Government that the media can cover with ease and can therefore act as a forum for publicising issues.
- MPs know how to attract national and local coverage and should be kept informed on issues if you want to limit the risk of damaging criticism. They may not have a powerful lobbying role in many cases but their PR power can be significant (and Parliamentary

Privilege means that they can say what they like about you during parliamentary proceedings).
- Ministers tend to be sympathetic to representations from MPs of all parties on genuine constituency issues.
- Ministers may use "the mood of Parliament" as an excuse for amending policy.
- Ministers often listen to their own MPs (and Peers) more than they do to the outside world. They all have MPs and Peers whose views they respect.
- Constitutional proprieties must be observed: changes to a Bill may be agreed in negotiation between organisations and Whitehall Departments, but it may still be necessary for an MP or Peer to table an amendment in order that Ministers have something to which they can publicly respond.

MPs and Peers

Functions: the 659 MPs should be regarded essentially as a Citizens' Advice Bureau for their constituents - they represent voters' interests and concerns to all parts of the system. They also scrutinise and approve legislation and act as a watchdog over Whitehall. Peers also vet legislation and (less frequently than MPs) make representations to Ministers.

Significance: can be very helpful on constituency issues or in gaining publicity for causes. Their access to the media and ability to make statements in the House under protection of Parliamentary Privilege can make them powerful opinion formers. Relatively little current influence on policy or legislation (more with a small majority) but officials and Ministers are nervous of criticism in the House under any circumstances. Peers can force through amendments to legislation, but most are reversed in the Commons. Can help to secure meetings with Ministers. They can promote Private Members Bills, although the chances of success are low.

Department of Trade and Industry
Organisation Chart

The Rt Hon Stephen Byers MP
Secretary of State for Trade & Industry

Alan Johnson MP
Parliamentary Under Secretary of State for Employment

Dr Kim Howells MP
Parliamentary Under Secretary of State for Competition and Consumer Affairs

The Rt Hon Richard Caborn MP
Minister for Trade

Patricia Hewitt MP
Minister of State for Small Business and E-Commerce

The Rt Hon Helen Liddell MP
Minister for Energy and Competitiveness in Europe

Lord Sainsbury
Parliamentary Under Secretary of State for Science

Sir Michael Scholar KCB
Permanent Secretary

Parliamentary Branch

Office of Science and Technology

Chief Scientific Adviser & Head of Office of Science & Technology
Sir Robert May FRS
Also reports directly to the Prime Minister

Director General of Research Councils
Dr John Taylor OBE, FRS

Director Transdepartmental Science & Technology (TDST)
Jo Durning

Director Science & Engineering Base (SEB)
Martin Earwicker

Seven Research Councils

Chief Executive British Trade International
Sir David Wright KCMG, LVO

Director Policy, Resources and Personnel (PRP&D) Co-ordinator Transition Team
Quinton Quayle

Markets and Sectors (MP)
Mark Gibson

Infrastructure and Energy Projects (IEP)
John Rhodes

Export Promotion Middle East, New East and North Africa (XP1)
Susan Haird

Export Promotion Asia Pacific (XP2)
Mike Cohen

Export Control & Non-proliferation (XNP)
Roger Hawthorne

Director General Trade Policy
Tony Hutton CB

Director European Policy
John Alty

Trade Policy (TPE1)
John Hunt

New Trade Issues & Developing Countries (TPE2)
Charles Bridge

Trade Facilitation & Import Policy (TPE3)
Alec Berry

International Economics (TPE4)

Export Promotion Business in Europe (XP3)
Keith Lewinton

Export Promotion Former Soviet Union (FSU) Central & Eastern Europe (XP4)
John Lewison

Export Promotion The Americas (XP5)
Michael Arthur

Export Promotion Sub Saharan Africa & South Asia (XP6)
Vincent Fean

Sectors Services Outward Investment (XP7)
Robert Lind

Export Services
Alan Reynolds

Director General Industry
Alastair Macdonald CB

British National Space Centre (BNSC)
Vacant

Biotechnology (Dti Business & Posts Sector) (IGBP)
Vacant

Engineering Industries (IED)
Drew Stevenson

Innovations, Policy & Standards (IP1)
Robert Foster

Innovation Unit

Environment (ENV)

Communications & Information Industries (CII)
Bill Macintyre OB

Industrial Sponsorship
Martin Berry

Industry, Economics & Statistics Unit (IES)
Nicholas Owen

Director General Energy
Mrs Anne Walker CB

Deputy Director General and Director Energy Policy, Analysis, Gas, Electricity and Coal (EPTAC)
Neil Hirst

Energy Utilities (ENU)
Jonathan Green

Engineering Inspectorate (EI)
Brian Fenwick

Nuclear Industries (NID)
Helen Liddell

BNFL, PPP Team (BPT)
Stephen Sisaroof

Oil & Gas (OG)
Geoff Dart

Reform of Energy Regulation (RER)
Keith Long

Director General Enterprise & Regions
David Durie CMG

Deputy Director General and Director Business Links (BL)
Peter Waller

Regional Policy (REG P)
David Smith

Regional European Funds (REG E)
Vacant

Regional Assistance (REG A)
Andrew Steele

SME Policy (SMEP)
Callum Johnstone

Management Best Practice (MBP)
Kenneth Poulter

SME Team (SMET)
Richard Abpress

Chief Executive Invest in Britain Bureau (IBB)
Andrew Fraser

Director General Corporate & Consumer Affairs
Dr Catherine Bell

Consumer Affairs
Stephen Haddrill

Employment Relations (ER)
Paul Savage

Company Law & Investigations (CLI)
Richard Rogers

Competition Policy & Utilities Review Team (CP URT)
Roland Anderson

The Solicitor & Director General Legal Services
David Nissen CB

Legal Services A (Legal A)
John Stanley

Legal Services B (Legal B)
Philip Bovey

Legal Services C (Legal C)
Alex Brett-Holt

Legal Services D (Legal D)
Fred Jonathan

Legal Resource Management & Business Law Unit
Carl Warren

Director News Room (NEWS)
Matt Tee

Chief Economic Adviser
David Coates

Director General Resources & Services
Jonathan Spencer

Staff Policy and Pay (SPP)
Barbara Haddrigan

Staff Personnel & Operations (SPO)
Rob Wright

Senior Staff Management (SSM)
Katherine Elson

Estates & Facilities Management (EFM)
Michael Cookson

Information Management & Process Engineering (IMPE)
Dick Wheeler

Finance & Resource Management
Jonathan Phelps

Knowledge Management Unit
Tim Soane

Internal Audit (IA)
Roger Louth

Office of Science and Technology

Director General of Research Councils
Dr John Taylor OBE, FRS

Director Competitiveness (Central) Directorate (CD)
Dr David Evans

Business Environment
Sarah Chambers

Future Unit
John Reynolds

Enterprise Unit
Mark Higson

Director Policy and Internal Communications (PIC)
Peter Burke

Current as of 9th August 1999

* IEP reports directly to Director General Energy on UK matters

The Chamber

Functions: where debate takes place, oral questions are answered, statements are made by Ministers on the most important policy issues and some legislation is considered by the House as a whole.

Significance: criticism of an organisation by MPs (through comment in debate, in an oral question, in a "Private Notice" question – on urgent matters: very rare – or through a Ten Minute Rule Bill – a publicity device in which an MP seeks a balloted slot and if successful is given ten minutes to advocate his cause) is often reported locally, occasionally nationally. MPs can therefore be a PR focus for those wishing to attack your interests. Ministers are invariably more concerned about enjoying the respect of the House than they are about the views of most outside interests.

Standing Committees

Functions: exist to scrutinise legislation line by line. In the Commons, they typically have 15-20 members (some, such as the Finance Bill Committee, may have more), appointed by a Committee of Selection (following the advice of the Whips) on the basis of interest expressed at Second Reading, loyalty and availability, split to reflect the relative standing of the parties – currently 11 Labour, four Conservatives and two Liberal Democrats for a 17-strong committee. They always include a Minister and Opposition spokesman, plus a Whip and a PPS on both sides. For all legislation in the Lords, and for parts of the annual Finance Bill in the Commons, Bills are considered by Committee of the Whole House, where any Member may participate. They may in a minority of cases take on a consultative role, holding hearings to take evidence from interested parties before considering a Bill in detail.

Significance: since the current (1999) Government's majority results in only six places being available to the Opposition, there is no practical prospect of Government legislation being amended unless Ministers are prepared to make a concession. In the rare instances where the Government allows a Standing Committee to take evidence or constitutes a special "pre-legislative" committee (which can include

---

THE MOOD OF THE HOUSE
AND HOW IT CAN MAKE A DIFFERENCE

It is rare for a Government with a large majority to pay much attention to the views even of a large group of backbenchers. However, in deciding how to handle the problem posed by the failure of RJB Mining, the owner of most of Britain's deep coal mines, to secure sufficient demand from power stations, a juxtaposition of events gave unusually high salience to parliamentary opinion:

- *Although the leaders of the move to modernise the Labour Party had long since ditched any allegiance to the NUM, there were enough senior Cabinet members concerned about their links with the grass roots, including the need to ensure that traditional Labour voters were not alienated, to represent a powerful voice in inter-ministerial debate.*
- *Many Labour Ministers were prepared to believe that the previous Government had destroyed the coal industry by making it easy for gas-fired generators to enter the market. In fact, it was the policy of the main coal-fired generators of keeping prices high that had encouraged more efficient operators to build power stations using a fuel that was both cheaper and cleaner, but the then Opposition referred to this as a "Dash for Gas". Furthermore, many of the new entrants were US-owned, prompting some senior Labour politicians and advisers to feel that a strategic industry would soon fall under foreign ownership if something was not done.·*
- *In addition, the current and former coalfield communities were well organised as lobbyists and could command the support of around 80 Labour MPs. While planned gas-fired power station developments would generate considerable employment in an appreciable number of constituencies, the prospective generators did not coalesce and in any event their MPs could never command comparable political weight to their opponents, who were so deeply allied to Labour's gut principles.*

As a result, when Labour took power there was a significant predisposition among Ministers against gas, regardless of market realities (it was made clear to them by officials and by most external experts that the economics of the coal industry would make it uncompetitive in the long term irrespective of any Government intervention). And it was further clear to them that any statement about the problem would have to be made to the House and that a large grouping of their own MPs would vociferously object if action to help coal was not announced.

---

members of both Houses – one such was appointed to consider the draft Financial Services and Markets Bill in early 1999), hearings can offer a useful opportunity to secure TV and press coverage for a cause.

Select Committees

Functions: to scrutinise Whitehall and to act as a parallel to it in examining policy issues. In the Commons, 18 committees each shadow a single Department, and the Public Accounts Committee scrutinises spending by Whitehall and other public bodies as a whole. Other committees examine Deregulation Act Orders (see p.154), European legislation and the machinery of government. The members of departmental committees (11, split pro rata to the parties' standing in the House, decide on the subjects they want to cover (through requests for written evidence and invitations to the key players - usually including officials/Ministers from the Department - to answer questions in person) and have clerks who administer their programmes, consulting with the Chairman on the witnesses they wish to call, liaising with them and drafting reports. Departmental committees may appoint specialist advisers for some inquiries; the PAC can draw on the resources of the National Audit Office, which audits all Departments and public bodies. The Lords has a series of committees and sub-committees which examine EC proposals and science and technology policy.

Significance: depends on the type of Committee. The PAC's findings, which are often highly critical, carry great weight and are traditionally accepted without amendment, but private sector organisations will only be involved if the issue being investigated concerns the system's dealings with them (eg mismanaged contracts). Departmental Select Committee reports may occasionally capture headlines, but while Departments take great care over preparation of their written and oral evidence they tend to ignore the subsequent recommendations. Tough scrutiny can occasionally prompt a rethink from public bodies if not from Whitehall. Lords committees examine legislation while it is being developed; they work without the coverage generated by their Commons counterparts (which are often televised) but are respected within the system and their recommendations can influence the UK's negotiating stance in Brussels.

Backbench and All Party committees

Function: Backbench committees are Party-based fora for Labour and Conservative MPs and Peers to discuss issues of interest. Meetings (usually monthly for Labour committees and weekly for the Conservatives) may invite outsiders to make presentations. Senior members may represent backbench opinion to Ministers. All Party Groups, which cover either subjects (ranging from road safety to beer) or countries (eg All Party Turkey Group) are often formed on the initiative of outside organisations, many of which may run their group's secretariat.

Significance: Backbench committees – limited except on politically highly charged issues, where backbench views may be relevant and the opportunity of a presentation should be sought by contacting the secretary (a list of officers of backbench and All Party Groups is available from the Public Information Unit in the House – 0171 219 4272). All Party Groups – not regarded as influential, but they provide a useful register of MPs and Peers with an interest in an issue. Warning: groups run by some outside organisations may refuse access to their membership lists by any interest hostile to their sponsors.

The Libraries

Function: one for each House, plus SPICE, their equivalent in Scotland. Produce research briefs on Bills and other issues of interest (available on the internet through the Houses of Parliament site) and undertake dedicated research for MPs, MSPs and Peers. Staff are given subject responsibilities (home affairs, economics etc).

Significance: their researchers cull the material that is most readily available to them. They should be sent a brief (not more than 10 pages) on your lobbying issue if it is likely to attract a measure of parliamentary interest.

Parties

Function: select parliamentary candidates; direct rank and file policy views towards Ministers; head office research departments brief backbenchers; can have a significant influence over the early stages of party policy development.

Significance: not decision-makers in their own right, but an influence on Ministers, Opposition spokesmen and MPs. Views of constituency party organisations can determine MPs' voting intentions.

WESTMINSTER'S SELECT COMMITTEES

Agriculture
Culture, Media and Sport
Defence
Deregulation
Education and Employment
(with separate Education and Employment sub-committees)
Environment, Transport and Regions
(with separate Environment and Transport sub-committees)
Environmental Audit
European Legislation
Foreign Affairs
Health
Home Affairs
International Development
Public Accounts
Public Administration
Science & Technology
Scottish
Social Services
Trade and Industry
Treasury
Welsh

EU Institutions

As a first step to understanding the dynamics of the EU system, consider the following:

- The institutions derive their powers and duties from the treaties establishing them - primarily the Treaty of Rome. Everything they do has to have a treaty basis, meaning that the system is more legal-istic than ours.

- Power is more evenly balanced than in the UK. While most legis-lation and policy decisions originate from the Commission, the European Parliament plays a more active role than ours in modify-ing legislative proposals and the Council of Ministers may reject the Commission's views. Nonetheless, whether you are seeking to monitor or to lobby, the Commission will usually be your starting point.

- "Subsidiarity" is much misunderstood. In short, it means that deci-sions should wherever possible be left to national governments and should not be imposed on them by EU institutions. Lobbyists may need to stress this dictum when they want to stop the Brussels machine. It also dictates the need, even when policy is set central-ly, to lobby within (usually several) Member States - EU legislation cannot be passed unless most (or, in some cases, all) of the Council members vote for it.

- There is no established culture of organised lobbying in most European countries. The normal method of representation is through large trade associations, rather than by individual organisa-tions, and this means that the Commission in particular attaches more weight to views from pan-European collective bodies. That should not inhibit single companies from dealing with Brussels where they can provide detail or clarity that may be lacking in the line of a trade association, which may have to reflect the lowest common denominator: indeed, in competition cases a unilateral approach may be the only way.

- UK Departments usually try to canvass views, sometimes through forming an informal advisory group of the leading players, before negotiating on EU proposals. But you may not be included, or your views, if advocated through officials, may be emasculated or at least modified to accommodate wider "national interests".

The Commission

Function: the EU's Civil Service. 23 Departments (called Directorates-General) staffed by officials from Member States draft annual "work programmes" covering legislative proposals, initiatives designed to encourage action in key areas (eg development of renewable energy pilot projects), grant and aid facilities (eg for depressed regions or for cross-border R&D collaboration) and administration of long-term requirements such as the Common Agricultural Policy. They also regulate, either directly (eg the Merger Task Force) or through panels of national officials or technical specialists (eg the Scientific Committee for Food).

DGs are structured like Whitehall Departments, with a Director-General (A1 level, equivalent to a Permanent Secretary) and other grades running from A2 (Deputy Director General) to A8. As with Whitehall, the key levels are A3 (Director, responsible for a directorate covering a broad sector, for example capital goods industries in the Enterprise DG), A4 (Head of Unit, which might cover aerospace, rail and other guided transport systems, and defence within that same directorate), A5 (Deputy Head of Unit, who will support the Head) A6 (Principal Administrator, who would cover aerospace) and A7 (Administrator, covering aspects of aerospace).

An important difference, however, is that there are far fewer political controllers. The 20 Commissioners (collectively known as the "College") are nominated by Member States for one or two five-year terms and are usually ex-Ministers, although they are required not to pursue any particular national interest. They have extended Private Offices, called Cabinets, each comprising a Chef de Cabinet and a number of "special chefs" who cover the policy areas for which the Commissioner is responsible and who operate on similar lines to the No 10 Policy Unit (they play a role both in stimulating policy and in influencing the work of DGs) but who also meet collectively every week, with support from line officials, to decide on the items to be put to the Wednesday morning conclave of all Commissioners: proposals cannot be put to the Council of Ministers or to the European Parliament without collective approval. As with UK Ministers, they are answerable to the Parliament, but its complex composition prevents them from developing a power base.

Like the Council, the Commission's work is administratively coordinated by a Secretariat-General, which handles everything from personnel to relations with the Council and Parliament. However, for practitioners a more important unit is the Legal Service, which advises DGs on whether proposals conform with the Treaties.

Widespread changes to the number and responsibilities of Commissioners are expected at the end of 2000. It is possible that they will be divided into two tiers, with only six or seven Commissioners and a lower cadre of decision makers.

Significance: the most important institution. It is the only body that can initiate and draft legislation (although the Council and European Parliament can ask the Commission to produce proposals), hand out money, put pressure on Member States to comply with the Treaty and implement EU legislation. Its regulatory function operates independently of Council/Parliament. Usual first stop for information on current/planned activity (although see Permanent Representations below).

EP COMMITTEES

- *Agriculture/rural development*
- *Budgets Budgetary control*
- *Citizens freedoms, justice & home affairs*
- *Constitutional affairs*
- *Culture, youth, education, media*
- *Development & cooperation*
- *Economic and Monetary Affairs*
- *Employment and social affairs*
- *Environment, public health and consumer protection*
- *External economic relations*
- *Fisheries*
- *Foreign affairs, human rights, common security and defence*
- *Industry, external trade, research and energy*
- *Legal affairs and internal market*
- *Petitions*
- *Regional policy, transport and tourism*
- *Rules of procedure/credentials*
- *Women's rights*

Council of Ministers

Function: political decision-making body. Divided into some 25 councils, which meet monthly or less frequently. Their chairmanship, known as the Presidency, changes every six months (eg Finland chaired all the councils in the second half of 1999) during which the incumbent will also host a heads of government summit to discuss major items. The incoming Presidency publishes its priorities for the work of each council (ie which legislation and other issues should be at the top of the agenda) around one month before its term starts. As with Whitehall, much of the negotiating work is handled by national officials through Council working groups. These, and other important elements including preparing revisions to legislative proposals

EUROPEAN COMMISSION DGs AND COMMISSIONERS (MARCH 2000)

President of the Commission	Romano Prodi (Italy)
Vice-President, EU reforms	Neil Kinnock (UK)
External relations	Chris Patten (UK)
Trade	Pascal Lamy (France)
Economic/financial affairs	Pedro Solbes (Spain)
Enterprise	Erkki Liikanen (Finland)
Competiton	Mario Monti (Italy)
Employment, IR, social affairs	Anna Diamantopolou (Greece)
Agriculture	Frans Fischler (Austria)
Transport and Energy	Loyola de Palacio (Portugal)
Development	Poul Nielson (Denmark)
Enlargement	Gunter Verheugen (Germany)
Justice and Home Affairs	Antonio Vitorino (Portugal)
Personnel/administration	Liikanen
Education and culture	Viviane Reding (Luxembourg)
Environment	Margot Wallstrom (Sweden)
Research	Philippe Busquin (Belgium)
Information Society	Liikanen
Fisheries	Fischler
Internal market	Frits Bolkenstein (Netherlands)
Regional policy	Michel Barnier (France)
Taxation and Customs Union	Bolkenstein
Budgets	Michel Schreyer (Germany)
Financial control	Prodi
Health and consumer protection	David Byrne (Ireland)

and compromise texts, are coordinated by the Council Secretariat, which is divided into a Legal Service (which, as with its Commission counterpart, has a central role given that all Brussels regulation must be based on powers and duties contained in a legal instrument, the EC treaties) and ten Directorates General, most of which cover the work of more than one Council. The Presidency usually works closely with the Commission to produce proposals which seek to achieve consensus but in the event of deadlock an issue may be left to Ministers to decide in a Council meeting. In addition to formal Councils, Presidencies stage a series of informal discussions in their country. Although these cannot take binding decisions, they may be used to cement agreement on issues for other Council meetings.

Significance: legislation or policy cannot get through without its agreement. Secretariat officials supporting each Council can be a useful source of information on discussions in working groups or Council meetings. Informal Councils, often held in the Council Presidency's own state, are often used to showcase the host's achievements: organisations can approach the coordinating unit (usually in the Foreign Ministry) within states due to hold the Presidency with an offer to hold or sponsor presentations or visits during informal meetings.

ORDER OF PRESIDENCIES (January–June; July–December)

1999	Germany; Finland	2002	Spain; Denmark
2000	Portugal; France	2003	Greece; Italy
2001	Sweden; Belgium	2004	Ireland; Netherlands

European Parliament

Function: the other approval body for legislation. 626 members, elected roughly pro rata to each Member State's population, and divided less by nationality than by party groupings (the two main ones are the European People's Party, including 36 UK Conservatives, and the Party of European Socialists, including 29 UK Labour MEPs).

Committees, which meet in Brussels every three weeks or so, consider legislation in detail by appointing a "rapporteur" from their membership to consult and to draft a report for them to consider. Once approved by the Committee, all MEPs vote on the report in their monthly plenary sessions (usually held in Strasbourg). Committee members may also produce reports, either on their own initiative or with the committee's sanction, on road policy issues. These are often critical of Commission or Member State action/inaction and tend to be ignored. Committees can summon Commissioners to explain themselves. A series of "Intergroups" correspond to the UK Parliament's All Party Groups; and 34 country "Delegations" are similar to Westminster's Country Groups except that they have restricted membership.

Significance: an increasingly important part of the system - arguably more significant, because the Commission and Council cannot count on its agreement, than the UK Parliament. In fact, keen to demonstrate its power, it often actively seeks to reach a distinctive position on legislation. The Commission used to dismiss its amendments but has had more respect since the Maastricht Treaty introduced a "co-decision" procedure (see p. 138) which balances power more evenly: a good proportion of EP amendments are now accepted by the Commission and the Council. MEPs also have much better access to Commission officials than MPs have to Whitehall. The EP tends to take a more radical view, particularly on environmental issues and relationships with third countries, than the UK Parliament. MEPs can press their own national Ministers on items affecting their constituency or on the national dimension of EU issues.

Permanent Representations

Function: every Member State has a team of officials in Brussels to act as the day-to-day liaison point with the Commission, Council and other institutions. Most legislative drafts, consultation papers and other communication between the Commission/Councils and Member States pass through the Perm. Reps, as they are called (ours

37

is UKRep). Their senior officials sit on the Committee of Permanent Representatives (COREPER) which meets weekly to agree on whether proposals are ready to be discussed by Ministers in Council meetings. UKRep has about 40 officials and is divided into seven sections:

- Institutions: European Parliament, liaison or issues that cross sections
- Agriculture and Fisheries
- Legal
- Industry: industry, internal market, consumers, transport
- ECOFIN: Economic and Finance Council, Customs, budget process
- External Relations: foreign, security and trade policy
- Social, Environment and Regions: Social Affairs and Environment Councils, regional policy, health, education, culture.

COUNCILS

Agriculture	*Health*
Budgets	*Industry*
Consumer affairs	*Internal Market*
Culture and audio visual	*Justice*
Economic and Finance	*Regions*
Education	*Research*
Employment	*Social Affairs*
Energy	*Telecommunications*
Environment	*Transport*
Fisheries	*Youth*
General affairs	

Significance: useful source of information on Commission and Council activity, briefings on national negotiating positions, and documents. However, most Perm. Reps wait for papers to arrive from the Commission and Council Bureau and you may find it quicker to approach the institutions yourself. Should be kept informed of your views (and, if your position is consistent with that government's line, your lobbying activity).

EUROPEAN PARLIAMENT POLITICAL GROUPINGS (1999-2004)
(in order of size)

European People's Party (PPE)
Party of European Socialists (PSE)
European Liberal Democratic and Reformist Party
Greens
European United Left/Nordic Green Left
Union Group for Europe
European Radical Alliance
Independents for a Europe of Nations Group
Non-attached

European Court of Justice

Function: ultimate forum for complaints about breach of the Treaty by governments or organisations.

Significance: in the main, to be used only if complaint to the Commission fails (unless the Commission itself has failed to follow the rules. Judgement timescale too lengthy (around two to three years) for most commercial needs.

Local Government

Function: Local authorities are structured as a streamlined version of central Government. Instead of officials, there are officers, who handle service delivery and provide the infrastructure for the committees of councillors which make most of the decisions. Full council meetings, which generally take place every six to seven weeks, formally endorse committee recommendations.

There are currently three tiers of local government in England:

• County Councils, whose responsibilities include Structure Plans, schools, social services, police and fire services, waste disposal, and

some consumer protection
- District, Borough or City Councils, responsible for local planning and development control, environmental health, housing, refuse collection and leisure centres. London boroughs also cover schools, social services, all planning, consumer protection, and local roads.
- Parish and Town Councils, of which there are around 10,000 in England. They have only minor responsibilities but must be consulted about planning applications in their area and often carry out limited duties in relation to the local environment.

Although the trend is to combine the top two tiers into "unitary" authorities, some local authorities have moved to a new style of management in which committees, instead of being run as distinct and independent entities, are controlled by a "cabinet" of chairmen.

Significance: apart from obvious roles - planning, trading standards, significant procurer of social services, educational, and environmental services (enhanced by a new requirement to secure "Best Value" in service provision), they also play a role (not least by providing grants) in attracting inward investment. Council Leaders and some councillors may have useful central Government links which could be exploited if a local issue also has central Government implications.

Devolved Government

Much of the legislative decision making for Scotland, Wales and Northern Ireland is now handled in Edinburgh, Cardiff and Belfast. Since the middle of 1999, Scotland has had a Parliament and Wales and Northern Ireland an Assembly (although at the time of writing Irish Ministers had not yet been appointed, the Northern Ireland Office had not been reorganised and power had not been fully transferred).

Scottish Parliament and Welsh Assembly members are elected partly on a first past the post basis for constituencies (73 in Scotland; 40 in Wales) closely following Westminster boundaries, with a further list of multi-member constituencies, based on European Parliament boundaries and elected by PR (56 in Scotland; 20 in Wales). The 108

SCOTTISH EXECUTIVE DEPARTMENTS

NEW DEPARTMENT	DEPARTMENTS IT REPLACES/RESPONSIBILITIES	MINISTERS' TITLES
Justice Department	Home Department and Courts Administration	Cabinet: Justice and Home Affairs (Deputy First Minister) / Deputy: Justice
Education Department	Focus on children, primary and secondary education as well as culture, the arts and built heritage	Cabinet: Children and Education, Culture and the Arts / Deputies: Children and Education / Culture and Sport
Health Department (and community care)	As old Health Department which also looked after community care	Cabinet: Health and Community Care / Deputy: Community Care
Rural Affairs	As old Agriculture, Environment and Fisheries	Cabinet: Rural Affairs / Deputy: Rural Affairs (fisheries)
Enterprise and Life-long Learning	Industry section of the Education and Industry Department and higher education section of old Education Department	Cabinet: Enterprise and Lifelong Learning / Deputies: Enterprise and Lifelong Learning / Highlands and Islands/ Gaelic
Development Department	As old Development Department - Housing, local government, transport and Euro Social Inclusion, Equality and Voluntary Sector structural funds	Cabinet: Communities / Deputies: Local Government
Finance	As before	Cabinet: Finance
Corporate Services		
Secretariat		

OTHER MINISTERS
Cabinet: Lord Advocate
Deputy: Solicitor General for Scotland

Cabinet: Minister for Parliament and Chief Whip
Deputy: Business Manager and Whip

Cabinet: Minister for Transport and Environment (straddles Development and Rural Affairs Departments)

SCOTTISH PARLIAMENT COMMITTEES

- **European**: Proposals for/implementation of European legislation, and any EC/EU issue.

- **Equal Opportunities**: Equal opportunities issues.

- **Finance**: Executive reports/documents on budgets, public expenditure, or tax-varying resolutions; committee reports concerning public expenditure; and Budget Bills, and (discretionary) legislative timetable for such Bills and handling of financial business.

- **Justice and Home Affairs**: Administration of justice, law reform and other matters within the responsibility of the Minister for Justice.

- **Transport and the Environment**: Transport, the environment and natural heritage and other matters within the responsibility of the Minister for Transport and the Environment.

- **Enterprise and Lifelong Learning:** Education, Scottish economy, industry, tourism, training and further and higher education and other matters within the responsibility of the Minister for Enterprise and Lifelong Learning.

- **Culture and Sport:** School/pre-school education, arts, culture and sport and other matters falling within the responsibility of the Minister for Children and Education.

- **Social Inclusion**: Housing and Voluntary Sector Health and Housing and the voluntary sector and other matters within the responsibility of the Minister for Communities other than local government

- **Community Care**: Health policy and the NHS in Scotland and other matters within the responsibility of the Minister for Health and Community Care.

- **Rural Affairs**: Rural development, agriculture and fisheries and other matters within the responsibility of the Minister for Rural Affairs.

- **Local government**: Administration of local government.

WELSH CABINET AND DEPARTMENTS

Under a Permanent Secretary (who has direct responsibility for finance and for the NHS Directorate), the Welsh Assembly has the equivalent of two Deputy Secretaries, respectively handling economic affairs, transport, planning and environment (divided into the Economic Development and Transport, Planning & Environment Groups and the Industry & Training and Agriculture Departments; and social policy and local government (divided into the Health Protection and Improvement Directorate, Local Government and Social Services & Communities Groups and the Education Department.

Apart from the First Secretary, who has overall control, and the Business Secretary (Chief Whip), Assembly Secretaries are responsible for these elements as follows

- *Finance Secretary: Finance Group*

- *Agriculture and Rural Economy Secretary: Agriculture Department*

- *Health and Social Services Secretary (incl food safety): NHS and Health Protection & Improvement Directorates and Social Services and Communities Group*

- *Environment, Local Government and Planning Secretary: Transport, Planning & Environment and Local Government Groups; and CADW*

- *Economic Development Secretary (incl tourism): Economic Development Group; Industry and Training Department (Industrial Development and Business Services Divisions)*

- *Education Post-16 and Training Secretary: Education Department (Further & Higher Education and Culture & Recreation Divisions) and Industry and Training Department (Industrial and Training Policy and Training and Finance Management Divisions)*

- *Education Under 16 Secretary: Education Department (Schools Administration and Schools Performance Divisions)*

There is considerable overlap between the responsibility of Assembly Secretaries: for example, the responsibilities of the Health and Social Services Secretary cross with education under 16 (children's health; children and social services; fluouridation; infectious disease control); the Agriculture Secretary (food); and the Environment Secretary (environmental health; fluouridation).

Northern Ireland representatives are elected by proportional representation. All three countries have an Executive or Cabinet, led by a First Minister or First Secretary, to which the former Scottish, Welsh and Northern Ireland Offices report. They have taken over the former functions of their Secretaries of State but there are differences in the extent to which they have been freed from Westminster control. Scotland and Northern Ireland have complete licence to legislate in the areas reserved to them, but Wales only has control over secondary legislation.

The national Secretaries of State now represent their countries in Cabinet and where policy responsibility has not been devolved. They also have the task of reconciling cross-border policy differences in cases where a coordinated position is desirable. However, although Whitehall Departments produced notes for   public bodies and others on the concordats they expected to reach with Scotland, Northern Ireland and Wales almost a year before the 1999 devolution elections were held, giving effect to them depends on cooperation between the Secretary of State, national Executive and Parliament in each case. A number of Whitehall/Edinburgh liaison committees at ministerial level have been established to coordinate policy development in distinct areas such as the knowledge economy, but they have not pleased Opposition MSPs. Small majorities, or a difference in political outlook between London and Holyrood, could create difficulties for bodies with UK-wide activities.

The main distinctions between Westminster and the devolved institutions lies in the enhanced role given to committees in each of the new bodies and in the streamlined legislative process. The Scottish Parliament and the Welsh Assembly both have:

• A Business Committee (called the Parliamentary Bureau in Scotland) which proposes the business programme and the remit, membership etc. of the committees and decides which, if any, written motions should be debated. The Parliamentary Bureau comprises the Presiding Officer, who convenes the group and has the casting vote; representatives of each Party with more than five

Members (Labour, Conservative, SNP, and Liberal Democrats); and a group representative of Parties with less than five members (Scottish Socialist Party, Green Party and Dennis Canavan in the 1999–2003 Parliament).

- Audit and Finance Committees to examine Executive spending, with a similar remit to that of the Public Accounts Committee.
- A Members Interests Committee to police ethical standards.
- Subject Committees shadowing their departments (Scotland: Finance; Justice and Home Affairs; Transport and Environment; Health and Community Care; Enterprise and Lifelong Learning; Rural Affairs; Social Inclusion, Housing and Voluntary; Local Government; and Education, Culture and Sport. Wales: economic development, agriculture and rural development, local government and environment, pre-16 schools, education and early learning, health and social services, and post-16 education and training. Northern Ireland: Agriculture, Environment, Regional Development, Social Development, Education, Higher Education. & Employment, Enterprise, Trade & Investment, Culture, Arts & Leisure, Health & Social Services, Finance & Personnel).

As in Strasbourg, the subject committees conduct inquiries and scrutinise legislation and financial proposals – there is no distinction between Select and Standing committees, a significant contrast with Westminster – and they can also initiate legislation. Each committee has around ten members (11 in Scotland, except for the European Committee, which has 13; nine in Wales; 11 in Northern Ireland, split on party lines and coordinated by the Business Committee. In Wales, there are also Programme Committees which look at issues, such as public health strategies, that may straddle more than one Subject Committee; "Task and Finish" working groups, to develop policy programmes in areas such as European legislation, equal opportunities and sustainable development; and Regional Committees, covering the North, Mid, South West and South East (and which meet in various locations around each region), designed to reflect economic and cultural differences (especially language) in response to

Opposition party pressure to curb the power of the Labour dominated Valleys. Regional Committees do not have a party balance. Because the Welsh Assembly incorporates government departments (in contrast to Scotland, where there is a more traditional separation between Executive and Parliament), its committees spend much of their time considering memoranda on policy issues that are submitted to them by officials. The Northern Ireland Assembly committees are regarded as a strong check on the Ministers they shadow, and given the coalition nature of Northern Irish politics there is no guarantee that a Minister will be able to push legislation through a committee which may be dominated by opponent parties.

Note that the committees' ability to summon witnesses, either for subject inquiries or during legislative scrutiny, is not confined to devolved areas: the Scottish Parliament could, for example, call the Financial Services Authority for questioning on Scottish aspects of financial regulation reserved to Westminster.

The process of scrutinising legislation is simpler than that at Westminster and is closer to the European Parliament's model. Subject Committees conduct pre-legislative examination of Executive/Cabinet proposals (they can introduce their own Bills, but most measures emerge from the Scottish, Welsh and Northern Ireland departments) through rapporteurs and hearings. As in Westminster, there is then a debate in plenary session to agree the principle of a Bill and the Committee proceeds to consider it line by line, but Report and Third Reading are combined into a single final stage. Welsh SIs, known as Assembly Orders, are mainly considered by the relevant subject committee after they have been procedurally vetted by the Assembly's Legislation Committee. They are then voted on in plenary, which (unlike its Westminster counterpart) can table amendments to them. However, Orders involving expenditure are not scrutinised by committees and go straight to plenary for debate; as do those that have to be approved by Westminster (although these items cannot be amended). Four year legislative programmes are announced at the start of the life of each Scottish Parliament but are revised annually; and the committees will normally operate on the basis of a rolling twelve month work programme.

In other respects there is little difference between the way devolved and UK institutions work. The roles of the Civil Servants, Ministers, and backbenchers are identical in each of the four systems.

The Northern Ireland Act allows its Assembly to incorporate Northern Ireland provisions in UK-wide legislation passed by Westminster, particularly on devolved issues (such as social security and company law) where parity is normally maintained. In fact, before devolution there were hardly ever more than three UK Acts and twenty Orders devoted to Northern Ireland in any year.

In England, nine Regional Development Agencies, covering areas corresponding to Government administrative regions, were established in April 1999 with the role of producing regional economic development strategies and coordinating their implementation across local authority boundaries. Although they do not handle planning, they have responsibility for policy in relation to

- investment
- setting a regional skills agenda
- advising Ministers on and administering EU structural funds land
- Regional Selective Assistance
- land use, including site reclamation
- transport
- housing
- tourism
- cultural and sport infrastructure projects

Each has a board with members drawn from the private sector, local authorities and rural interests. The intention is that they should work with assemblies or chambers which would represent interests in the region. Government is at present leaving it to the regions themselves to take the initiative in establishing these bodies, but no direct elections have taken place and at the time of writing they are dominated by local councillors,.

Although Government has not made it easy for outsiders to determine the dividing line between RDAs, Government Offices for the

DEVOLUTION—THE THREE SYSTEMS AT A GLANCE

Scotland

Powers of First Minister

Power to remove Lord Advocate. Head of Scottish Executive; ppoints its members. Represents the Parliament in discussions on European proposals and at international meetings. Advised by a Policy Unit and a group of Special Advisers

Other Ministers and Departments

9 Scottish Ministers and 11 Deputy Ministers: Justice, Education, Health and community care, Enterprise and Lifelong Learning, Development, Rural Affairs, Secretariat and Corporate Services DepartmentsImplements EU obligations on devolved matters. Involved in UK policymaking on EU matters and has to take the UK line once it has been agreed. Scottish Ministers can speak for the UK in EU Councils.

Powers of Secretary of State

Minimal powers. Represents Scottish interest in Westminster Cabinet for non-devolved matters.

Legislation and reserved powers

Can initiate and pass primary and secondary legislation in all devolved areas and will also scrutinise European legislation.

DEVOLVED: economic development/inward investment (including administration in Scotland of European Structural Funds; Scottish Enterprise, enterprise companies, and financial assistance to industry, subject to common UK guidelines); ports, harbours, provision of freight shipping and ferry services, Highlands and Islands Airports and airport planning/environmental issues; environmental protection, water and sewerage; agriculture; natural and built heritage and arts; powers and duties relating to electricity supply (including consents for construction of power stations or overhead lines); Lottery distribution in Scotland; setting of gaming hours and some licence fees.

RESERVED TO WESTMINSTER: DSS, employment, transport regulation, macroeconomic policy, defence, financial services regulation, competition, consumer protection, company law and insolvency, intellectual property, Home Office matters such as asylum and immigration (not police), broadcasting and some film matters, energy and telecoms regulation, and trade policy/ECGD, air traffic control. Sets the framework for local government, quangos and health bodies and vets/scrutinises UK-wide quangos relevant to Scotland (eg Offer, HSE, BBC).

Legislative process

Legislative programme published at the start of each four year parliamentary term; revised annuallyDepartment drafts proposals as in Whitehall (incl. production of Regulatory Impact Assessment). Subject Committee considers draft Bill (may hold hearings) then sends it to Plenary (general principles debate). Bill returned to subject committee for line by line scrutiny

Plenary considers committee amendments, final vote. Bills can roll over between sessions. SIs - as at Westminster, except that proposals to reject SIs are put to the Committee examining them. Bills can be introduced by Executive, private members ("Members Bills") or committees ("Committee Bills").

Start date and date of next Election

Parliamentary year runs from 12 May. Located in Assembly Rooms (will move to Holyrood)Four year fixed term. Next election: first Thursday in May 2003

No. of Members

129: 73 directly elected for single member constituencies following Westminster boundaries; rest elected by PR for multi-member constituencies following European Parliament boundaries. .Parliament Members titled MSP

Parliamentary timetable

Monday 2.30-5.30. Friday 9.30-12.30. Other days 9.30-5.30. Committees sit on Monday/Tuesday/Wednesday am and Friday am. Plenary sessions Wed pm, all day Thursday. Question time: First Minister, then all Departments at random - Thurs pmSummer recess: mid June-end Aug. 12 half-day sittings to discuss committee work; 15 half-day sittings to consider Opposition motionsConsideration of draft budgets in the late autumn and of the Stages of the main Budget Bill in January/February

Committee sructures and remit

Mandatory Committees: Business, Standards, Procedure, Finance, Audit, European, Equal Opportunities. Delegated Legislation, Public Petitions 9 Subject Committees shadowing each Department, with power to summon witnesses, scrutinise and propose legislation.Standing Committees ad hoc - scrutinise Bills and shadow departments.Expected to hold sessions around Scotland.Scottish Select Committee will remain at Westminster11 members (European Committee has 13)

Dispute resolution mechanism

Presiding Officer consults with law officers on remit of Assembly. Judicial Committee of the Privy Council evaluates whether Assembly is operating beyond its remit. Concordats between Departments in Scotland and Westminster.

Tax-raising powers

+/-3p in the £1 Control over local authority budgets, rates and transport charges.

Access to Information

Daily Business Bulletin, Official Report and Minutes of Proceedings, and weekly What's Happening in the Scottish Parliament available at 8am on the Scottish Parliament website (scottish.parliament.uk and scottish.parliament.uk/ webcast for live broadcasts). Live coverage available of all proceedings on website. Parliament number 0845 278 1999; Public Information 0131 348 5000

DEVOLUTION—THE THREE SYSTEMS AT A GLANCE

Wales

Powers of First Secretary

Head of Welsh Assembly Cabinet. Represents Assembly at international meetings, including the British-Irish Council and on European issues

Other Ministers and Departments

Cabinet comprises eight Assembly Secretaries, including a Business Secretary and a Finance Secretary. Former Welsh Office Departments now report to the Assembly and are split into Finance, Economic Development and Transport, Planning & Environment, Local Government, and Social Services & Communities Groups; the Industry & Training, Agriculture and Education Departments; and the NHS and Health Protection & Improvement Directorates. Advised by central Policy Unit.

Powers of Secretary of State

Represents Welsh interests in Westminster Cabinet on non-devolved matters. Introduces primary legislation. Must consult Assembly on UK Government legislation. Attends Assembly at least once per year.

Legislation and reserved powers

Power to draft and pass secondary legislation in all devolved areas

DEVOLVED: agriculture, heritage and tourism, culture and sport, economic development, education and training, environment, health and social services, highways and transport, housing, industry, local government, and planning

RESERVED TO WESTMINSTER: foreign affairs, defence, Social Security, Treasury, financial regulation, air traffic control, trade and industry (except inward investment), food standards, criminal law, prisons, legal aid and Home Office issues such as asylum and immigration, broadcasting and film

Legislative process

Following departmental consultation and full regulatory appraisal1. Legislation Committee checks for vires etc, 2. Subject committee consideration, 3. full Assembly debateWhere expenditure is involved: 1. Legislation Committee, 2. full Assembly debate and vote Draft Orders can roll on to the next session.Westminster SIs passed by Affirmative Resolution can be "fast tracked" in Wales by using Negative Resolution procedureOrders mainly introduced by Assembly Secretaries; ballot for backbench SIs.

Start date/date of next election

Official opening: 26 May 1999, located in Crickhowell House. (Later moves to dock site) Four year fixed term. Next election: first Thursday, May 2003.

No. of Members

60 members - 40 elected for single member single member constituencies following Westminster boundaries; rest elected by PR for multi-member constituencies following European Parliament boundaries.. Assembly Members are titled AM/AC

Parliamentary timetable

Plenary Tues-Wed. Sessions: 9am-5pm; questions to First Secretary Tues 2pm-2.30pm; to other Ministers Wed 2pm and 2.30 (two Departments each week, each Assembly Secretary faces questions at least every four weeks). Short balloted debates held at end of Tuesday business. Legislative timetable published each yearCompulsory annual debates on

•Annual report of the First Secretary

•Allocation of the Budget

•Reports submitted by subject committees

•Reports by the Audit Committee

•The Government's legislative programme

•Annual report on the local government scheme

•Annual report on arrangements for co-operation with business

•EU matters

Committee structures and remit

Mandatory Committees: Legislation, Audit, Business, Equality of Opportunity, European Affairs and Standards of Conduct. Regional Committees: North Wales, Mid Wales, South West Wales, South East Wales. Membership reflects local party strengths. Must meet in their region at least twice a year. Subject Committees (10 members, including the relevant Minister) consider legislation and scrutinise departments, First Minister and Non Departmental Public Bodies. Rolling 12 month inquiry programme. Welsh Select Committee will remain at Westminster.

Dispute resolution mechanism

T.B.A. Concordats between Government departments in Wales and Westminster.

Tax-raising powers

None

Access to information

Verbatim reports within three working days. Bilingual Order Paper and Record of Proceedings available on the internet (wales.gov.uk).

DEVOLUTION—THE THREE SYSTEMS AT A GLANCE

Northern Ireland

Powers of First Minister

Head of Northern Irish Assembly Cabinet. Represents Assembly at international meetings, British-Irish Council and on European issues.

Powers of Ministers and their departments

Deputy First Minister plus ten Ministers: Agriculture and Rural Development, Environment, Regional Development, Social Development, Education, Higher and Further Education and Employment, Enterprise/Trade/Investment, Culture/Arts/ Leisure, Health and Social Services, Finance and Personnel. Allocated on basis of number of seats each Party holds

Powers of Secretary of State

Represents NI interest in Westminster Cabinet on non-devolved matters. Attends Assembly by invitation.Important role as go-between with Assembly and Irish Parliament.

Legislation and reserved powers

Can draft and pass primary and secondary legislation in all devolved areas:

Devolved: agriculture and rural development; forestry; environment; waste management; local government; mineral resources; transport planning; rail and road; ports and airports; energy; water; housing; education; employment services and law; economic development; tourism; health and safety; culture, arts and leisure; health; social services; fire authority.

Reserved to Westminster: foreign affairs, defence, Social Security, Treasury, financial regulation, air traffic control, trade and industry (except inward investment), food standards, criminal law, prisons & Home Office, including RUC, broadcasting and films

Legislative process

Can opt into UK legislation.Decisions via parallel consent or weighted majority Bills must conform to human rights requirements set out in the Northern Ireland Act 1998Following departmental consultation and full Regulatory Impact Assessment, Assembly debates general principles; Bills then allocated to Subject Committee, Plenary debates Committee amendments), final voteBills can roll over between sessions. Can be introduced by Cabinet, private member or committee

Start date and date of next election

2 December 1999. No date for next election

No. of Members

108 by STV (Assembly Members titled MLA)

Parliamentary timetable

To be established at time of writing. Legislative timetable published each year

Committee structures and remit

Subject Committees: Agriculture, Environment, Regional Development, Social Development, Education, Higher Education. & Employment, Enterprise, Trade & Investment, Culture, Arts & Leisure, Health & Social Services, Finance & PersonnelOther ad-hoc CommitteesPower to introduce and odify legislation, call witnesses, consider budgets & subjects.Statutory committee on equality which will interpret all proposed legislation

---

Dispute resolution mechanism

Concordats between Belfast/Whitehall departments and through Council of the Isles

Tax-raising powers

None

Access to information

Verbatim reports on website (ni-assembly.gov.uk). Others TBA.

---

regions, local authorities, Training and Enterprise Councils and Business Links, it will help organisations if they can obtain RDA support (expressed either directly to Ministers and local authorities or in their regional economic strategies) for major planning applications, in particular those that may be subject to call in or other determination by Whitehall, and for other development projects. Contact details are available on the internet at http://www.local-regions.detr.gov.uk/rda/index.htm. Regional Assemblies may also be lobbied on these issues, either direct (the DETR regional liaison section has contact numbers and addresses) or through local authorities where there is a need to emphasise a case to Ministers (for example, if the regional office of a regulatory agency is felt to be acting unreasonably but is close to its Whitehall officials).

...AND HOW TO WORK IT

- *How decisions are made*
- *The passage of UK legislation and regulation*
- *Local government policy-making*
- *EU policy-making and legislation*
- *How pressure groups can influence the system*
- *Special issues: Budget, competition and procurement lobbying;• Regulatory Impact Assessment*
- *The ethics of lobbying*

How decisions are made

In this section, we will try to open the green baize door and show how the system deals with the work most relevant to organisations:

- Policy decisions
- The passage of UK and Scottish, Welsh and Northern Ireland legislation and regulation
- Local government and EU policy-making and legislation
- General liaison with outsiders (correspondence, meetings, visits)

How new is the "New Labour" style of government?

The arrival of a new Labour government in May 1997 introduced a number of changes in the system's approach to decision-making which must guide lobbyists:

What has changed

... And what hasn't

Ministers have shown greater dependence on their Special Advisers for policy advice. There

...but, while some Special Advisers wield an influence over policy that their Conservative predecessors

was initially a degree of wariness of being captured by the Civil Service

never enjoyed, Ministers are still-swamped with work and continue almost totally to rely on their officials to sift information, handle most dealings with outsiders, administer consultation exercises, make recommendations and write their letters and briefs on 90% of issues. Labour introduced a thicker political layer in Whitehall, but it has thinned and decisions are made through several components working together - lobbying which aims only at politicians is likely to miss tricks

Greater use of outsiders (eg well-known businessmen, scientists, friends of Labour) to consult and produce policy recommendations

...but the mentality of the system has not changed. Policy proposals, whether generated internally or by outsiders, are still subjected to the Standard Whitehall Test (see p. 78). The key to persuasive policy/legislative/regulatory lobbying still lies in understanding and preempting that test. In any event, the Task Force concept became criticised because of over-use

With a large majority, Ministers cannot be pushed around by Parliament

...but although their prime considerations are to get their programmes through, they are concerned to look good in the media and among their parliamentary colleagues. They want to feel that their decisions are popular in the House

Years of being ignored in opposition made them more sensitive to views of long-term allies. "What you know" is still the key, but "Who you know" is a factor.

...but, while those with developed relationships will have "Call Back Factor" and may enjoy easier access to politicians, Ministers and their advisers will not do anyone favours - fear of the media and accountability at the Despatch Box ensure that.

THE INFLUENCE GAME

	Influence	Strengths	Weaknesses
Prime Minister	10/10	• Total control	• Too broad an area of responsibility to cover small issues
Ministers	8/10	• Ultimate decision makers • Can expedite official action • Can overturn official advice	• Have to depend on officials • Room for manoeuvre limited by ongoing policies and pragmatic constraints • May be moved regularly between departments
Commissioners	7/10	• Ultimate decision makers within Commission • Power to choose their own Cabinet gives them greater control than UK Ministers over flow of information	• Can be thwarted by Council and Parliament
Council of Ministers	8/10	• Key EU decision makers	• Difficulty in securing agreement can stall progress on legislation for years
Commission officials	7/10	• Prepare legislation, • Administer (and often stimulate) EU initiatives • Vet most legislative representations	• Strongly corporatist - often resistant to individual representations • National quotas mean quality can vary
Whitehall officials	8/10	• Command of facts/files • Advice to Ministers often conclusive • Ministers can't survive without them • Draft and formulate legislation • Control consultative processes, • Put words into Ministers' mouths	• Often defensive • May have poor commercial understanding, • Must work within overall manifesto/ministerial brief
PPSs	3/10	• Ministers' eyes and ears in the House • Direct line to Ministers	• No guarantee of further promotion
Policy Unit	7/10	• Direct advice to the Prime Minister • PM's progress chasers with Departments, • Ability to re-evaluate issues and resolve interdepartmental conflicts, • Significant contribution to manifesto	• Dependent on the information they get from Departments and outsiders

	Score	Strengths	Weaknesses
Commissioners' Cabinets	7/10	• Gateway to Commissioners • Negotiate agenda for weekly Commission meetings • Alternative source of advice for Commissioners • More powerful than UK Ministers' Private Offices	• Overworked. • Over-concentrate on issues of the nationality of their Commissioner
Special Advisers	6/10	• Close and regular contact with Ministers • Alternative conduit to Ministers on policy issues • May be used by Ministers to second guess officials • Sensitive to media issues	• May just be speechwriters or media managers - few are policy specialists
MPs/Peers as a group	4/10 (can rise to 6 if small majority or major public interest issue)	• Public debate. • Ability to embarrass Ministers	• Easily overridden by Executive. • All talk, no action • Manifestation of democracy rather than democratic force • Peers can't deal with money matters
European Parliament	6/10 (can rise to 7 on Co-decision making issues)	• Co-Decision Making makes it a real check on Commission/Council	• Ineffective at questioning Commission. • Resolutions, own initiative reports achieve little
Individual MPs	1/10 (3 on genuine constituency issues)	• Respected by Ministers on constituency issues • Representations on individuals' problems, • Can draw attention to issues • Some power if majority small • Privileged access to Ministers • Ability to criticise organisations in public	• Whipped; ignored by the Executive • Harassed, poorly serviced and briefed

		Advantages	Disadvantages
Individual Peers	1/10	• Privileged access to Ministers • Less inclined to be lobby fodder • Easier to get debate time than MPs • Senior ones can command great respect	• Ministers consider them to be politically unaccountable
Individual MEPs	2/10	• Access to Commission officials	• Little influence unless they are rapporteurs
Select Committees	3/10	• Can publicise issues • Ministers may use them as alternative sounding board on policy	• Often regarded as an inconvenience by Whitehall • Recommendations are rarely adopted
EP Committees	5/10	• Assess legislation • Influence voting on legislation • Chairmen have considerable influence • Can summon Commissioners	
Backbench committees	2/10	• Represent MPs' views to leadership • Direct access to Ministers • Can take up individual cases	• Don't examine issues in depth • Secretaries control access, may use position for their own purposes • Quality of chairmen variable
All Party Groups	1/10	• Can mobilise support on occasions (eg threat to impose VAT on books)	• Too influenced by pressure groups • Country groups seen as beano hunters
Euro Parliament Intergroups	2/10	• Access to officials as well as Commissioners • Largest groups (eg Land Use and Food) carry real weight.	• Variable quality
Scottish/Welsh/ N Irish Assembly Members	1/10 (3 on genuine constituency issues)	• Ability to criticise organisations in public	• Same limitations as MPs.
Assembly committees	4/10	• Scrutinise departments and legislation • Handle some consultation,	• If Executive can command a majority in Plenary, they can be rolled over. • Can initiate legislation.

The policy agenda does of course bear the stamp of the Government of the day even though the great majority of issues roll on from Government to Government. Three distinct themes run through Labour's approach: social exclusion, implying a greater need to tackle disadvantage; regionalism, which will encourage organisations (particularly public bodies) to be seen to be establishing regional decision-making structures; and a broad populist thread, which could be read as meaning "people's policies" - a greater readiness to take the side of the consumer against the retailer or the passenger against the rail operator. Lobbyists must be prepared to recognise and, wherever possible, to incorporate these aspects of the political mind-set in the style and substance of their representations.

The mechanics of decision-making

As a rule of thumb, decisions in the system

- are rarely single-faceted - they are the product of a complex coalition of forces, with two or more Departments, Cabinet Committees, Parliament, public and media opinion, the Policy Unit, Prime Minister and declared party policy all acting as pressures on the lead Minister in each case
- are usually shaped and taken by several people - the idea of Ministers, Council committee chairmen or European Commissioners deciding everything themselves is misleading
- are often heavily influenced at a relatively low level. Real power rests far further down the Civil Service than is often believed. The crucial grades are G3-G7. And ministerial decisions often do no more than endorse the letters, briefs and draft legislation produced for them by officials. This should not surprise anyone - it is how most large corporations operate
- are usually evidence-driven - pressure sometimes has a role, but (almost) all decisions have to be justified on their facts
- are usually negotiated - high profile campaigns are the exception and are usually unnecessary
- do not follow a universal template - attempts to influence issues

OPEN GOVERNMENT?

A private sector company wants to investigate the possibility of providing services to the NHS. At present, these services (let us take medical equipment or liability insurance) are handled by public sector organisations, the NHS Supplies Authority and the NHS Litigation Authority. Both of them, like other public sector trading bodies, publish accounts; but how to find out whether a better service could be provided at lower cost? The company considers five options:

- *Approach the Authorities direct? It will be met with a flat refusal on grounds that information on cost structures, funding of claims etc is commercially confidential. The approach will be regarded as a threat.*
- *Contact departmental officials (in this case the NHS Executive)? They will be completely reliant on the trading bodies for their information and will immediately inform them of the approach. The company will receive the same answer.*
- *Persuade an MP to table questions seeking the data the company needs? The answers will either reproduce annual report figures, which will be less than transparent, or will restate the "commercially confidential" mantra.*
- *Persuade an MP to organise a presentation to Department of Health Ministers? But how can it present a case if it does not know what it has to beat? Even if it is prepared to take a chance by offering a formula guaranteeing savings and service standards, the Minister will have in front of him a very plausible brief prepared by the Authority and setting out performance improvements and five year plans. Message: it would be premature, Minister, to engage in a market testing exercise, with all the disruption that involves (ie extra work for officials), until the current plan has been completed. Market testing now would not offer a realistic comparison since the efficiency improvement programme agreed with Ministers will not have been fully carried through (public bodies can remain "in transition" for years).*
- *Persuade the Health Select Committee to run an inquiry in the hope that the bodies may be put on the spot? If the bodies give evidence, they will offer the line they gave to the Minister: no objection to market testing, but a fair comparison can only be made once the current transition programme (or whatever) has been completed. The company could forearm the committee and, with cooperation from the media, the right report. could prompt Ministers to accelerate market opening or could make NHS Trusts more receptive to an approach from the company. However, the Committee will need some information before it can decide whether there are grounds for an inquiry - Catch 22 again.*

The company probably has only two courses open to it - approach the NHS Federation, which represents the Trusts who are the customers for both bodies; or, more likely, to find an individual Trust prepared to discuss costs and service levels and to run an informal market test. The company will eventually need to put its case to Ministers and to policy-level officials, but the data it needs in order to do is only likely to be obtained through a circuitous route. These areas are of course excluded from the ambit of Freedom of Information legislation. However, another lever exists. The Code of Practice on Access to Government Information (available from the Freedom of Information Unit, Cabinet Office Room 65d/1, Horseguards Road, London SW1P 3AL, 0345 223 242, www.cabinet-office.gov.uk/index/search.htm) requires the system to provide

- *Analysis considered relevant and important in framing policy proposals and decisions*
- *Explanatory material (rules, procedures, internal guidance to officials, and administrative manuals)*
- *Reasons for administrative decisions to those affected by them*
- *Information relating to policies, actions and decisions*

However, there are several exclusions:

- *Material relating to defence, security or international relations*
- *Proceedings of Cabinet and its committees*
- *Internal opinion, advice and consultation*
- *Analysis of alternative policy options and information relating to rejected options*
- *Confidential communications between Departments and public bodies*
- *Information relating to legal proceedings or covered by Privilege*
- *Information which could prejudice the commercial position of a Department or public body*
- *Commercial confidences*

Failure to provide information under the Code can be taken up with the Parliamentary Commissioner for Administration (see Challenging Legislation, p116) Naturally, the system has kept the existence of the Code a secret.

through political lobbying alone may only put the cart before the horse.

Policy decisions

The great majority of representations to central Government concern the power of Ministers and officials to take action under existing provision; or proposals for the amendment or maintenance of legislation.

MULTIFACETED DECISIONS

From time to time, the threat has arisen of VAT being applied to books and newspapers. The departmental relationships on this issue are typically complex:

- *• The Budget is formulated by the Treasury*
- *• But VAT is the responsibility of Customs & Excise*
- *• And the implications for education fall to DfEE, the Scottish and Northern Ireland Offices*
- *• And public libraries are sponsored by DCMS*
- *• Lastly, DTI sponsors the publishing, bookselling and printing industries*

Similarly, policy on genetically modified foods would involve MAFF, on behalf of farmers and the food industry; DETR, responsible for environmental implications, DoH - impact on health; DTI, which sponsors the biotech industry; the Cabinet Office, coordinating policy across departments; and possibly Treasury if compensation is being considered.

It is normal for the lead Department on an issue to have a long circulation list. Take a Brussels proposal on misleading advertising. DTI's Consumer Affairs Directorate would be the sponsor in the UK, but others involved and possibly keen to comment would include

Foreign Office	*Northern Ireland Office/Executive*
Treasury Solicitors	*Office of Fair Trading*
Lord Chancellor's Department	*Cabinet Office*
Home Office	*Scottish Executive*
Wales Office/Welsh Assembly	

Bear in mind, however, that conflicts arise within, as well as across Departments. DETR should support the Channel Tunnel Rail Link because it sponsors the construction industry and railways; but it is also responsible for assessing the implications for the Kentish environment and it sponsors other transport sectors - aviation, ferries and hovercraft - which opposed the Channel Tunnel.

In any one day, Whitehall will have to take a mass of routine decisions (for example, supplementary credit approvals required by public sector bodies); it will be working on the implementation of manifesto and other politically driven commitments; and it will be assessing the viability of ideas put forward by outside bodies (for example, that the Northern Ireland herd should be exempt from BSE restrictions). The generic influences on the system are straightforward:

- There is no option but to act: for example, if another country imposes exceptional restrictions on UK exports.
- Party influences: the manifesto, or views developed within the Party machine - a reflection of rank and file opinion from the Chairman of the Conservative National Union or ideas produced by Labour Party officers or researchers, for example.
- Media influences: consistent media highlighting of an issue such that the system is unavoidably called to account. Ministers are usually very good at judging whether a story will run or not - if the latter (and if they have not generated the coverage themselves as a means of justifying their proposals) they will usually discount attempts to lobby them through the media.

DO CONTACTS HELP?

Yes, because it makes it easier to get through Ministers' and Special Advisers' doors and to obtain acceptances to invitations to receptions, visits, lunches etc.

Yes, because Labour politicians have developed strong relationships with those who dealt with or were loyal to them in Opposition.

Yes, because officials are more likely to speak candidly to those who have worked with them.

No, because you still have to understand the system, play by its rules and have a strong case. They may talk to you but they will not do you favours.

Generally speaking, develop your relationships in peacetime, but do not expect them automatically to support you when problems arise. The most respected politicians take cases on their merits regardless of how professional - or how generous - you are.

- Weight of evidence: research initiated either by the system itself or by outside lobbyists which shows that there is a strong case for action - a mass of reports from respectable sources suggesting that a toy may be unsafe, for example.

- Weight of numbers: proposals, whether initiated by the system or by outsiders, need to command a broad body of support.

- The "mood of the House": even with a large majority, Ministers and officials will want both to avoid criticism from Government backbenchers and the creation of hostages which the Opposition can exploit through the media. A fundamental point to remember when dealing with MPs is that, apart from genuine constituency issues, where Ministers will almost always listen to them regardless of their party, as a group they only carry influence if enough Members who are regarded as heavyweights walk into the Whips' Office and say they are worried.

- Other Departments or public bodies: views from other parts of the system are generally given more weight than those presented by outsiders. A proposal from one Department may be circulated to a large number of others, either because their work may be affected by it; because it may affect their territory (eg Scotland); or for protocol reasons (eg the Cabinet Office will see a lot of these) before views of external organisations are considered. And inter-departmental disagreements, which may be factual (a DTI policy proposal may make it harder to implement a Foreign Office programme) or personal (where two Ministers are rivals) may be resolved either through collegiate discussion in Cabinet committees or through the Prime Minister acting as tie-breaker.

- The calendar: it may not be possible to take action because the legislative programme is full or because other events make it inadvisable. Most obviously, the system grinds to a halt in the three weeks or so before the annual round of ministerial reshuffles in July; and decision-making can be paralysed for months in the run-up to General Elections. Similarly, there is no point in calling in August for primary legislation to be included in November's Queen's Speech when the bidding process starts the December before; but timetabling constraints can be more subtle:

International Networks Corporation is a regulated UK telecoms group with growing multimedia interests. In September 1997, shortly before the Competition Bill is due to start its parliamentary stages, it decides that it wants to lobby to secure a restriction on the right of Oftel to regulate its activities in new communications areas falling outside the formal definition of telecommunications. Unfortunately, although the Bill appears to be an appropriate vehicle for the clarification INC needs, this is a measure inherited from the previous Government and the present administration does not want to delay it further by introducing new issues on which consultation (which would not be straightforward - INC is always clashing with Oftel and other utilities would be certain to pile in with their demands) would be needed.

That is not all. Officials advise Ministers that this is both a utility regulation problem - and, concurrent with the Bill, they are running a review of this area: raising INC's point in the Competition Bill would prejudge the outcome of the review, which may not lead to legislation until Autumn 1998 - and a cross-media issue, on which a DTI/DCMS consultation exercise on common regulation of broadcasting and telecommunications is due to start in the first quarter of 1998 and run for a year, meaning legislation not before Autumn 1999. Only exceptional factors, such as the need to address rapid restructuring of the market, will persuade the system to act earlier.

SEVEN QUESTIONS TO ASK YOURSELF BEFORE YOU LOBBY

- *Who will make the decision in reality (not always Ministers)?*
- *Who or what will influence them in this case?*
- *How do the arguments look on both sides?*
- *Who is likely to be lobbying them on this issue? Who are our allies and opponents?*
- *Is this a media issue; or are we unlikely to generate enough coverage to worry the system?*
- *If the system's (unwelcome) plans involve expenditure, will we be able to highlight the costs?*
- *If our ideas involve expenditure, are we likely to be able to make them a policy priority?*

- Money: any proposal involving cost must be negotiated with the Treasury; and one Department's gain is often another's loss. Good but costly ideas without a compelling political rationale (Labour's Welfare to Work Scheme was considered so fundamental that it was felt to justify a utility windfall tax to pay for it) is likely to be given a lower priority.
- The system's friends: some bodies or individuals will always be more "inside" than others, and Ministers and officials do listen to their friends and family.
- Therefore information does not always reach the system systematically or through a formal process of consultation.

As an illustration of these principles at work and of how you can take account of them in your lobbying, we will look at an example (part fact, part fiction), of the system considering its own ideas. In the next section, which explains how legislation and regulation is produced, we will consider what happens when outsiders seek to influence policy decisions. Given the time it can take for policy to be produced, we have taken a case history that crosses two administrations.

Taxing Aviation Fuel

As a result of persistent environmental campaigning, which has slowly influenced a fair body of public opinion, all political parties believe that capturing the Green agenda is electorally desirable. International pressure is also putting them under increasing pressure to consider means of restricting industrial emissions. However, officials advise Ministers that adopting a Green programme could significantly damage our competitiveness and there is further concern over the implications for consumer costs. It is agreed that a Royal Commission on Environmental Pollution should be established.

The Royal Commission eventually recommends that aviation fuel, which at that time, unlike fuel for road transport, is not taxed because carriers have to purchase it in so many different countries, should bear an environmental levy in recognition of the pollution caused by aircraft emissions. Concurrently, the European Commission, stimulated by an enthusiastic Environment Commissioner, starts work on a programme which includes aviation fuel tax proposals; and in the UK a new, environmentally aware Secretary of State takes over at the Department of the Environment. He asks his Private Office staff for a brief on the issue, and they in turn contact three different but linked parts of the Department: the Office of the Chief Economist, which coordinates DoE's position on tax issues; the Environment Protection Group; and Air Quality Division..

All this takes place before the

This is the time to be targeting the system with a detailed submission to the Royal Commission. If at all possible, do not wait until Government has considered its own views - seek to shape, rather than respond to them.

Ditto with Brussels. You will have to work much harder to stop the machinery once it has gained momentum.

Ministers will receive views from many sources other than the Civil Service - friends, people they sit next to at lunch, Party insiders and other MPs and Peers. They will usually use officials to check this information but it may influence their gut feeling at the outset. You therefore need at the outset to have a clear idea of who will make the decision on your issue and who will shape their opinions.

1997 General Election, and the Departments of Transport and Environment are still separate bodies pursuing separate agendas. Although it would be normal for Departments to liase on issues that cross their boundaries, and DoE might be expected to contact Aviation and Environment Division (AED) in DoT to compare studies, in this case the assumption within DoE is that DoT will treat the airlines as its clients and will wish to protect them and the Secretary of State wants as far as possible to present his transport counterpart with a fait accompli. In requesting the brief, Private Office hinted that the Secretary of State has been lobbied by one of his Special Advisers, who was recruited from the Green movement, and is keen to approach Treasury (whose approval, informed by Customs & Excise, is essential to any proposal to tax fuel) if the data supports the adviser's views.

DoE officials have already been sent research by a respected consultancy which corroborates the Royal Commission's findings. However, a G7 in Air Quality Division is deputed to search for other studies and to

Many policy proposals spend years in gestation. Although we have changed the facts slightly, this one is typical of many which started under one Government and continued to be developed by another.

Try to learn as much as you can (from MPs, journalists, Special Advisers and other businessmen) about those who are relied upon and respected by Ministers and officials. You can then decide whether they are accessible and how to tailor your advocacy to their sensitivities.

The workhorses on such issues are the HEOs and G7s. They control information and should not be ignored in favour of more senior officials who will only go back to them to corroborate your story.

call Customs & Excise and other bodies known to officials to check figures on fuel duties and relative pollution levels. A brief is assembled for his Assistant Secretary to send:

To: Secretary of State

From: XXXXXXXXX

Environmental levies – aviation fuel

Subject

While the style varies slightly from Department to Department, this is typical in layout and content to the note officials might send to Ministers. It makes sense to adopt Whitehall style in producing submissions: material in a familiar format is more likely both to be read and to be incorporated into their memoranda.

The Secretary of State has requested a brief on the logistics and implications of imposing an environmental levy on aviation fuel. The following appendices are attached:
1. Status of current EU and international environmental taxation proposals.

Ministers do not have the time to read lengthy papers. Officials therefore summarise content and advice and leave as much as possible to attachments.

2. Comparison and breakdown of fuel taxation borne by UK road, rail, shipping and air transport operators.

3.Extracts from the Royal Commission on Environmental Pollution's report on transport and the environment.

Recommendation

1. There is unlikely to be strong opposition to a proposal to impose an aviation fuel levy provided we reassure the industry that agreement would have to be sought internationally. The airlines are not forceful campaigners, preferring to negotiate at official level, and they do not have a record of commissioning detailed research. It will therefore, we feel, be difficult for them to rebut the Royal Commission findings; nor will they be able to argue that competition will be distorted. There will be some concern over the impact on demand

The system will take a view on whether outsiders

- *are "professional" (they understand how to work the system and how to deal with us - could be dangerous)*
- *are "unconstructive whingers" (representations consist of little more than unresearched or uncorroborated assertions)*
- *have friends in high places ("we need to be careful about these, but while Ministers may see them they will not do them any favours in case the media finds out"). Contacts help a sound case to be heard; they (usually) cannot substitute for poor arguments.*

70

of further cost increases, but Customs & Excise inform us that despite two years' experience of Air Passenger Duty, passenger numbers are increasing.

Officials like to feel that they have done their prep but they are only as good as the information they receive. Has the industry checked the C&E figures in case they are incorrect?

2. We recommend only qualified support for the Dutch proposal that an aviation fuel levy be imposed on an EU-wide basis in advance of wider international agreement. This would not be in the interests of UK airlines seeking to compete with US and other non-EU carriers.

Timing

3. If the Secretary of State wishes to progress this matter, papers for HMT, DoT and DTI will have to be prepared by 3 March since UKRep reports that the Dutch intend to raise the issue at the 10-11 March

Transport Council and the first working group to settle our line for the December Kyoto World Environment Summit will meet on 19 March.

Background

3. The data available to us indicates that a distortion does exist between road and air transport since petrol and diesel taxation includes an environmental element whereas aviation fuel is untaxed.

4. Information supplied to us by the Society of British Aerospace Companies suggests that new generation engines are being developed by Rolls Royce and Pratt & Whitney with the capability of reducing NOx emissions by 28%; these engines could be available from the end of 2005. In principle

This may have been obtained either direct or from aerospace officials in DTI. By taking this initiative, the engine manufacturers gained the initiative. Lesson: never let the lobbying of competitors or pressure groups go unchallenged.

at least, the taxation of aviation fuel may encourage airlines to modify their fleet purchase plans in favour of aircraft fitted with more efficient engines.

5. The Royal Commission on Environmental Pollution's Eighteenth Report (1994) recommended that growth in demand for air transport should be curbed by making passengers face the cost of the damage aviation causes to the environment. Although the report admits that there is little conclusive data on the extent and impact of aircraft emissions, it reported the International Energy Authority's estimate that 176m tonnes of aviation fuel (which, according to a World Wide Fund for Nature study translates into 122m tonnes

This area was not a high priority for the industry in 1994. In hindsight, it should have put itself in a position rapidly to question the areas of uncertainty in the report and to rebut its conclusions by pointing out to DoE/DoT/DTI/HMT the impracticality of curbing demand and, if possible, by showing that a levy would be unlikely significantly to influence fleet purchase plans

of carbon) were burnt in 1990 and recommends that a fuel levy be negotiated on an international basis to encourage transfer of passengers to high speed rail travel. This approach is echoed in a 1994 paper in Transport Policy.

6. The European Commission's Fifth (1995) Environmental Action Plan refers to the need to consider the use of economic instruments to reduce transport pollution. We expect the 10 March Transport Council to request the Commission to produce a report on the effects of intro-ducing a kerosene tax by the end of this year. The Dutch are expected to table a proposal to tax kerosene on an EU-wide basis; at present, only Belgium and Austria are likely to support action other

than on a global level. Should the issue proceed at EU level, the final decision will have to be made jointly by ECOFIN and the Environment Council. However, the development of international action would best be left to the International Civil Aviation Organisation (ICAO) on which DoT represents the UK.

The Economic and Finance Ministers' Council

7. There are, however, a number of counter-factors to take into account:

a) The rationale for the current untaxed status of aviation fuel is that international airlines have to buy fuel in several countries and tax accounting is therefore complex.

b) Furthermore, were the UK or the EU to impose an environmental levy without

The system seeks to anticipate the arguments that will be used by outsiders. As a fundamental principle of lobbying, never assume that the system or your opponents will not spot holes in your arguments. Always pre-empt the concerns and rebuttals of Government, or of others lobbying against you, before the system has the chance to consider its own response. Your aim is to give them no alternative but to accept your case by showing them that their caveats or alternatives are flawed. We cover this point further in the next case study.

wider international
agreement, our carri-
ers could be disadvan-
taged in comparison
with US and other air-
lines. It would also
be possible to avoid
the levy, at least in
part, by operating
some services via
Geneva or Zurich.

c) Airlines will
argue that the bulk of
their operations do
not compete with road,
rail or surface trans-
port; there is howev-
er the argument that
road, ferry and
Eurostar travel are
alternatives to domes-
tic and very short-
haul international
flights and that air
fares would be less
competitive if avia-
tion fuel faced compa-
rable tax levels.

*As you can see, officials follow the preemp-
tion rule themselves*

d) Airlines will
also point out that
the imposition of Air
Passenger Duty was
justified in the 1993

Budget on the grounds that aviation fuel was undertaxed. They will complain that the same argument cannot be used twice.

e)   They may suggest that, although the Royal Commission's aim was to encourage air-road transfers, these would only be possible on a small minority of routes.   In   other cases, passengers will simply have to bear higher fares with no compensating improvement   in   emissions. RCEP states that road traffic generates five times   more CO_2 than does aviation, which is   responsible   for less than three per cent of all man-made emissions. The reduction resulting from a fuel levy may therefore be insignificant even if a levy is set at a level which makes airlines   seriously consider the specification of lean burn engines.

f) Furthermore, under the Sulphur Directive refiners have since October 1996 been required to reduce the SO_2 content of gasoil by 0.2-0.05%. The costs of this are, we understand, passed on to airlines in the fuel price, which (mainly due to other factors) has risen by around 40% over the past five months. The industry could therefore claim that it currently bears a cost directly related to environmental cleanup.

Officials had been briefed by the airlines on this. Time spent in such work is never wasted provided your information reaches the system before its thinking has crystallised.

g) We assume that the airlines will demand that no decision on policy is made without consultation, which could reveal that the RCEP's impact data is vague. However, the fact that aero engines pollute, and that aviation fuel is favourably treated at present, is incontrovertible; the argument should therefore be not about whether a levy should be imposed but whether the level can be set equitably in relation to taxes on other modes of transport

The Secretary of State then holds a meeting with his junior Minister responsible for environmental protection. They are joined by the three Assistant Secretaries from OCE, EPG and AQD and by the environmental Special Adviser, who has already advised both Ministers that media response to a fuel tax is likely to be favourable. They agree to pursue the idea and the Secretary of State hopes to be allowed to announce the UK's support for an internationally agreed levy at the Summit. The subject is further discussed at the 9am "prayer meeting" at which all DoE Ministers, their Principal Private Secretaries, Special Advisers and the Department's

The political assumption will be that, in contrast with rail or road transport, aviation is not a 'public' issue and that it will therefore be both difficult for the industry to generate much media pressure on the Government and unlikely that the media itself will wish to take a populist stance on the levy.

Head of Information check diaries and discuss issues of the day (once a week, the meeting is treated as "political prayers", without officials but adding the departmental Whip and PPSs and the environment researcher from Conservative Central Office).

Whose work includes drafting Second Reading briefs for backbenchers.

OCE drafts a letter for the Secretary of State to send to his counterparts on the key Cabinet Committee, including Treasury, DoT, DTI, and the Foreign Office (the Summit is a diplomatic occasion). Other copies go to the Cabinet Secretary (the Cabinet Office is running the committee coordinating arrangements for the Summit) the head of the Downing Street Policy Unit and the foreign affairs P/S at No 10. It expands upon the earlier brief by including estimates of Exchequer revenue from a levy at varying levels, calculating demand impacts by reference to Customs & Excise data on the elasticity of demand for air travel. He also drafts a letter for the Secretary of State to send to his ministerial counterparts and to the environment and transport advisers in the Prime Minister's Policy Unit. Such a

On most issues, what the system wants is not broad papers sketching out policy concepts but detailed economic, administrative and legal thinking. Every claim, statement or view that you put to Whitehall and regulatory bodies, local authority and European Commission officials must be fully corroborated. Investing in this level of detail pays dividends; conversely, many submissions are simply filed because they do not address the system's forensic needs. Unless an issue is one where political considerations will override the facts, there is no alternative to thorough research.

wide circulation is common in
Whitehall; indeed, if an issue is
covered by a Cabinet Committee
a paper may be sent to over a
dozen Departments. As far as the
Secretary of State is concerned,
the more he involves other
Departments, the less chance
there is of DoT mounting effective opposition to his idea.

There are a number of telephone
discussions between the G7 in
AQD and his counterparts in
DoT, which is unable to adduce
any evidence to counter the
Royal Commission's conclusions. DoT officials do not tell
airlines about the proposal; nor
do they insist on external consultation. They agree to recommend the DoE line to their
Ministers as the one to follow for
the forthcoming Transport
Council. At this stage, it represents only agreement in principle
since no work has yet started on
models for taxation or likely
yield to the Exchequer.

Issues such as the line to take at
world summits and economic
measures are usually discussed in
Cabinet Committee (domestic-
only taxes are items for the
Budget and are not revealed by

This is not unusual. The system is not proactive on such matters - you have to go to them and ask the right questions if you are to get the information you need

the Treasury to other Departments until the day itself). This matter is covered by ENV, whose membership includes the Deputy Prime Minister, Chancellor, Foreign, Environment, Transport, Trade and Industry and Health Secretaries and 17 other Ministers, in a broader discussion on Kyoto Summit policy introduced by the Environment Secretary. The meeting agrees that there will be no need to announce the policy to the House. However, the Secretary of State's PPS is deputed to take soundings from officers of the Conservative environment and transport committees to see whether there is any risk that the proposed announcement will be unpopular with backbenchers.

The Environment Secretary believes that this is an issue on which he could benefit from publicity. His Private Office calls the Department's Head of Information and the line officials working on the issue, asking for an environment correspondent to be invited in for a briefing. In other circumstances, a press statement would be drafted and its

All Cabinet committees are preceded by a parallel meeting of officials. They produce a "Line To Take" for their Ministers, most of whom have only a peripheral involvement in many of the issues to be discussed. If you cannot make headway with the lead Department on your item, try to find an angle relevant to as many of the others as possible - it may result in an otherwise straightforward decision against you being taken to Cabinet Committee, where the lead Department might be outvoted

Ministers are most sensitive to coverage by political correspondents and Leader writers, largely because their comment is most keenly read by political colleagues. Specialist media is not ignored but it has less lobby potential.

timing would be cleared centrally. On the most political issues,
Ministers or their Special
Advisers brief lobby correspondents and political editors, sometimes privately.

We move forward four months.
Labour has taken over and has
merged the Departments of
Environment and Transport. It
believes that there is still strong
public support for an environmental agenda. On his first day in
office, "First Day Briefs" on this
and many other issues are presented to the Deputy Prime
Minister, who is in charge of the
new Department and, although
he has higher priorities, after
some weeks in which he has
been overruled on a number of
other policy issues, he turns his
attention to the environment as
an area where he can make his
mark. The fuel tax seems to him
to be an easy way to be seen to
be doing something with little
chance of any political repercus-
sions.

It takes the aviation industry a
little time to react to the pre-
Election press coverage: a heavily
regulated sector, it has to deal
first with other Government

*You will need to assess whether a brief on
your industry/sector would be appropriate for
a new Minister's early days; if so, produce
one in two sections:*

- *The XXX industry (facts and figures)·*
- *Key policy issues (regulatory structure, if
any; main concerns)*

related proposals likely to have a shorter term impact on their operations. The airlines do not have access to the documents prepared by officials but they are able to talk to those who drafted them, and three leading carriers ask the G5 who heads AED to arrange a meeting. They have met in advance and conclude:

1.that they should exploit the Royal Commission's indecision about the impact of aircraft emissions

This is designed to buy them some time. They will seek to show that no decision should be made until the impact has been fully assessed and compared with other transport emissions.

2.that they should highlight the fact that if, as the Royal Commission stated, aircraft emissions account for three per cent of all man-made pollution, a tax which might encourage a reduction in some very short haul services would only lead to a cut in the overall emission total by a small fraction of one per cent and that the tax would have to be set at a penal level in order to discourage enough passengers to necessitate the scrapping of a schedule. Against that should be set a possible increase in use of cars to travel domestically or across the Channel

This point will be used in 4.

They will seek to exploit the Government's requirement that regulatory proposals should not proceed if burden is likely to be disproportionate to benefit

3.that they should stress the recent sharp increase in fuel

prices and remind officials of the desulphurisation levy they now have to pay. They seek to show that this is a tax even though the money does not go to Government. They will also remind officials that the introduction of Air Passenger Duty was justified and introduced because aviation fuel was untaxed

4. that they should insist on production of a Regulatory Impact Assessment, a formal requirement of Departments under which the costs to industry of complying with a policy decision or measure are computed and set against the quantified benefits. Ministers are obliged to decide whether the assessed benefits are proportionate to the burdens and the decision to proceed should not be taken unless the "Proportionality Test" is satisfied. The airlines believe that the benefits are so limited that they will be outweighed by any reasonable assessment of costs and revenue impacts.

5. that as a fallback position they should reiterate at the meeting the necessity of the tax being imposed only with worldwide

Regulatory Impact Assessments are an important but underused lobbying weapon. All policy proposals should be accompanied by an comparison between the costs they will impose on business, and on SMEs in particular, and the benefits the proposal will create. Officials are obliged to consult a representative sample within the affected industry or sector in producing them and the assessment must be published

agreement

6. that there is no need for them to commission consultants to second-guess the research used by DETR or to propose a fair level of fuel tax. They suspect that another study could only conclude that if an aviation levy is to achieve its objectives, it must be set high. They believe it would be better in this case to make Ministers aware of the imbalance in cost:benefit both by direct representations and through the media. The latter is a calculated risk – they feel that the Green lobby will have more important things to do than to target them if they publicly claim that the environmental impact of aviation has been overstated and that thousands of UK business travellers could suffer. They do not, however, wish to demand that Government consults formally in case unanticipated evidence emerges that might go against them

Two of the four G5s attend the meeting, plus a G7, and the reasons for the UK's stance are explained to the airlines who have agreed among themselves to

Whitehall normally tries to match the number of outsiders coming to a meeting. The grade of official attending is geared to the breadth of the issue and the status of the visitors.

raise only 1,2,3 and 5. The officials accept that the airlines have information of which they were unaware about the proportion that the shortest haul flights bear to the total, but they suggest to the airlines that these flights are the most damaging since aircraft spend relatively more time climbing and descending through the lower atmosphere. They tell them that although they will take account of the points the airlines have made, they have not been presented with conclusive evidence to justify aviation fuel being untaxed and that the Government intends to seek international agreement to comply with its Rio Summit commitments.

None of this surprises the airlines, who then write to "their" official in AED. She has assured them that she will argue their case with her colleagues but the airlines also send copies direct to them. The letter is not adversarial but it does ask for sight of the Regulatory Assessment (knowing that one has not been prepared) on the grounds that they believe that the decision would have significant impacts on UK airlines. They also make the point that

The dice were cast some time ago. Officials have no alternative at this stage but to stonewall. They know that there is always the risk of the industry seeking to use friends in high places to trump their Minister, but believe that the airlines are unlikely to come up with compelling new evidence to alter the Government's political imperatives.

There is no point in exaggerating or expressing indignation.

How did they know? There was no consultation exercise, and the only time an Assessment can be prepared without one (and then only in outline) is for highly sensitive items such as Budget announcements); and because a very junior official in

Government's decision overlooks the existence of Air Passenger Duty and of the desulphurisation levy.

They decide that there is little point in briefing MPs because this is not a matter of great political significance and there is no realistic prospect of generating enough parliamentary noise (either front of house or in quiet representations to Ministers) to worry the Government. Instead, they use an adviser well known to political correspondents to help them brief the media. The line they sell is that the Government has decided on a new tax on holidays without proper assessment. They preempt the likely rebuttal by telling the selected journalist and *Today* what Government will say about aviation fuel being undertaxed and then giving them bullet points covering the previous Government's statements justifying Air Passenger Duty; fuel price rises; and the levy they already bear.

The Chairmen of a number of UK airlines request a meeting with the Deputy Prime Minister. They are referred to the Aviation Minister but insist on seeing the

Environment Protection Division revealed it in response to an apparently innocent enquiry.

Ignore the emphasis the media places on MPs' views - they are simply the easiest part of the system for journalists to access. Take a realistic view on who will carry influence on each issue.

It pays to inure the media to Government's (or your opponents') likely response by getting your retaliation in firs

senior Minister, whose Private Office relents on grounds of the businessmen's seniority (and concern that they might complain to the PM) and allows them 45 minutes. They ensure that at least 48 hours beforehand Private Office and line officials are sent a clear agenda covering the items they intend to raise and they call the latter to ensure that the brief officials will prepare for the meeting accurately reflects the industry's case and data. At the meeting, to which one chairman and two chief executives come, the Deputy Prime Minister is surrounded by the Aviation Minister, the G3 who heads Aviation Directorate, the AED G5, the Chief Economist and one of the two EPG and AQD G5s who have been dealing with the fuel tax. There is also a minute taker from Private Office. The officials have prepared a two page brief for Ministers and spend ten minutes before the meeting taking them through it. They have done some more digging since meeting the airlines and have unearthed two studies which suggest that aircraft emissions have a quantifiable pollution impact. They have also

The status rule applies here. The top people in large organisations are dealt with by more senior officials.

Minutes can, of course, say what the Department wants them to say, so never go to such meetings alone. Very rarely is there a dispute about what was said, but if there is you must make sure that you have a witness to your account of events.

compared the fuel tax burden borne by road, rail, shipping and aviation. They tell Ministers that a Regulatory Assessment is being produced, feeling safer in the light of their new information, and the Deputy Prime Minister's view is that the airlines are unable to come up with any new pegs on which to hang further media coverage. The airlines are experienced enough to know that they should take up no more than seven minutes in presenting their case to the two Ministers – they want as much time as possible to be devoted to Government explaining itself (and their 45 minutes may be squeezed to 35 because Ministers often run late). What they hear is a concession on the regulatory assessment and an assurance that the UK would seek a low level of tax; but also a clear comparison in tax burdens that they will have some difficulty in dismissing. They also suspect that Ministers could easily mobilise the road and rail lobby against them.

It is most likely that the outcome of this case will be determined by three factors: timing; bigger issues and the nature of the subject. Because Ministers

Unless you are seeking a private ministerial meeting through the Minister's PPS or another backbench MP because you are being blocked further down the Department, ask their Private Office which officials will be attending and brief the junior one on your organisation and the issues you wish to raise. The brief prepared by G7s and HEOs for such meetings will give details of the lobbyist, its case and the line to take are summarised. Always contact those officials and ask whether they have all the information they need. Keeping your case a secret until the day usually leads to sterile meetings; and discussion can reveal the other side's rebuttal for you to counter. If you cannot influence officials' brief for the Minister, you are unlikely to influence him.

The seven minutes (or less) rule is very important. You are unlikely to get a second chance and if you fill up the meeting with your 'presentation' you allow the Minister to listen, tell you it was interesting and go to the next one content that you have not put him on the spot. Furthermore, assume that although officials will note everything, only one or two points will be remembered by the Minister. Do not enter the room with a long agenda.

had already committed themselves before the airlines found
out about the Government's
plans; because the Government
knew it would very publicly be
on the hook over its progress in
implementing the Rio commitments (aviation was just a dispen-
sible victim within the larger
agenda); and because it became
almost impossible to turn the
lobby into any more than one
day's media embarrassment for
the Government (and only a
minor story at that; furthermore,
the Opposition could not exploit
it because this was their policy
too) the lobbyists' chances were
always likely to be slim.

This case may seem complex, but it is a reasonably typical example of
the way the system makes policy decisions. What lessons can be drawn
from it?

- First, the balance between Ministers and their advisers. Ministers
  may set broad political parameters, but control of content is largely the province of officials or policy-geared Special Advisers.
  Pressure or friends in high places can get you a ministerial meeting or make the system look twice at a marginal case but it rarely
  forces the system to set aside (what it sees as) a compelling argument.

  This is perhaps the most frequently misunderstood and misrep-
  resented aspect of lobbying; and in truth it can be difficult to judge
  when it is necessary and appropriate to seek to take a case to
  Ministers. Four further examples may help to explain the balance
  of power:

TAKE IT TO THE TOP?

"A smallish engineering company wanted ECGD cover in order safely to tender for a Tunisian export contract. It contacted ECGD, who told it that cover for Tunisia was 'exceptional'. Assuming that this meant insurance would not be available, the MD wrote a furious letter to the Prime Minister complaining that the British export drive was being thwarted. The PM's correspondence secretaries followed normal procedure in sending the letter to DTI and ECGD. The junior official, who knew that 'exceptional' simply meant that special conditions would be imposed and therefore saw no reason to criticise ECGD, produced a draft reply which, because the PM was involved, was approved by senior officials and sent back to No 10. By the time the MD received the letter telling him what he could have found out by talking to the right organisation instead of unnecessarily trying to bring political pressure to bear, the tender deadline had passed."

Former DTI Deputy Secretary

If the company had met, say, the Prime Minister's Political Secretary at a reception and she had offered to help, the same circuit would have been followed. She could not risk wading in without "calling for papers", which would be produced by the same officials and would still suggest that there is no problem. In other words, unless you can get to the root of the problem at source, it may serve little purpose to use politicians or senior officials as unblockers. However, if you have followed the "correct" route and are still getting nowhere because officials are either demonstrably uncooperative, unreasonably slow or misleading in their responses, MPs and sympathetic Special Advisers can help. You do have to be sure of your ground, though: allegations of delay, obfuscation or sharp practice will always reach the people about whom you complain, limiting your chances of future cooperation if you may need it.

Metadioxin

While all *Yes Minister* scripts offer excellent - and in the main minutely accurate accounts - of the reality of decision-making within Whitehall, this example is perhaps the clearest in showing how technical and political factors interrelate. With apologies to the authors for the poor summary, the plot of the Metadioxin case went like this:

The British Chemicals Corporation proposes a significant expansion of its Merseyside factory to manufacture Propanol, which contains Metadioxin, an inert compound which sounds like Dioxin, the chemical released in the serious Seveso incident some years ago, but which is considered by scientists to be harmless. The factory was under threat and the saving of jobs and the promise of export orders makes this seem like a good news story. Just to be absolutely sure that public concerns will be allayed, Whitehall commissions an independent scientific assessment of Propanol; the report will soon be published.

WORKING THE INTER-DEPARTMENTAL NET

Glasgow-based Yummee Sausages is one of only five sausage casing manufacturers in the UK; the others are all foreign-based. Yummee has 85% of the home market and it wishes to take over one of its competitors in order to expand in the US. Because of the size of the deal, the high market share and the removal of a competitor in the UK, OFT is examining the case. Yummee believes it has good arguments to explain its dominance and to show that the market is competitive and will remain so.

Instead of relying only on its representations to OFT, it also targets the Scottish Executive, seeking to persuade officials to support Scottish industry, and the Ministry of Agriculture, which has oversight of food manufacturing and which would be relied upon by OFT to provide it with a neutral assessment of the extent of competition in the UK sausage casing market.

Finally, Yummee seeks to direct its leading customers towards OFT and MAFF if they are unconcerned about the implications of the deal. OFT respects the views of other Departments, believing them to be more objective than those of the parties to any deal, and it is also influenced by supplier and customer opinion.

The constituency MP (who happens to be the Prime Minister's PPS) hears rumours about BCC's plans. She seeks assurances from the Minister that Propanol is safe. He believes that environmental groups only represent a few votes in her constituency. She reminds him that the seat is marginal.

Suddenly, the Minister is worried. What if Propanol turns out not to be safe after all?

The Propanol scheme leaks to environmental pressure groups. The TV news broadcasts feature mothers demonstrating outside the plant and talking about risks to children etc. Although the advance draft of the independent assessment agrees that Metadioxin is safe, the Minister takes issue with Sir Humphrey: "it's harmless chemically, but dynamite politically." Political considerations dictate that the report is buried and the project cancelled.

The political trigger points that overcome pure reason are clear in this case. Had *Yes Minister* been written today, Metadioxin might well have been transformed into genetically modified foods, where Ministers have recognised that there is no point in flying in the face of public fears regardless of their foundation, or the Brent Spar case, which taught lobbyists the importance of inuring the system, and those that might influence it, to trouble ahead. Government does not react well to surprises: forewarn officials, Special Advisers, and constituency MPs if you are about to make a sensitive announcement or if a potentially difficult issue is likely to be the subject of a forthcoming campaign against your interests or could otherwise feature in the media. While confidential information given to Departments or DGs will be treated as such, MPs may leak but it is still possible to tell them of closures, restructuring plans and takeover bids a few minutes before public statements are made (if possible, call their offices the day before to establish a fax or telephone number on which contact can definitely be made when necessary. If a number of MPs or MEPs are involved, use commercial multifax facilities to ensure that the message reaches everyone at the same time.

Kingston Telecoms

Hull is the only part of the UK with its own telephone system. The company, which was owned by the local authority, wanted to be privatised. But pure financial considerations would not decide the issue. The local authority was opposed, and the support of central Government would be determined as much by the Department of Trade and Industry's view of whether Kingston Telecoms would be more effective in the public sector, or even the Trade and Industry Secretary's own views, as by the fact that the Deputy Prime Minister represented one of the Hull constituencies and his Department had the power to licence the local authority to run a telephone system. On the other hand, political enthusiasm would have been effectively countered by reports from departmental officials and the telecoms regulator that Kingston Telecoms was not financially strong enough to maintain customer service as a plc.

<hr>

TECHNIQUES MUST FIT THE ISSUE

A proposed merger between two major airlines was being considered by the UK and Brussels competition authorities. A competitor made all the usual detailed submissions to officials and Ministers but also decided to take a series of full page advertisements in the national papers to set out its case for tough restrictions to be placed on the deal.

What were they seeking to achieve?
- *Pressure on officials? They already had a lengthy dossier from the company and were not going to learn anything new from the advert. If new facts had been included, officials would have wondered why they had not been told through the usual channels.*
- *Pressure on Ministers? The issue was not one likely to attract public interest and the chances of the ad. generating a volume of powerful letters to Ministers were slim.*
- *To promote themselves? If so, why not just advertise their company? In another case, a leading vehicle manufacturer with a strong safety image hired consultants to help it tell MPs and others how safe it was. What was the point? In the eyes of its targets the company had nothing to prove.*

<hr>

Medical devices company

A medical equipment manufacturer has developed a new test kit that could save the NHS considerable treatment costs. However, such items have to be subjected to a testing process before the Department of Health will allow GPs to be reimbursed for using them, and for reasons unknown to the manufacturer it cannot get the system to review the kit. The company secures a meeting with the Health Secretary through its constituency MP. The meeting is attended by a series of officials, who pre-brief the Minister on the product and the process through which it would have to go. The way they put it, it all sounds quite reasonable and the company is just making a fuss. They advise him to be non-committal since it would be wrong for him to prejudge the outcome of an approval process that is meant to be free of political interference; and in any event he lacks the technical knowledge to make such decisions.

The company gives a first class presentation, clearly explaining the product's cost effectiveness. The Secretary of State is clearly impressed and the company leaves his office convinced that it has made a breakthrough. Unfortunately, officials always have a short debriefing session with Ministers following such meetings. They reiterate that the product's merits still have to be evaluated fully and that to make an exception by agreeing to a shortcut would create a potentially difficult precedent. Although the Secretary of State is able to insist that the kit be regarded as desirable in principle, he dare not substitute his judgement for the specialist knowledge of the experts. The company has won political favour but it is still at Square One.

If you are genuinely blocked by the system, either in negotiation or in finding out how things work, contact the Minister's PPS (if he has one) or your constituency MP and ask them to raise the problem with the Minister privately. However, you must be absolutely sure that you need to go over officials' heads, because when the Minister asks for a brief from officials - as he will do, because he will not take an MP's third party account as gospel - it will look convincing. You must therefore anticipate and preempt that brief and show that the issue of concern to you cannot be resolved, wholly or partly, at official level. If Ministers rather than officials are the barrier - for example where a decision really depends on them and they refuse to consult you, and in particular where several Ministers with conflicting views are involved in an issue - the Prime Minister's Policy Unit can intervene effectively.

• The emphasis on detailed research. Think of the system as a three legged stool (Parliament, public/media opinion, advisers,). Your aim is either to remove those supports for an unacceptable policy or to get them to support your replacement idea. You can only tackle the Civil Service leg by providing them with better information than they can command and by anticipating and preempting their "ah, but..." responses. Officials will not only ignore poorly argued cases; they will have less respect for you if you have to deal with them on another issue. Winning arguments, other than in the relatively few instances of largely political decisions, can be expensive not because of the amount of lobbying activity in which you may have to engage but because it pays to use respected (meaning respected by

A GENUINE BLOCKAGE

TRADE AND INDUSTRY DEPARTMENT SEEKS TO AVOID CONFLICT OF INTEREST WITH COMPANIES INVOLVED IN BIDS

DTI accused of closing doors to companies

David Wighton, Political Correspondent

Some of Britain's leading companies have complained to Downing Street about a clampdown on access to Department of Trade and Industry ministers and officials following Stephen Byers' appointment as secretary of state last month.

Companies say they have been told they cannot meet DTI ministers or officials to discuss any issue if they are involved in a bid in the UK or abroad. Those affected so far are understood to include British Telecommunications, Vodafone, Scottish Power and National Grid.

One company was so surprised at being denied a meeting it appealed to Downing Street, which knew nothing about the new ban and demanded the company be seen by a DTI minister.

"If strictly applied, this would mean most companies could not talk to the DTI about anything. This hardly fits in with the government's claim to be open and business friendly," said one executive.

The clampdown is believed to have been agreed by Mr Byers after competition policy officials stressed the need to avoid any perceived conflict with his quasi-judicial role in merger decisions.

A colleague of Mr Byers confirmed he was anxious to avoid giving "ammunition" to John Redwood, the Conservatives' industry spokesman, who waged a campaign against Peter Mandelson, Mr Byers' predecessor.

Some senior DTI officials have told companies they are unhappy about the move. Insiders say it has further undermined department morale following Mr Mandelson's resignation last month. "Mandelson's drive and enthusiasm gave the department the new sense of purpose it needed. It is early days, but Byers is seen as much more cautious and conservative," said one official.

The DTI said that there had been no change in the official guidelines on access for companies involved in bids subject to the UK competition authorities. These bar meetings with either the secretary of state or the competition minister. In theory, it applies to any bid notified to the Office of Fair Trading, even if it is overseas.

The DTI denied companies' claims they were now being barred from meeting officials in the DTI's "sponsorship" divisions dealing with particular industries such as telecommunications or electricity. "They must have got the wrong end of the stick," said one official.

DTI sponsorship officials are understood to be unhappy companies that remain free to talk to other departments, such as the Treasury. British Aerospace executives claim to have had trouble meeting DTI defence industry officials following its proposed purchase of GEC's Marconi. But the companies briefed officials at the Ministry of Defence and met the prime minister, before the deal was announced.

(Financial Times, 30 January 1999) For the result, see the next box

the system – if in doubt, ask them for advice) economists, lawyers, environmental consultants and other experts to produce or give an imprimatur to your submissions. And reports by independent organisations can also be newsworthy.

NAMING AND SHAMING

We concentrate in this book on techniques of reaching solutions by working with the system wherever possible. But there are times when Ministers or officials refuse to meet you or where apparently constructive proposals are rejected. Only experience will tell you whether taking the gloves off would persuade Government to listen or act as a deal-breaker; but there will be times when you need to use the media to complain about high-handedness or obtuseness. The system is highly sensitive to suggestions that it has failed to consult, that it has blocked access or that ideas that appear to be in the public interest have been ignored.

The FT piece in the previous box is a good example of a well-judged briefing of a respected Lobby correspondent. A week later, the same journalist reported that

"Stephen Byers, the trade and industry secretary, has ordered the DTI to maintain an open-door policy towards companies involved in bids, amid concern about a crackdown on access to ministers and officials.

Mr Byers has made it clear there should be no tightening of rules designed to avoid potential conflicts with the DTI's role in scrutinising merger decisions."

It can work, but the tactic must be carefully measured.

• The importance of getting in early and of spending as much time as possible on monitoring the system (see Monitoring Checklist, p.286) even though you may not feel you have a problem at the time. As the example shows, once policy emerges it is likely to have been considered in some depth. You may either be presented with a done deal or by a consultation exercise which in most cases is only designed to ask you what tyres you want on a car that has already been built. Those who seek to influence the questions asked during consultation usually do best. It is not always easy to follow this advice: you may have more pressing priorities and may not have the resources to keep on top of policy planning all the time.

LOBBYING THROUGH THE MEDIA

Politicians see relatively few newspapers and see or hear even fewer programmes. The key media are

- *political correspondents, commentators or Leader Writers - the articles politicians read first*
- *The Times (and the Scotsman and Glasgow Herald in Scotland and Western Mail in Cardiff)*
- *Daily Mail - thought to have a line to Middle England and to women*
- *Sunday Times - only time they have to read a paper thoroughly*
- *Sun - seen as a line to the CDEs*
- *Today programme (and Scotland Today - sets agendas*
- *World at One - Ministers may listen to it in the car just before lunch*
- *Evening Standard - Ministers read it on their way to meetings. And because the Scottish Parliament closes at 5.30pm, the Edinburgh Evening News can run reports at the end of each day.*
- *GMTV - Prime Minister's early morning favourite*
- *Breakfast with Frost - long enough to preclude sound bites and allow political debate on Sunday*
- *Ceefax - viewed by Ministers and in their Private and Information offices*

- There are times when you may have to acknowledge that you cannot achieve all your objectives because Government's political initiative is so strong. Always, therefore, consider your strategy in terms of options, with one being mitigation of damage. Officials like to give Ministers alternatives to consider and the system does not respond well to 'There Is No Alternative' lobbying. In the above case, the industry's fallback arguments (agreement only on a worldwide basis; low level of tax) would have been adopted anyway, but as a general principle Government will often negotiate provided a compromise is not likely to be seen by others as a climbdown.

- Government is always conscious of the way the media will react but in most cases it feels it is better than outsiders at managing PR. It also knows that in only a few instances is an issue sufficiently newsworthy for its profile to be raised to an uncomfortable level (example: the Government needs legislation in order to restructure and reduce electricity prices. Drafting has fallen behind and there is a risk that the Bill may miss the Queen's Speech. Public exposure by a heavyweight lobby correspondent of the risk that prices may not be reduced will usually galvanise the system into meeting its deadline). Only experience will tell but, where a story could be made to run, try to find an angle that will interest the Lobby and concentrate on the (surprisingly few) outlets to which the system is sensitive. Do not underestimate the need for stamina: it may take a stream of items over several months to have any effect.

The passage of UK, Scottish, Welsh and Northern Ireland legislation and regulation

Before considering the process of evolving, drafting, passing and campaigning on legislative or regulatory changes, four basic principles need to be highlighted:

- While the Queen's Speech is always full of Bills and new regulation is being tabled daily, governments will only legislate if a less time-consuming option is unavailable. The preference is a policy decision; if that is not possible, secondary legislation (Regulations or Orders made under existing statutory powers). Only where completely new powers are needed will primary legislation (Bills) be considered.
- Departments have a stock of pet proposals (either their own or recommended by the Law Commission) which officials may present to new Ministers year after year - you should similarly not expect to succeed first time. There is also considerable competition between Departments for space in the annual legislative programme and many proposals are rejected. Departments will have a notional quota, so it is almost impossible for, say, the Home Office to be allowed five Bills in a year. You either have to displace the Government's own priorities (by giving it something it will see as offering greater advantage) or give it no alternative but to do

something about your issue (this is very rare and only really applies to responses to exceptional circumstances - firearms or dangerous dogs bans, for example).

- Furthermore, the passage of most measures takes a long time. Ideas are fed into the system, considered internally, consulted upon, turned into White Papers, turned into draft Bills or regulations by the draftsmen and put through the usual parliamentary stages. While it is possible on rare occasions for all this to be compressed into a few days, the process of seduction, conception, gestation and birth is more likely to take at least two to three years. It is not surprising, therefore, that lobbyists are always advised to deal with the system early, on the basis that it is harder to correct an error than to prevent it from happening. For example, although Whitehall issues many proposals for public consultation, by that stage officials and Ministers have often decided what they want to do and only need to know whether they have missed anything. The advantage is held more by the organisations which seek to influence the questions than by those who only provide answers. Similarly, it is very difficult to amend Bills and Regulations once they have been published: by then, four fifths of the process has been completed and only minor points or technical errors are likely to be considered.

- In seeking to influence the system, whether on policy or legislation/regulation, bear in mind the two types of lobbying:

Advocacy-led lobbying, based on careful case-assembly and quiet representations or negotiations. Appropriate in the bulk of cases, particularly where the issue is technical, complex, unlikely to attract political concern or where public debate could be counter-productive; or

Pressure-based lobbying, which seeks to harness and direct public opinion towards Government. Relevant if Government does not want to act (or is determined to do so and you need to stop it), if the issue could be politically sensitive and if it is newsworthy.

Always look to the first before you consider the second: you are more likely to get your way by talking to people than by shouting at them, and lobbies which start with pressure techniques may find themselves in a trench war that can only be won by attrition. There may of course be no alternative - many pressure groups depend for their effectiveness on campaigning by bringing to the public's attention issues which they want to move up the political agenda.

In our second case history we seek to show how primary and secondary legislation is produced and how outsiders can shape it.

Telecommunications masts

ComCo UK relays services for radio and telecoms operators through 120 masts across the country. Originally a nationalised industry, it was privatised in 1994 and although it is no longer a monopoly provider it is regulated by Oftel and the Radiocommunications Agency under powers contained in the Wireless Telegraphy, Broadcasting and Telecommunications Acts. It plans to use its UK sites to expand into direct provision of information superhighway services and at the same time to move into relay provision in Eastern Europe and Russia.

ComCo's relationship with its regulators has always been a difficult one. They have indicated that they will wish to examine any diversification on the basis that their powers allow it to regulate ComCo "in the provision of telecommunications network services" and because it has a duty to ensure that ComCo invests adequately in provision of relay facilities.

ComCo feels that the regulator should only be able to cover its core business and its bankers are concerned that a perception of regulatory risk may increase the cost of the funding required to implement the expansion programme. It therefore decides that the powers of the regulators must be clarified.

Alongside this issue, four others have to be considered:

• The Government has for some time been considering reform of competition law to incorporate Treaty of Rome principles into UK legislation. ComCo and the other privatised utilities see this as an opportunity to secure changes to regulators' powers to deal with

IDENTIFYING AND CONTACTING OFFICIALS AND
SPECIAL ADVISERS

First, work out which Department or Brussels DG will have responsibility for the issue in question. There may be more than one, or day-to-day work may be handled by an agency, with officials only acting as a liaison point for Ministers, but whichever body you contact should be able to direct you to the lead Department or to the one that responsible for your matter.

Telephone numbers and addresses are available from the Civil Service Yearbook (at the time of writing, counterparts for Scotland, Wales and Northern Ireland had not yet been published) Vacher's European Companion or from the European Commission offices in the UK (for details see p.177). The published guides do not list every official, and although some UK Departments make their full functional and telephone directories available at a small cost, the numbers and names frequently change. Furthermore, officials assume you have telepathic knowledge of the extension you want; they are notoriously reluctant to transfer calls if you have dialled the wrong number - and it is often far from easy to work out where to go; and transfers often result in the line going dead. You may therefore have no option but to ring the main switchboard number and ask for Enquiries. The Yearbook lists enquiry points for every Division, but they are often unmanned or staffed at a very junior level. Avoid them unless you have no option.

Do not assume that all decisions are made at the top. If you need information or seek to make representations, the most productive entry point is at Grade 5 or 7 (A 5-7 in Brussels) level - usually the latter. Ask for the "head of the section dealing with XYZ". Only go higher on the biggest issues.

A first meeting with officials should normally take place in their Department, although it may be relevant for them to come to you if, for example, it is important that they see something or meet a team of people. Do not seek to entertain them on first contact. Special Advisers are at the beck and call of their Ministers and may have to break a meeting to run down the corridor at any time. It is safer to try and meet them on Fridays, when their masters may be in their constituencies.

It helps to send a brief before the meeting: if you seek to surprise them they will either check their files afterwards or, if the issue is unfamiliar to them, take longer to understand you. However, if you are targeting Special Advisers because you have made no progress with officials, it may be preferable to leave detail to the meeting itself; they normally "call for papers" from officials, who would then be alerted to your meeting over their heads, if they are aware of the subject. Better to condition them before they get the system's version.

anticompetitive behaviour.

- DTI is also considering a review of utility regulation with the likelihood that legislation will be produced within two years. Terms of reference have not yet been announced but the Minister's ideas were trailed in Opposition. ComCo had a number of pre-Election meetings with him and his adviser to ascertain his thinking and to give him views on relaxation of supervision in its sector.
- Furthermore, it is widely recognised in the industry that new technology has blurred the distinction between telecommunications and broadcasting and another review, this time of communications policy, has been talked about, with the likelihood that it will be lengthy and that consequent legislation may not be in place for almost three years. ComCo was among those who had lobbied Opposition spokesmen and their advisers to support a review and this issue was mentioned in a pre-Election party policy document. The matter had been considered by the then Government through a multi-media task force, although ComCo's expansion plan was not drafted until shortly before the Election.
- Lastly, a number of environmental groups have objected to ComCo's siting of new relay masts in areas of natural beauty. MPs have raised these concerns with Ministers and protests by local communities have been covered on Today and Newsnight and in the Sunday papers.

ComCo believes that it has three options:

- To seek clarification of the regulators' powers in the forthcoming Competition Bill.
- To seek inclusion of the regulators in the review of utility regulation with the aim of securing a delineation of powers by secondary legislation (the relevant sections of the legislation allow the Secretary of State to make changes "by Order".)
- To do the same in the context of the communications review.

Before we consider ComCo's strategy, we will run through the procedure and timescales for legislation on competition. We have simplified the process in some places.

1. Decision on whether something needs to be done. Influenced by views from internal (Office of Fair Trading, Competition Commission, DTI Competition Policy Division) or unsolicited - expressed at informal meetings or following a difficult or controversial policy decision - outside (lawyers and their bodies, academics, companies, European Commission) sources. Alternatively, new Governments may insist that the system works on manifesto commitments.

Either the DTI Secretary of State or Corporate Affairs Minister would initiate a meeting with the head of Competition Policy Directorate or officials would produce a paper for Ministers to consider. The input to this might be discussed casually with, for example, the Law Society, the CBI, National Consumer Council, departmental advisory committee or companies, all of which Ministers and senior officials would be expected to meet in

You can make your case for legislative change before the system has taken any action by

- *Sending a submission to the head (G3/5) of the relevant unit, coupled with a request for a meeting*
- *(if the issue has a clear political element) to Ministers through either their Party research department desk officer or their Special Advisers.*

It helps to have the support of a trade association, representative body or (if one exists for the issue in question) a Departmental advisory committee.

105

the course of their work. The factors to be covered at this stage are.

- How deficient is current provision?
- What are the broad options for addressing the deficiency?
- Who is likely to benefit or be damaged by those options?
- Can we do anything (eg EC legal constraints)?
- Will we need primary or secondary legislation? (Secondary legislation is always preferable – it need not be included in the Queen's Speech and takes up very little parliamentary time)
- Likely timescale (Bills covering complex legal issues may take many months to consult upon and draft before they get to Parliament. In this case, 18 months of preparation are anticipated)
- Will other Departments be involved? (Complicates matters)
- Will it cost anything? (Treasury will have to be persuaded) In the case of competition law, it is decided that there needs to be greater consistency between EC and UK principles; that the bulk of

If you seek to propose new legislation, you will have to cover these areas. Officials in London and Brussels apply what we call The Standard Whitehall (and Commission) Test to proposals submitted by outsiders:

- *Can these ideas be made to work? How?*
- *What is wrong with them?*
- *Yes, they are good, but will they be squeezed by a weight of countervailing opinion (eg the Big Battalions?)*
- *They have told us what is wrong with our new policy proposals, but have forgotten that we have publicly committed ourselves to take action. Do they have a constructive and workable alternative?*

Much better, therefore, for you to preempt that test by doing it yourself. Your aim should be to put yourself in the position of being able to say "There is no reason for these proposals not to be accepted", or alternatively "There are good reasons for not changing the status quo.

legal practitioners and large corporations to whom Ministers and officials have spoken favour this (albeit that "legal" Bills usually involve lengthy argument about fine detail); that the changes needed are sufficiently fundamental to require a Bill rather than Orders; and that other Departments (apart from the Scottish Executive and the Welsh and Northern Ireland Offices, which have to be consulted on anything affecting their territories) will not be involved. However officials (including the Department's lawyers, who will be closely involved on such a Bill) advise that the Bill should apply to the utility regulators (which do not include the Radiocomms Agency) since they have the power to act to promote competition. As insiders, the regulators will be closely consulted alongside the OFT and the Competition Commission.

2. Having gathered informal views, the Secretary of State seeks policy approval by writing to his colleagues on the

relevant Cabinet Committee. DTI then has two options: to produce a "Green Paper", setting out the problem, suggesting options for change and inviting comments; or to seek views on a draft Bill. The latter is rare but is more appropriate here since officials acknowledge that in this area considerable drafting expertise lies outside Government and that the real discussion is likely to cover interpretation rather than concepts. However, since legislation is drafted by Parliamentary Counsel, who work outside the Department, permission to brief the draftsmen must be sought from the Queen's Speech and Future Legislation Cabinet Committee

A team in Competition Policy Directorate (typically one G5, one or two G7s, three junior staff and two lawyers) is assigned to the Bill. A memorandum is produced for the Parliamentary Counsel setting out the principles, powers and other elements that will have to be included. To the draft Bill is added several pages of background comments and

While Parliamentary Counsel are unlobbyable, the content of the memorandum from the Department can be critical. Organisations have found that an agreement reached during consultation is not reflected in the Bill because the brief to the draftsman was changed at the last minute.

requests for comments on specific issues.

The system does not want to be tripped up by suggestions that it has failed to consult significant sectors of interests, so Ministers may trail the document in speeches to trade associations. Officials prepare a consultation list covering every relevant organisation of which they are aware and will usually send copies to trade publications.

They will always include you if you ask them.

As expected, a large number of comments are received and a revised draft Bill is sent out. (However, in most cases a Green Paper would be followed by a White Paper, in which firm intentions are stated - it may be debated in the Commons)

Officials usually summarise responses at all stages in the form of a grid. In responding to consultation proposals, produce a summary sheet to make officials' task easier for them. They may choose to put your summary into Ministers' Red Boxes as an example of views received.

3. In December of that year, DTI submits its preliminary bids for legislative slots to the Cabinet Office. It is felt that the Bill will be ready by the next autumn and that it is sufficiently important for DTI to include in its shopping list for the April meeting of the Future Legislation Group, the Cabinet Committee that

decides on Queen's Speech priorities and sanctions drafting of the Bill itself. Further meetings are held in September and October. Although Ministers and the Bill Team, as the group of officials dealing with the project are now known, continue to be lobbied heavily over the Summer, the system becomes increasingly resistant to change as the final two FLG meetings approach. FLG also decides on whether Bills should start in the Commons or Lords. Business has to be split between both Houses to avoid overload, and it is often considered that Bills likely to attract many amendments should start in the Lords. Because of the mass of legal detail, this is one such.

4. The Bill Team now has four main tasks:

• To agree a date for parliamentary introduction of the Bill, known as First Reading, and to discuss a provisional date for Second Reading, a major debate in which the principles of the Bill are covered and the clauses are outlined

Bear in mind that unless you are a major player yourself, your views - no matter how sensible - may be ignored if they conflict with those of the big boys.

If the story could be newsworthy to the media to which the system responds (see LOBBYING THROUGH THE MEDIA, p. 99), take it to them; or use your constituency MP(s) to take your points to Ministers but bear in mind the importance of proving that the greater good is served by your ideas rather than those on the table. If a proposal could have an impact on you that has not been anticipated, use the Regulatory Impact Assessment rules (see box, p. 162) to make officials consider it.

Your proposals must be timed to match the legislative calendar. Keep an eye on this by staying in contact with the Bill Team. If you need to brief MPs or Peers, you will want as much notice as possible.

• To ensure that the Bill is printed on time. They are normally published just after First Reading

• To draft Ministers' speeches opening and closing the Second Reading debate and to prepare files with answers to all the points likely to be raised by Opposition spokesmen and backbenchers

• To produce Notes on Clauses, an explanatory memorandum for Committee Stage, which follows Second Reading.

These are made available to any MP or Peer and usually to outsiders on request. They are useful because they contain the system's view on purposes and interpretation of each clause.

5. At Second Reading, the Minister or Government spokesman in the Lords introduces the Bill and takes the House through its clauses in outline. The Opposition spokesmen respond and there is then time for around 15 Peers to speak before another Government spokesman winds up by replying to comments made during the debate (the same procedure is followed in Commons, except that MPs vote on the Bill whereas Peers do not. In only one case in recent history - Sunday Trading - has a Bill been voted down at Second

Reading. Nonetheless, by tradition account must be taken of the "mood of the House" in the Lords).

MPs and Peers use Second Reading:

•   to make broad comments for or against the Bill. These can be discounted

•   to raise specific points on behalf of outsiders, in some cases because they want to be considered for a place on the Standing Committee. They may indicate that they will seek to table amendments at Committee or later stages

6. There are normally two sitting weekends (ie excluding parliamentary holidays) between stages. After Second Reading, two things happen:

•   If the Bill is in the Commons, the Committee of Selection meets immediately to appoint a Standing Committee. In practice, the Whips decide this (for composition of Commons committees, see p. 27).

•   Amendments are tabled, by any Peer in the Lords but only by members of the Standing Committee in the

Meaning that if you can get a number of respected Peers to advocate your case on a cross-party basis, there is some chance that Government may agree to look again at the arguments.

If you need to lobby during a Bill's parliamentary stages, contact MPs or Peers with relevant interests (see below how ComCo did it) well in advance to see whether they are interested in your case and willing to speak on your behalf at Second Reading and to put themselves forward for Commons Standing Committee (in the Lords, Committee stage is open to any Peer).

MPs with relevant paid outside interests are likely to be excluded.

112

Commons. They take the following form:

The Lord Jimmy
Baroness Nargs

You may want to show that your amendment has broad support by finding two or more sponsors across the House.

Clause 14, page 11, after line 4, insert

Bills have numbered lines.

"(6) The Secretary of State, before exercising his powers under this section, shall consult the body or bodies specified in section 21."

Always use quotation marks to define the amendment

Amendments can be disallowed if they are improperly drafted or if it is decided that another covering the same subject with better wording is to be preferred.

Standing Committees cannot amend a Bill such that its main principles are destroyed: those will have been agreed at Second Reading.

As soon as the amendments are down, officials prepare detailed rebuttals for Ministers and the Government Whips assess whether there is likely to be any strength of support for them. This is now academic in the Commons because the Government side dwarfs the Opposition, but defeats are possible in the Lords, although reduction in the number of hereditary peers entitled to participate and vote in debate will make this less likely.

You will need the support of the Opposition Party Whips and of several Peers across the House who are prepared to speak and to persuade their colleagues to be present and to vote for you.

Amendments may be tabled for three reasons

• Most obviously, to seek a change in the Bill. This will require either a concession from the Government, which is only likely if there has been a drafting error or a key issue has been overlooked or mis-understood, or a defeat in a vote.

Government will usually itself table several amendments to correct drafting errors; these are the easiest to get accepted.

• For probing purposes, designed to elicit an explana-tion or assurance from Government.

You may only need to persuade one MP or Peer to raise your point, but it helps to give notice to the Department beforehand.

• As a matter of propriety, where Government has agreed in negotiations to look again at an issue but needs a formal prompt in the House. It may then table its own amendment at a later stage.

Government may still need to see that the issue is of concern to several respected MPs and Peers before it agrees to this. Direct rep-resentations outside the Chamber by former Ministers and accepted experts will help.

• There is a further reason; to delay debate on other amendments to which excep-tion has been taken; but in our view this is unethical.

At Committee Stage in both Houses, the clauses are taken in order. In the Commons, once all amend-ments on a clause have been taken it is also possible to debate broader issues under a procedure called "Clause

Bear in mind that tabling an amendment involves quite a commitment for a Peer - apart from speaking to it, the amendment's sponsor should by convention be present when the Minister winds up. On major issues this could be some hours.

Stand Part" in which time is allowed before the Committee votes on whether the clause should stand as part of the Bill. Amendments only have a realistic chance of success if they have been negotiated in advance with the Department but clarifications are often given. Nonetheless, you should take the view that once a Bill is in Parliament it is hard to change: the Government's aim is to keep to its timetable and it can always use its Commons majority to get its way.

Accept that if you have already received a firm No on the record, you are unlikely to get Government to change its mind in the House unless you can marshall massive media and parliamentary pressure. Only one amendment in 20, other than those tabled by Government itself, succeeds.

7. Most amendments are withdrawn by their sponsors following the Government's response in Committee, not because the explanation is satisfactory (it rarely is) but because if an amendment is pressed to a vote and is defeated, the issue cannot be raised again at the final two stages, Report and Third Reading. In the Lords, these are little different from Committee Stage; in the Commons, they are taken in the Chamber and any MP can participate. At the conclusion of the Bill, the Commons considers, and

On a very contentious Bill, Report Stage may take two days; on the other hand, if there are few amendments Report Stage and Third Reading may be combined. As a Bill reaches its later stages and the timetable tightens, the chances of the Government giving way on amendments shrink appreciably.

usually votes down, any amendments (other than those agreed by the Government) made in the Lords.

8. Most primary legislation contains "enabling" powers, meaning that the Act, instead of setting out precise powers, rights and duties, gives power to Ministers to do so in secondary legislation (Regulations and Orders). As we mentioned, the Radiocommunications Act contains such powers, and implementing Regulations are often drafted (by departmental lawyers rather than Parliamentary Counsel, possibly with the assistance of one of the many departmental advisory committees) while the originating Bill is proceeding through Parliament. Since MPs and Peers distrust clauses that allow Ministers to act as they see fit, the Department may produce an explanatory memorandum outlining content and form. Whenever they are considered, draft Regulations will be sent to interested parties in the form of a consultation document, the responses to which may

The important point to bear in mind is that secondary legislation must derive from primary legislation. You cannot seek Regulations unless there is a statutory right to produce them.

However, they can be produced at any time. The system prefers them to primary legislation because the process is simpler and less parliamentary time is required. Note that unlike primary legislation they can be challenged in the courts if, for example, Ministers have exceeded their powers.

116

lead to amendments. Ministers have little part to play in this. Officials assess views and produce the end product without political guidance.

All Regulations must be approved by Parliament. During a Bill's passage, it will be agreed whether they should come into force "Affirmatively" (only if Parliament agrees, meaning that a short debate would be held within 28-40 days from tabling in the House) or by "Negative Resolution" (automatically unless MPs or Peers object within a set time limit, usually 40 sitting days, which excludes periods in which Parliament is in recess for more than four days).

The primary legislation process in Scotland and Northern Ireland is much simpler. In Scotland, Bills fall into three types

• Introduced by Committee
• Executive
• Introduced by Members (who must have at least 11 other supporting MSPs)

Bills initiated by the Executive progress through a consultation process similar to that in

Apart from mainstream Bills, there is also provision for Consolidation or Codification (bringing existing law up to date), Statute Law Revision (reviving spent provisions) and Statute Law Repeal Bills, each of which is designed to implement recommendations of the Scottish Law Commission.

Whitehall. However, the parliamentary stage starts (Stage 1) with submission of a Bill to the relevant subject committee (Scottish committees combine Select and Standing roles) or committees, if the Bill crosses departmental responsibilities, in which case one will be designated as lead committee. Within the committee, one or two members will be appointed as rapporteurs on each Bill, and in some cases the committee may also establish a group of external experts to assist it.

The committee produces a report which is debated in plenary session – the equivalent of Second Reading at Westminster. The Bill is then (Stage 2) sent back to committee, which gives it line by line consideration to a set timetable. MSPs who are not members of the committee may participate in the debates but may not vote, and a final single plenary stage (Stage 3), at which any MSP may table amendments with two days notice, follows.

The Executive can also introduce Emergency Bills where all the stages are taken in one day.

A subject committee can hold an inquiry into whether there is

Committees have a more influential role in Scotland than at Westminster.

As with the European Parliament, the rapporteur (called reporter in Scotland) is the focus for representations. However, unlike EP or Westminster committees, any MSP may attend committee meetings as an observer and may participate in proceedings – Ministers have been known to go along to answer questions informally.

a need for legislation on a particular topic. Any member of the committee may submit to the Parliamentary Bureau a draft proposal for a Bill. A report is then set out explaining the need for the Bill and the committee's recommendations on content. If the Parliament agrees to the proposal, the Bill is then drafted. At Stage 1, instead of going to committee, the Bill goes straight to Parliament for consideration.

Scottish secondary legislation (usually Statutory Instruments) is first checked by the Subordinate Legislation Committee to see if it is within the Parliament's remit. The lead subject committee may then if it wishes discuss it for no more than 90 minutes. The lead committee will report and make a recommendation to the Parliament within 40 days. A short (six minutes, including the proposer and the Opposition) debate then takes place.

Affirmative Motions (usually Orders) are submitted to the lead committee, which debates them for no more than 90 minutes. The committee reports within 40 days of the instrument being laid. A six minute debate follows in Plenary.

It is also possible for instruments/orders to be debated in Parliament for 90 minutes.

Motions for annulment are not made – any MSP may propose to the lead committee that the instrument should not be made or should be annulled within 40 days of the instrument having been laid.

Wales only has power to introduce secondary legislation. All Orders must be proposed in a draft form.

The Assembly Secretary then decides whether or not to carry out a regulatory appraisal (the equivalent of Regulatory Impact Assessment – see pp 162, 252-263). A draft of the Order and a memorandum explaining the intended effect and financial implications is submitted to the Business Committee; it allocates the draft Order to a subject committee which has between 2-8 weeks to report. In parallel, the Legislative Committee considers whether or not the draft definitely falls within the Assembly's remit. The Assembly then considers the principles of the legislation. Amendments can be considered if tabled by a minimum of three AMs at least two days before that part of the draft is to be considered and if they are accompanied by an explanatory note. Amendments are taken in the same order as they appear in the text of the draft legislation. If amended by the Assembly, a revised draft is produced and again the Assembly Secretary must consider whether a regulatory appraisal is required in light of the amendments. The draft Order is then approved by resolution of the Assembly. It is signed by the Presiding Officer and First Secretary (or a Secretary).

Orders involving expenditure bypass subject committees and go straight to debate in plenary once the Legislation Committee has confirmed that they are procedurally and legally correct.

It is possible for a draft Order to be implemented without consideration by the Assembly. In such cases, AMs have 40 days in which to oppose the Order and table a motion for it to be revoked. The Assembly must then vote on whether or not it should be revoked.

In cases where Westminster secondary legislation also applies to Wales, a draft is laid before the Assembly, which then considers whether to agree to the draft. No amendment may be made. The relevant Assembly Secretary then notifies the Minister of the Crown of the Assembly's decision.

It is possible to petition against subordinate legislation which would otherwise be subject to special parliamentary procedure. In such cases petitions are invited and a special committee of between five and seven Members is established to hear the views of the petitioners.

There are also powers to consider local SIs. The Assembly must be given at least ten days notice. If at least ten Members table a motion opposing the proposals, it is examined in the normal fashion (see above). In addition, those SIs deriving from local authorities or Government bodies will allow ten days for AMs to oppose the Secretary's intention to confirm or approve them. If at least ten AMs oppose, the SI is debated by the Assembly.

In the case of subordinate legislation not made by SI, the draft is published and the Assembly Secretary decides whether it should be considered by the Legislation or subject committees or referred to the Assembly plenary meeting to be considered in the same way as other SIs. If the Assembly is to consider the draft, the Assembly is given at least ten days notice.

The Northern Ireland legislative process had not been established at the time of writing.

ComCo's three key executives on this issue, the Director of Corporate Strategy, who is responsible for implementing the expansion plan, the Chief Counsel, who also handles all regulatory affairs, and the Head of Government Affairs, who is responsible for all other dealings with officials and politicians, meet to consider their strategy.
Their conclusions are as follows:

MEMORANDUM

TO: Chief Executive

FROM: Director of Corporate Strategy/
           Chief Counsel/Head of
           Government Affairs

Expansion plan - regulatory concerns

Background

We have three opportunities to secure the objective of containing the regulator's powers so as to ensure that he will not be able to exercise jurisdiction over us in the new markets we intend to cover:

Seek to amend the forthcoming Competition Bill to give further definition to the competition powers of regulators: we have come to this very late, since it is due to start its parliamentary stages with Lords Second Reading on 9 November. However, while we may not be able to persuade Government to agree to changes since it has made it clear that it does not want to introduce new items for debate (and this one would be considered a fundamental new concept which falls outside the scope of the current draft); and an ambush in a Lords vote would probably only be reversed in the Commons, it may be possible to achieve recognition on the record from Government that our concerns are reasonable and that they will be addressed during the

Utility regulation review: DTI informs us that an announcement of terms of reference will be made next week and that there will be 10 weeks in which to submit views. Conclusions should be announced just after Christmas. We are not sure whether our concerns will be covered by the review (hence the possible need to press Ministers during the Bill) although we have told the G5 responsible for utilities in Competition and Consumer Affairs Directorate that there are no grounds for excluding them. The difficulty lies in the imminence of the

Communications review: there is a danger that DTI will feel that the issue of the extent of regulatory control must be considered in the context of this exercise. The review will be very complex, seeking as it does to splice telecoms, broadcasting and multimedia regulation and we would be well into our diversification programme before any conclusions were reached on regulators' powers. We must avoid any move by DTI to deal with our concerns through this forum

---

DON'T PUT IT IN WRITING

Everyone has seen media scoops fuelled by the leak of lobbying strategy memoranda from organisations or advisers. Do not commit any strategic advice to writing unless you would be happy for its content to appear in public without incriminating you. This is particularly important if an issue could end up in the courts and discovery of documents could be demanded.

We conclude that we should

- Seek to meet the Competition Bill Team and Communications and Information Industries (CII) Directorate officials to see whether they would be prepared to recommend to Ministers that the Bill be amended to restrict the exercise of regulators' powers to those areas which would not otherwise be covered by the Office of Fair Trading - in other words, to our core business only - or at least to acknowledge that our case has some merit and that it will definitely be considered during the utility regulation review. We should seek to show that uncertainty over regulators' powers to interfere in areas not envisaged by the originating legislation applies across the board. We should not, however, press the point too hard as it would be better to withdraw than to get "No" on the record.

- Assume that we will initially not get the response we want. We should seek the support of the most commercially-minded Law Lords (our legal advisers have given us a list of the five most likely to be interested in competition and utility regulation). They will feel constrained from tabling or even speaking to amendments as they cannot be associated with an attempt to change the law, but the Lords Second Reading debate would allow them to express views since only general principles are covered at that stage. We should send them a two page brief explaining that this is an area of legal uncertainty; that it is an issue that could come before them for determination; and that it would be best to preempt it by statutory clarification. Their views, whether expressed to the House or privately to Ministers (preferably both) will carry great weight and we would hope that, combined with approaches to all sides of the Lords, we might persuade Ministers that they should offer us some assurances.

- Brief the DTI Special Adviser responsible for regulation (the Secretary of State relies on his views) on the problems and hope that he will recommend clarification of the regulators' powers.

- At the same time, seek to interest [one of the Sunday Times political or business correspondents] in a prominent news piece, coupled with a business leader, on "regulatory creep" and concerns being expressed by the City over the cost of regulatory uncertainty.

IT'S NOT OVER TILL IT'S OVER

The campaign to deregulate Sunday Trading in the early 1980s thought it had succeeded when Government promised legislation. It therefore relaxed and stopped lobbying. Its opponents did not, and through hard work they were able to persuade enough backbenchers to vote against the Bill for it to be defeated at Second Reading, something that was almost unprecedented. The lesson for lobbyists is to pack up only when it is impossible for anything to derail the decision you want.

• Lastly, we will liaise with BT, Transco and Centrica and the water and electricity sector to see if they will raise this point in their utility review submissions and add their weight to lobbying in the Lords. If they can back us, the risk that this problem will be seen as ComCo-specific and left to the communications review should be avoided.

ComCo has obtained a copy of DTI's internal directory (available on request, or use the less explicit Civil Service Yearbook, which covers all Departments - available from the Parliamentary Bookshop or HMSO and calls the Special Adviser's secretary, the G5 responsible for competition and the utilities (whom ComCo feels would be more sympathetic to the case than the hard-pressed head of the Bill Team) and its regular contacts in CII to seek meetings at which it can explain its problem and discuss the scope for amendment of the Bill. This covers both official and ministerial ends of the Department. It also has a brief ready to fax to DTI to explain why it believes a change to the Bill would not be controversial (and would therefore not disrupt the timetable) or inconsistent with the explanatory memorandum attached to the front of the Bill; and the impact on its diversification plan if the regulators' competition powers are not clarified.

MINISTERIAL MEETINGS – DOs and DON'Ts

Don't go to Ministers unless

- *The issue is one where Ministers really make the formal decision and you have reached agreement with officials on principles and detail*
- *You have no prospect of squaring things at official level*
- *You have a clear agenda and have set it out in your letter requesting the meeting*
- *You have asked Private Office which officials will be attending and you brief them beforehand*
- *You have assumed you will not get another meeting: this one will be the clincher and everything must be in place*
- *You can keep your opening remarks brief. Giving Ministers a long and complex presentation (unless they have requested one) allows them to think of other things while you talk and avoids the need for them to say anything. Keep the opener to two or three minutes and cover no more than two or three issues*

Courtesy meetings achieve little or nothing, and may use up a line of credit that may make it harder to get a meeting when you really need it.

ComCo is careful in the conversations with officials to make them aware of its understanding that they do not want further interference with the Bill and that it is only contacting them at this late stage because the plan has only just been agreed; because it believes this would be compatible with the Bill's objectives without risk of opposition (other than from the regulators); and because other opportunities for considering the problem would be unlikely to offer the City the regulatory certainty it needs in time.

ComCo does not expect a positive initial response and it asks only for an informal oral view as a letter from the Department would be regarded by DTI as an expression of policy. A flat "No" in writing would leave little way forward. The G5 in charge of the utility review has heard the arguments in favour of regulatory consistency and limitation before and confirms that the general question of regulators' discretion will be examined in the course of the review but he is guarded about making promises: he cannot be seen to prejudge the outcome and officials must tell outsiders that Ministers make all the decisions. As expected, the Bill Team takes the view that ComCo's concerns fall outside the intention of the Bill and that any attempt to amend it at this stage could invite a raft of further amendments from other utilities. Had the matter been raised some months earlier, they say, it might have been possible to consult all utilities and their regulators, but with Second Reading upon them they fear that valuable time could be taken up in the House without the prospect of an agreed solution.

HOW IS COMCO DOING?

Apart from starting very late in the Bill process, ComCo has got it right:

- *It has taken a realistic view of its chances of changing the Bill - too late to do that, and ideas that fall outside the scope Government envisages for a measure are always unlikely to be accepted.*
- *It has a number of alternative strategies - negotiation with officials (no change of a technical nature could be agreed without their approval); pressure in the Lords, both in debate and direct to Ministers behind the scenes; lobbying the Special Adviser; and pressure through one of the few newspapers Ministers have the time to read.*
- *It is seeking to enlist allies and to broaden the case in order to maximise its muscle and to avoid the charge of special pleading.*

However, while the memo shows awareness of officials' possible advice that ComCo's case should most appropriately be considered in the communications review, it does not second-guess the reaction of the Agency (whose views DTI will canvass) or of ComCo's potential competitors. ComCo must consider whether probing amendments or press coverage might provoke an unwelcome reaction - and how to head it off.

CII officials are more sympathetic. In advance of the meeting with them, ComCo sends them (on a Commercial in Confidence basis – officials will respect this) its market research on the extent of competition in the superhighway sector, together with analysts' reports endorsing the company's regulatory thesis that the sector is highly fragmented and that there is little chance that even a national network such as ComCo's could capture a dominant market share. It also produces a paper explaining how expansion outside the UK could be funded without prejudicing investment in domestic infrastructure. Officials read all this carefully: they do not like to go to meetings unprepared. However, because ComCo does not want them to liaise with the regulators beforehand, it has only told them it wants to discuss its development plans.

Part of CII's brief is to promote the development of the industry; it will tend to act as the industry's advocate in Whitehall and the company has always ensured that the Directorate is kept up to date with financial and other information. However, while exercising primary responsibility for policy parameters in this area, officials leave the detail to the regulators. ComCo is careful to acknowledge this in the meeting; it also preempts the obvious comment that if it is confident of its case on competition and investment it should have nothing to fear from the regulators by stressing the need to avoid the City's concern that any diversification will be prefaced by a regulatory face-off. Officials take this point and agree that they will send a minute to their Minister and to the Deputy Secretary in charge of the regulatory review (their Deputy Secretary does not report to the Minister covering the review and they must therefore move through a series of zig zags). They are less convinced, however, about the suggestion that the limits of regulators' anti-competitive powers should be spelt out in the Competition Bill: after the meeting, in which ComCo tells them that this is a concern shared by all regulated utilities and on which they all intend to lobby, the CII officials speak to their counterparts and find that the other utilities have not recently contacted the Department on this point. Lesson: you cannot just tell the system you have the support of others; you must prove it.

The Special Adviser agrees to see ComCo because he is one of the new breed of Labour advisers who is also a technical specialist. A former Civil Servant, he is turned to by Ministers as a parallel source of guidance on regulatory policy. Nonetheless, ComCo recognises that his portfolio is wider than that of any policy official (there are only two Special Advisers in DTI) and concentrates on the two aspects that it hopes will appeal to his political sensitivities: concern in the City (to which Ministers pay attention), and asking for his advice on what the utilities (note: not just them; ComCo uses language designed to stress the broad-based nature of the problem. "Special Pleading" is a term often used by the system to dismiss representations) should do. Because of his knowledge of regulation, he does not call for papers beforehand, but in any event ComCo tells him of its representations at other levels to prevent him from referring the matter downwards. Once again, his view is that ComCo has not shown that the issue could be introduced into the Bill without other utilities piling in with their demands; but he hints that he has not received any calls on the subject – meaning calls from the Whips about possible difficulties in the House if the point is not considered; or from City editors reflecting dissatisfaction with "regulatory creep". In other words, that is what ComCo needs to address if it is to move Ministers on the Bill or, more likely, in their decision on the outcome of the review.

A SIMPLE GUIDE TO ASSEMBLING YOUR CASE

- *Every pound spent on research is worth ten spent on lobbying*
- *Source every statement and fact; and anticipate the arguments against yours and deal with them there and then.*
- *Do not try to sweep inconvenient information under the carpet: assume that officials (either through their own research or from your opponents) will find out so get your rebuttal in before they draw the wrong conclusion.*
- *Always think "why should they want to know this/deal with me/read this?"*

The three executives have anticipated this advice and have arranged 20 minute briefings with eight Peers, two of which are prepared to mobilise additional support. However, unless a vote is involved, numbers are often less important than the status of the Peers involved – hence the letters sent from ComCo's Chief Counsel to its selected Law Lords. All ComCo wants at Second Reading is an indication to Ministers that the issue will be raised in Committee and, as a fall-back, confirmation that it will be considered during the regulatory review.

IDENTIFYING AND CONTACTING MPS AND PEERS

ComCo identified its parliamentary targets through five sources:

- *It trawled through Dod's Parliamentary Companion (see p.277), which lists the background of every Peer, for current spokesmen, former Ministers responsible for competition or telecoms/technology, legal specialists or City heavyweights.*
- *It consulted the Lords Register of Interests which, although voluntary, lists the business interests of many Peers.*
- *It then looked at the Lords attendance list, available from the Lords information office (0171 219 3107) and ruled out those who rarely came to the House.*
- *It researched those who had tabled Lords parliamentary questions and participated in debates on competition, radiocommunications, IT and the superhighway. ComCo used a monitoring agency, since this can be time-consuming, but you can get Hansard yourself from the Parliamentary Bookshop, 12 Bridge Street, London SW1A 2JX and fairly recent Hansard is on the internet (HMSO - parliament.the-stationery-office.co.uk) but access is not user-friendly*
- *It asked for recommendations from those whom it contacted from the resulting list.*

Had it met a relevant Select Committee member, ComCo would have checked on the internet whether this or a similar issue had been investigated by the committee during the time its target had been a member.

Either write, explaining why you want to meet them and showing that you understand their relevance to your issue, or telephone their secretary or researcher (the switchboard number is 0171 219 3000 but you may still be asked to write unless there are extenuating reasons such as short notice). Letters should be addressed to Joe White Esq MP (the convention is that initials are not used) House of Commons, London SW1A OAA or to The Baroness Green, House of Lords, London SW1A OPW. Check in the standard directories (see p.277) for other titles (knighthoods, Privy Councillors, QCs and Lords forms of address).

If the issue is primarily a constituency matter, contact by someone in the constituency is preferred, but whoever writes to them, get the job title right. Politicians want to feel they are being contacted either by someone whose job is tailored to them (eg "Parliamentary/Government/Regulatory Affairs") or by a senior executive who has the power to commit the organisation. Any suggestion of a corporate apologist should be avoided.

A model letter on the Competition Bill could be

Dear Lord Jimmy

Competition Bill: Second Reading 9 November.
Competition powers of utility regulators

ComCo is the UK's largest provider of relay services for radio and telecoms operators. We are regulated by the Radiocommunications Agency, which under
the Competition Bill will be given powers consistent
with Article 85 of the Treaty of Rome. We read your
speech in the debate on radio spectrum last May with
interest and wondered whether you were intending to
be present for Second Reading; we would be grateful
for your assistance in raising points on the extent
to which regulators can extend their anti-competitive powers into areas not envisaged in the original
utility legislation if we (or BT, water companies,
RECs etc) diversify.

I attach a one page brief setting out the problem
we face. If this is of interest to you, we would welcome the opportunity of a short meeting before Second
Reading.

*Remember at all times that they do not know as much about your subject as you do: be
clear and give them only what they need to know. Similarly, others have demands on their
time: if you can say it in 20 minutes there is no need to take up an entire lunch.*

*Have regard to their daily and weekly timetables. Most MPs are usually in their con-
stituencies between Thursday night and Monday lunchtime and the Lords does not sit on
Fridays. Take account of the sittings of any Select Committees they are on. Backbench
committee meetings are usually held in the late afternoons. Meetings are not advised during PM's Question Time (Wednesday, 3-3.30pm).*

The executives ask their Peers for advice on tactics (they will do
the same when the Bill starts its Commons stages) since gaining a feel
(for the procedures and culture of both Houses - for example, who
respects whom or when an amendment should be pressed to a vote)
requires considerable day-to-day experience.

One of the Law Lords agrees to meet the Chief Counsel. He
believes that he might be seen as committing his colleagues to a formal position if he were to raise the problem with the Government
spokesman in the Lords but accepts that it would be desirable if the
legal position could be clarified without reference to the courts and
agrees to take informal soundings on the Government's position. It
will not be possible for the Chief Counsel to press further so he can

only hope that in the course of contacting the spokesman, the Law Lord will hint that the demarcation line should be clearer without expressing a view on the merits of the argument.

The Chief Counsel's two colleagues now involve the head of Corporate Communications and Finance Director, who between them seek to set up non-attributable media comment directed at Ministers and the City (they target the Sunday Times and the FT Lex column for the week leading up to Second Reading) and contact the senior corporate finance directors and analysts with whom they are familiar, having concluded that raising awareness of the issue will not damage their share price since the diversification plan has not yet been revealed. The media line is that the Bill gives regulators new competition powers but does nothing to address the uncertainty over their application and that Ministers should draw clear boundaries without delay. The City strategy is to stimulate personal representations to Ministers and to the Special Adviser from the leading institutions. ComCo knows that the City meets politicians constantly and two of the banks are due to be lunching the Government Lords spokesman within the next three weeks. Even more important, one of the heads of corporate finance is prepared to talk to the No 10 Policy Unit specialist on trade and industry issues, who works closely with the DTI Special Adviser and is sensitive to the PM's concern to keep senior figures in the City onside.

At the same time, the Head of Government Affairs drafts ComCo's submission to the utility regulation review. He adopts the Civil Service submission format (numbered paragraphs with the first line indented, ragged right hand margin, single line spacing) in preference to ComCo's house style in order to make the document look more familiar to DTI. In his conversation with the G5 responsible for the review, he had asked about the points on which the Department particularly wanted views and for an indication of the issues considered out of bounds. He is therefore confident that his submission will be relevant even if not all of it can be accepted by DTI.

In addition to being careful to observe the Standard Whitehall Test, he treats any submission he makes to officials, regulatory bodies and local authority officers as if it was a legal document:

TREAT POLITICIANS AND OFFICIALS AS INDIVIDUALS

They do not appreciate labels on envelopes or "Dear MP" letters unless you explain the reason (eg lack of resources) at the outset. If you are likely to deal with many MPs/ MEPS/members of national assemblies/ councillors on a regular basis, keep a stock of properly typed envelopes and buy a parliamentary mailmerge disc.

It pays to invest extra hours in writing personal letters: you probably do not like receiving mailshots and neither do they. Parliamentary secretaries can spot them a mile away and many envelopes (perhaps a quarter of a typical mailbag) are thrown away unopened.

Standard postcards (posted or via Email) which only require a signature from the sender are generally ignored because Government believes they involve little commitment on the part of the lobbyist. They do, however, have a use in cases where a lobby seeks to demonstrate the extent of support or opposition on an issue - the 1994 campaign against Post Office privatisation was able to get postal workers to send many thousands of identical cards and then tabled a PQ on the number of responses for and against the Government's proposals. The bald answer was used to show the media that the proposal had only a handful of backers.

If you must treat Government as a PR target (eg sending Press Releases to MPs or officials) always cover material with a short letter explaining why they are receiving it. They tend to assume that glossy brochures have been produced for general consumption, so if you go to trouble and expense to produce something for them, make it clear that it has been written and designed with them in mind - or the bin will beckon. Accept, however, that sending them your company newsletter is a waste of time: they will not read it and it should not be regarded as a convenient substitute for a personal briefing on issues they need to know about.

Keep parliamentary representations local wherever possible: MPs and MEPs would rather see a letter from a factory manager on constituency letterhead than from someone at head office (unless it is the chairman or chief executive of a household name).

And treat officials as you would analysts: industry analyses produced for the City could be very helpful to Whitehall or Brussels.

- He avoids emotion, hyperbole and vituperative criticism (even where Government has been pig-headed or has completely failed to understand an issue).
- He never makes a statement or lists a fact without producing a source and corroboration.

- He anticipates the questions that will be raised against his arguments and preempts them there and then: he cross-examines himself.
- He explains the effect – economic and practical – of his proposals/concerns on ComCo's sector, on others and on related policy areas. This is particularly important now that Whitehall and the Commission are required to produce Regulatory Impact Assessments or "Fiches d'Impact" (see pp252-263) with any proposal: this requirement may be carried out by officials on the basis of little research (in Brussels, it is often ignored) and it is possible to stall or modify Government's plans by showing that the financial and administrative impact on both industry and consumers will be greater than anticipated; or that actual benefits will fall short of those claimed.

> *Try to get your issue onto the agenda of the weekly meetings of crossbench peers through one or more of its members. The crossbenchers do not agree on a common line but they do discuss important representations made to the group or to its convenor (currently Lord Craig).*

He knows that in dealing with Whitehall and the Commission, content is far more important than packaging: indeed, attempts to overcome a weak case with PR are likely to be met by antipathy among officials. However, politicians are sensitive to some coverage, particularly by the heavyweight Lobby correspondents since Ministers know that their colleagues focus on the Lobby, and the Head of Corporate Communications is briefed to set up a story about the review in which the City concern angle is reworked.

At Lords Second Reading, ComCo's main advocates – the Conservative and Liberal Democrat spokesmen, two cross-benchers (one a former Cabinet Secretary) and, critically, a respected Labour lawyer – all mention its point. In winding up, the Government spokesman delivers the expected refusal to amend the Bill, partly because that would prejudge the outcome of the utility review, but he is able to confirm that the review will consider the issue. A partial success. The Bill Team, members of which are present at all stages of the Bill (the relevant officials sit in an area called "The Box" during all parliamentary proceedings in case Ministers need advice) notes the Peers' comments and prepares a rebuttal to the amendments to come.

ComCo has already instructed a Parliamentary Agent (addresses available in Dod's Parliamentary Companion) to draft amendments restricting the ambit of regulators' anti-competitive powers to core activities. Parliamentary drafting is an art best left to specialists, particularly since in this case consequential amendments will be required to all the originating utility Acts. They are sent to ComCo's supporters in good time (amendments must be tabled at least 48 hours before each stage) with a half-page explanation and an offer to draft individual speaking notes for Committee Stage (if you send the same speaking brief to several Peers or MPs, the first speaker may leave the others with nothing to say; and always send them on unheaded paper - your letterhead can be identified surprisingly easily from the gallery). Lists of Commons amendments are published in the daily Order Paper or are available for both Houses on order from the Parliamentary Bookshop.

The Committee Stage debate on ComCo's amendments passes without surprises. The Government Whips have asked the lead sponsor (the LibDem spokesman) whether he intends to press the matter to a division and, although an answer is not always given if the Opposition wants to maintain an element of surprise, in this case a discussion with ComCo concludes that there is no point in forcing a vote since it has not proved possible to generate enough support on the Labour benches and, equally importantly, it looks as though the amendments will not be reached until after 7.30pm - votes in the Lords after 5.30pm attract a far smaller turnout. This is not a failure on ComCo's part: it just has to be accepted that some issues have bigger constituencies and attract more interest than others. It is also a fact that most Lords defeats are overturned in the Commons.

The management team now takes the view that there is no point in tabling new amendments at Report Stage and Third Reading since they will only receive the same treatment (and as a Bill proceeds, the

DEVELOPING LINKS WITH OFFICIALS
The Example of the UK Lathe Association

The UK Lathe Association was formed a year ago to promote the image of the industry and to negotiate with and monitor Government on its behalf. In carrying out the last of these responsibilities, it concentrates on five Departments:

- *DTI - for information on the Department's attitude to the industry; progress on current policy planning; possible future policy developments; policy on some of the main industries using lathes; the motor, shipbuilding, aerospace, and power generation industries; future lines of credit and the Department's attitude to including lathes in future trade and aid packages; and export intelligence.*
- *DfEE - for information on changes in employment and training policy.*
- *DETR - regional policy.*
- *DFID - for information on international development programmes and to lobby for incorporation of lathes in development packages.*
- *Treasury - monitoring Budget planning, since the Association is seeking improvements to the capital allowances regime.*

In addition, it has to liaise with Regional Development Agencies to ensure that regional economic strategies recognise the importance of the lathe industry; with the Scotland, Wales and Northern Ireland Offices; and with the Health and Safety Executive.

The Association initially contacted each body at Grade 7 level, telling the officials who it was and stating that it wanted to ensure it was kept informed about any policy that could affect it. On first liaison, which was by telephone, it asked officials whether they were able to disclose whether anything was in discussion on a range of subjects and about progress on current policy developments. It ensured, in asking officials for this information, that it conveyed its understanding of the discretion Civil Servants have to exercise in disclosing information as yet unannounced publicly. In a meeting shortly afterwards with its sponsoring officials (requested by the Association) it was revealed that a Green Paper would shortly be published on a subject affecting the industry. The Association asked about its publication date and for guidance on the considerations of the Department in examining submissions. It later contacted the relevant Division to find out how many submissions had been made in response to the Green Paper. It ensured that it produced its own Regulatory Impact Assessment as soon as the details of the proposal were known and that the costings were negotiated with Whitehall; it also pressed officials to consult well before publication of the Green Paper on the methodology they would adopt in producing the official RIA.

The Association is careful never to ask officials, even those in Divisions with which it now enjoys regular and close relations, for information that could compromise that relationship. It does not ask for sight of documents while still in confidential draft form although it does ask if officials can tell it anything about their content on the basis that the worst answer it can receive is no. It has asked for, and received, information on a number of matters: on the decision-making structure, particularly where that structure is unrecognised - its members need to know about the composition of teams working on individual departmental procurement contracts; how the interdepartmental process will work on some of the issues affecting the Association; and on timing of statements; the White Paper following the Green Paper's consultation period; and the introduction of legislation.

The Association has found that it often has to make contact at Grade 5 level rather than with Special Advisers, who are less interested in the technical policy areas that are of greatest value to lathe manufacturers, for information about ministerial attitudes to the issues in which it is interested. Once again, it never pressures officials but makes them aware of the consequences to it of not being properly informed and of its awareness that officials may not be able to release all the information it needs. Its approach is invariably deliberately naïve when contacting Civil Servants with whom it does not have a close working relationship: having identified itself, it asks for help with a problem, states that problem, and then asks if the official can tell them anything about legislative timetables, departmental attitudes or concerns, consultation processes or whatever.

The Association learnt early that some officials are more cautious than others about providing information and that this problem is more evident at Grade 7 because of the frequent need to check upwards before responding.

Like many industry groupings, the UK Lathe Association has little money and therefore makes maximum use of free sources of information. It learns about the parliamentary timetable from the Monday and Friday papers; it studies those papers' Lobby gossip; it is on the mailing list for all of the relevant departmental press releases (and if it knows an announcement is going to be made, it calls the relevant policy officials to request a rapid copy by fax); it accesses Hansard, Select Committee information and departmental announcements through the internet every day (see p 286); and it consults the reference books in the library next door for lists of MPs. It takes the view that resources are not a great problem if the system of acquiring information is understood and the organisation knows how to target officials.

Government, becoming ever more conscious of the need to stick to its schedule, is increasingly unlikely to make concessions). Instead, it prepares a rebuttal to the Minister's rejection (published in Lords Hansard) and asks the LibDem spokesman, who is widely respected across party divides, whether he would be interested in organising a small delegation of Peers to see the Minister privately and without publicity (this last point might attract senior Labour Peers who would not want the media to suggest disloyalty. The spokesman also suggests a letter countersigned by up to a dozen senior Peers. In the end, Ministers' receptiveness to this lobbying will be governed by two factors:

- Will these people cause us/me embarrassment (public criticism from respected Peers/MPs and particularly from our own Party)?
- Are the claimed consequences of failing to address their concern (or at least addressing it now) well-founded?

ComCo has only partly succeeded on both grounds. The media coverage and City representations have been noticed, and officials have acknowledged that greater clarity would be desirable, but by announcing that the issue will definitely be covered in the utility review (which could be concluded before the Bill becomes law) Ministers believe they have kicked ComCo's lobby into touch.

The company does not completely ignore the Bill after this. At the outset, the Head of Government Affairs prepared a list, based on discussions with constituency MPs and other contacts including MPs' parliamentary researchers, many of whom network furiously, of the MPs regarded as closest to the Minister, who will be taking the Bill through the Commons and who is also responsible for the review. From that list, ComCo now selects lawyers and members of the Trade and Industry Select Committee, which has held an inquiry into utility regulation, and sends them an adapted version of the Lords brief. Many letters sent to MPs are simply mailboxed to Ministers, whose officials then prepare standard responses. ComCo avoids this by making it clear in its letters (drafted similarly to its initial Lords letters and based on thorough research into the relevance of each MP to the issue) that if a meeting is not possible it would prefer that the brief is not sent to the Department (this is important, and not just in this case. ComCo may wish to convey sensitive information to Ministers via MPs and could be embarrassed if the response to a mailboxed letter starting "thank you for your letter of XXX, enclosing a letter from

ComCo..." - a standard ministerial opener - were to fall into the hands of the organisation about which ComCo was seeking to complain via an MP).

GET YOUR DATA ON THEIR FILES

A major UK defence company was bidding for another contractor. The deal was highly sensitive in policy terms. The competition authorities sought views from the DTI division covering the company's sector. The company liaised with officials regularly but the only financial information they had on their files dated back three years, and at that time the company's performance was poor. It had improved markedly since then, but the tendency of Whitehall to rely on the material it has, instead of actively conducting research, meant that officials concluded the company might not be able to finance investment and might milk the contractor's revenue stream.

The error was spotted by the company at the last minute and the misconception corrected. That does not mean that every organisation must barrage Whitehall and Brussels with facts; but if the system is likely to have to produce briefs on your sector or company (for ministerial meetings and speeches, regulatory decisions, debates or answers to questions) make sure that its information is your information.

Three MPs have space in their diaries before Second Reading, although ComCo is by now less concerned that they should speak in debate - the politicians most respected by Ministers are unlikely to make a case to them in the Chamber - than that further pressure should be applied to the Minister to limit regulators' remit when he announces the conclusions of the review. However, there is little point in directing new people towards Ministers with the same arguments. The company therefore persuades one of its corporate financiers to join it for the briefings on the basis that views on the implications of "regulatory creep" will be met less sceptically if expressed by a third party than by a regulated body.

Throughout this exercise, ComCo has regularly contacted CII officials to keep a careful watch on the Department's reactions to the lobby, since there is a danger in doing too much and annoying the people they are trying to persuade. That might have been a risk had the other regulated utilities also majored on this issue, but their agendas for the regulatory review had higher priorities and ComCo found that, while they would raise the concern in their review submissions, they were not prepared to use up their stock of political capital by pressing Ministers on its behalf. But this can also be a weakness, since in the face of possible advice from officials (who, it must not be forgotten, also have very strong day-to-day links with the regulators, who are not without views of their own on this matter) that fettering regulatory discretion at this time may create the impression of going soft on the utilities, Ministers and their political advisers need to see signs of countervailing pressure at their end of the Department.

ComCo therefore tries its last two tactical moves: it contacts the Chair of the Labour Backbench Trade and Industry Committee to explain the problem it faces (it does not go into detail about its business plans - unlike officials, MPs can on occasions leak such information).

It hopes that he will either raise the point at the next meeting of the Committee and will then take a collective view to Ministers, hopefully implying to them that the parliamentary party will not demur if they are seen to be striking a balance between the need both for tough regulation and to allow regulated business to make decisions on the same basis as any other private sector company; or that ComCo will be invited to address that meeting.

ComCo also seeks a meeting with the Minister responsible for the review. You may be wondering why this was not activated earlier. It could have been, although not before the ground had been prepared with officials (and bear in mind that we are trying in this example to explain all the possible angles). How does ComCo get to the Minister?

- If it does not know him/her, it speaks to CII officials, who are most likely to be favourable to its case, and asks whether they would be prepared to recommend that a meeting should be scheduled (it is important to understand that requests for meetings are referred by Private Office to the relevant line officials for advice. They cannot force a Minister to accept an invitation, but if they express caveats

- for example because the organisation has a planning application sitting on the Minister's desk - it is unusual for Ministers to go ahead).

- It then writes to the Minister, explaining that it has a number of problems resulting from regulatory uncertainty which now need to be resolved with some urgency; pointing out that there has been full discussion with his officials to make Private Office, aware, Ministers hardly ever see such letters, that the right hoops have been passed through; setting out an agenda for the proposed meeting (this makes it easier for Private Office to decide which officials should be involved) and hoping that a meeting might be possible to discuss a solution.

- Ten days later, ComCo rings the Diary Secretary to see whether it has been possible to find space. This shows a correct understanding of Ministers' position. You either go to them in the same way as they would go to Cabinet - as the culmination of negotiations at a lower level - or because you are blocked below and have to go over officials' heads, but this can be dangerous; or because you want to sell them political ideas. It is possible to ring a Diary Secretary to establish whether a Minister would not be precluded by other commitments from considering an invitation for a particular day, but appointments are normally made only after a written request has been sent.

- If the request is unlikely to be supported by officials, either because they oppose ComCo's case or because they feel that nothing can be gained by reiterating it to Ministers, the Special Adviser may be prepared to help; or a helpful backbencher (it is easiest to approach your constituency MPs, regardless of their party, but if they are unwilling to help the alternative is MPs with a subject interest - the same principle applies Scotland, Wales and Northern Ireland) may agree to approach the Minister on the company's behalf: Ministers are much less likely to turn down such a request, but that does not mean it is preferable to sponsorship by officials since they will probably be present at the meeting and will certainly have drafted the Minister's brief (remember the Aviation Fuel Tax case).

143

A DAY IN THE LIVES OF A DIRECTOR GENERAL AND A G7

We interviewed two DTI officials, one close to the top of the Department; the other on a lower rung of Civil Service middle management.

X, a Director General: with 700 staff in his command, he sees his role in several ways: as a link between Ministers and the Directors (Grade 3) or Grade 5 officials in Directorates or Divisions; as a focus for the identification and (hopefully) resolution of conflicting divisional priorities; and as a point of contact for senior business and industry figures (such as Directors of major companies relevant to his area of responsibility). His working day divides roughly into thirds - policy advice, including coordination of the interests of his Directorates; management of staff and resource allocation; and representation of the Department at meetings and at functions

8.45am Read daily digest of press cuttings on all matters affecting the Department. See if he should speak to a colleague, or to the Minister's Private Office, about any item.

9.00am Read correspondence - mainly official papers such as copies of submissions to Ministers or notes of meetings.

10.00am Monthly meeting of the Department's Resource Management Group (consisting of the Permanent Secretary, all Directors General and the Head of Finance and Resource Management Directorate). The Permanent Secretary will then put the recommendations agreed by the meeting to Ministers.

11.30-12.45pm Meeting with two or three Directors (Grade 3) and some Grade 5s and 7s about, for example, the departmental approach to a merger proposal which is shortly to be discussed interdepartmentally. Alternatively, telephone conversations with industrial executives or officials in other Departments. These conversations either inform them of departmental intentions on policy issues or seek information from them.

12.45pm Lunch with a trade association or with a senior executive from a major company sponsored by one of his Directorates.

2.34pm Briefing meeting with the Secretary of State prior to a meeting with the chairman of a utility group.

3.00pm Attends the meeting, which lasts until

3.45pm The Secretary of State brings him up to date informally with developments on one or two current issues.

4.00pm Read various minutes; make telephone calls; handle correspondence.

5.00pm Meeting with Minister of State about the visit next day of an industrial delegation.

5.30pm Telephone conversations with colleagues in Directorates.

6.00pm Introductory discussion with a Grade 5 who has just moved to one of his Directorates.

7.00pm Home or (on two nights a week) attends a function hosted by a company, trade association or an embassy.

Y, Grade 7: she has three specific responsibilities within her Branch: general policy on her subject area, including speeches, coordinating briefings, parliamentary questions, ministerial enquiries, review and development of policies relating to her subject; international policy, particularly involving the EU and OECD; and performing a sponsorship function in relation to a specific industrial sector. She sees her role as providing policy advice to senior officials and Ministers, administering departmental support schemes, often involving a high degree of financial responsibility, and ensuring that the interests of the sector she sponsors are reflected in policy decisions. In particular, she regards herself as the first point of contact between Whitehall and the companies for which she is responsible.

9.00am Works on correspondence and papers. Prepares draft replies to parliamentary questions and letters to her Minister.
10.30am Weekly meeting with her Director (Grade 3) to review progress and to alert him to developments or problems arising in her sector.
1.15am Meeting a company to discuss an application for departmental support.
12.15am Prepares brief for an international meeting.
1.00pm Lunch with executives from her sponsored industry.
2.15pm Meeting with the Minister and a group of local councillors concerning a local problem involving her industry.
3.00pm Meeting with other DTI officials on international policy coordination in preparation for an overseas meeting.
4.15pm Brief her Grade 5 on a visit he is paying to a major organisation. Discuss with him the first draft of a policy paper that will eventually be submitted to Ministers.
4.45pm Telephone conversations with a number of companies including a discussion with an organisation with a significant problem which DTI can help resolve.
5.00pm Draft notes on these discussions including a minute seeking departmental agreement to a policy line intended to resolve the company's difficulties.
5.45pm Draft letters for the Minister to follow up the meeting with councillors.
6.45pm Leave.

Their advice on dealing with officials

- *Clear the ground at G5/7 level before seeking a meeting with a Grade 2 or higher. These grades always handle the follow-up of work and senior officials rely on them for advice on the quality of outsiders' representations.*
- *If you cannot persuade G5s and 7s of the merits of your case, your chances of securing acceptance over their heads may not be good.*
- *Some organisations presume that a letter to a Minister, either directly or through an MP, is enough to win a battle. It is not.*

People underestimate the extent to which their representations may be probed by officials. More than anything else, therefore, develop a good, well-corroborated case.

An MP can request a private meeting, but these are really only meant for instances where party political or official miscarriage issues are to be discussed.

- If ComCo does know the Minister (this means more than having met him for five minutes at a large reception) or if its size and Chairman's status merit special attention, it can write using the Minister's first name. It may be shown to him, but Private Offices are wise to all the ploys and will usually put the request to him with all the others at their regular diary meetings. However, friends are important: while Ministers will do an outsider no favours if they seek preferential policy decisions, it helps to have friends if you want to shorten the odds of claiming space in their diaries – they receive up to ten requests for every slot.

POLITICIANS' BOREDOM LEVEL

Politicians are good listeners, but they also like talking. Avoid opening statements to Select Committees and keep your answers short and to the point; restrict presentations to 7-8 minutes; and introduce your problem in meetings simply and briefly. "Lobbying By Listening", meaning making your points in response to their questions, is as good a technique as any.

Do not, however, assume that materials you might produce for others with short attention spans (such as journalists) are appropriate for politicians. Brochures and videos are regarded as too slick and almost always go straight in the bin. Ordinary paper, and information that can be assimilated within three minutes without the need to be re-read, is usually best.

Let us assume that ComCo is lucky. Often getting through the door is the easy part for organisations; knowing what to do when they are in the Minister's office is the problem, even if they do not realise it. The four most frequent mistakes are not giving officials full information beforehand (much better to start the meeting running rather than to have to explain things from scratch; and ComCo will want to have a chance of influencing the Minister's brief); not giving Ministers time to talk (so many organisations prepare half hour "presentations" which take up most of the meeting and allow Ministers to sit in silence); over-complicating the meeting in an attempt to cover as many issues as possible – Ministers should be left with no more than three short points to think about; and failure to consider the What's In It For Them test. ComCo knows that it can explain its development strategy and the concerns over uncertainty in five minutes, allowing most of the allotted 40 minutes for exchanges. The company is aware that Ministers cannot, for fear of Judicial Review action (it could be alleged by other parties that they prejudged the outcome of the utility review), give it the categorical assurances it wants in advance of making their statement at the end of the process, so it can only seek to persuade them that the problem is genuine and that resolution on the lines ComCo suggests would both be technically reasonable and need not be seen as a climbdown by the regulatory system.

MEETING MINISTERS: BEAR IN MIND...

If you want Ministers to make visits outside London (or Edinburgh and Cardiff), it is best to offer a Friday date since parliamentary business makes it difficult for them to travel during the rest of the week

The Chief Secretary to the Treasury and the Financial Secretary have to spend a considerable amount of time in the Finance Bill Standing Committee between April and June of every year. Their availability will be limited during this period.

If you want to entertain Ministers, understand that some tell their Private Offices that they do not want more than X evenings a week away from their families; others (the Chancellor for example) prefer breakfast meetings. Check with Private Office before writing.

What conclusions can we draw from this second example?

• First, if you want to have the best chance of influencing legislation, start well before Parliament becomes involved. Changes can be made behind the scenes, but a public reversal or admission of omission is unwelcome. The amount of thinking that takes place before Whitehall is ready formally to consult outsiders is extensive: as a

A VISIT TO THE SWANWICK AIR TRAFFIC CONTROL CENTRE

The legislation allowing Government to privatise the operator of the air traffic control system creates a new management body, ATCO, which will be part of the private sector but with a Government "Golden Share" to allow it to insist on operational safeguards for emergency defence and other reasons. Liaison between ATCO and DETR officials is constant in the first few months of its existence and Ministers will have received a number of minutes from the Grade 5 in charge of [the branch responsible for ATC].

Eventually, ATCO decides that it is properly restructured and it invites the Secretary of State to open its new ATC centre near Southampton. Having contacted the Minister's Diary Secretary to establish that he is not engaged on the day (for something as important as this, any day will do, but otherwise Fridays are considered easier for Ministerial visits out of London unless they are undertaking a regional tour or are looking for useful photo opportunities during local government or parliamentary election campaigning). ATCO writes to him.

The letter is seen by the Principal Private Secretary, who will read all correspondence not marked "Personal" (and possibly some that is). He asks the Minister whether he wishes to accept. In this instance his approval is a formality but in most cases Private Office will seek views from the relevant officials, who will produce a note on the advisability of a Minister committing himself to a visit or a meeting. For example, it may be regarded as a bad idea for there to be ministerial contact with a company tendering for a contract supervised by the Minister's Department. In other cases, if the date is specific and a senior Minister is unable to avoid a clash of commitments but departmental approval is recommended, the invitation may be passed to a more junior deputy.

In the six weeks or so before the Secretary of State travels to Swanwick, his officials will prepare a brief on ATCO; progress since privatisation; liaison between DETR and ATCO; and, if ATCO has notified the Department (either Private Office or its line officials) of the people the Minister will meet, potted details on the guest list. ATCO knows the ropes and does this for them. Since they are always short of time, briefs for Ministers are presented on no more than two summary sheets with attachments in case they want more detail. Most of the time they will be briefed by their Private Secretary (a Principal or Assistant P/S will accompany Ministers to all but the most private engagements) in the car only a short time before arriving but, since it has been decided to make a major policy review speech at the opening, the Secretary of State will be briefed in advance and will concentrate on reading his script, which may have been written by officials, his Special Adviser, or both, on the way.

At an early stage the MP for Swanwick will have been informed, since it is regarded as discourteous for an MP to undertake official business in the constituency of another without prior notice.

We have already mentioned that someone from Private Office accompanies a Minister everywhere. He may also bring one of the sponsoring officials - indeed, organisations may find it useful to have them there. In this case, the Director General, Aviation; the Director, Airports Policy; and the Grade 5 and 7 officials responsible for ATC ask to attend, and ATCO ensures that their opposite numbers are on hand to make the most of the opportunity to talk business with them.

Lastly, the Department's Information Office is told of the visit. It advises that there is likely to be considerable media interest and in turn is advised by Private Office of the significance of the speech in order that, at the weekly meeting of departmental information officers, DETR can try to ensure that no other major speeches or Government events clash with the opportunity to obtain coverage for a statement on its success in bringing private sector management to the ATC system. DETR will liaise with ATCO's PR department to ensure that the same press and broadcasting targets are not invited twice and ATCO and DETR will exchange drafts of their respective press releases. They will also cooperate in organising a press briefing on site. If ATCO has an announcement it wants the Minister to make in his speech, it will similarly ensure that line officials, and possibly the Special Adviser, are approached at least 48 hours beforehand. The Central Office of Information, which distributes departmental press notices to the media and to other subscribers, would be briefed to expect the announcement on the day of the visit.

Compared with the organisation behind it, the visit itself is simple. The only role performed by the Minister alone is delivering his speech.

former Permanent Secretary put it "by the time a Green Paper is published, we're usually only looking to see if there is anything we have got wrong or forgotten. In effect, at that stage we have pretty much built our car: we're just offering the option of chrome or black bumpers." The lobbyists who make the greatest impact on the system are the ones whose investment in early warning allows them to discuss issues with the system before views have hardened, and often before their competitors have become aware that Whitehall (or Scotland and Northern Ireland) is considering policy options.

• Second, it is not enough just to respond to consultation if you want your view to prevail. You need to harness third party support, anticipate and beat off countervailing political pressures, and in some cases capture the media's agenda.

149

- Third, you either need to explain why others' views are wrong as well as showing why yours are right (and that a decision in your favour can be defended publicly if the others express concern) or, as always, you need to gather a coalition of interest behind you.
- Fourth, work within the procedures appropriate to each stage of the process.
- Fifth, understand how parts of the same Department can work for you and against each other.
- Sixth, the sequence in which buttons are pressed is important. ComCo knew when to play the City card and use the media; when to approach Ministers; when to call it a day on its Bill lobbying; and it considered carefully the order in which it should approach various officials and political advisers.
- Seventh, if you seek to persuade the system that legislation is needed, be mindful of the timescale and timetabling problems. Demand heavily outweighs supply and you may have to work for years even to secure secondary legislation unless the need can be shown to be pressing. And the annual bidding schedule must be met.
- Lastly, if you make representations to MPs, MEPs or Scottish, Welsh and Northern Ireland representatives, ask their advice but understand that they prefer it if you know exactly what you want them to do for you. They are too busy to think deeply about your problem and will usually know less than you about what is happening within Departments or DGs.

There are two further options for those wanting to promote legislation:

- Private Members' Bills, which follow the same stages as other public Bills, can be introduced by any MP or Peer at any time or through the November Commons ballot, from which the top six or seven MPs will have a strong chance of being given enough parliamentary time to get a Bill through. Government may ask the higher placed backbenchers to sponsor a Bill for which there is no space in its own programme, in which case its Whips will ensure it has enough support, or in rare cases it may take over the Bill itself

A PLEA ON BEHALF OF MPs

Although a large number of MPs are career politicians, they are still treated as gifted amateurs. Many have only a secretary, who may not even work in the House, and although a large number also have research assistants, the office resources of any MP hardly compare with those of a Congressman, who may have a staff of between 20 and 150. Yet they receive around 20,000 letters a year and send 10,000; they are expected to understand the hundreds of issues thrown at them by constituents and lobby groups; and they are required to work unreasonably long hours in conditions that no corporate executive would accept. Perhaps half the mail sent to an MP is consigned to the bin by his secretary. Around a quarter of the rest is likely to come from constituents and is given priority treatment. The rest may be parliamentary and party circulars, invitations, requests to table Parliamentary Questions and more precisely targeted lobbying material. Faced with the volume of mail that arrives daily - their bundle is forwarded during recesses - and their inability to research most issues or corroborate representations himself, an MP's normal response to a constituency problem or lobbying letter is twofold:

- *It is sent with a short note to the relevant Minister or local authority department, whose staff process the enquiry (unlike MEPs, who can deal direct with Commission officials, MPs must make departmental enquiries only through Ministers). If it is a Whitehall Department matter, the Minister then corresponds with the MP who passes the Department's response to his constituent; or*
- *He sends a letter back on the lines of "I have read your letter with interest. Rest assured that when this matter comes before the House I will take full account of your concerns"*

It is possible for them to do this because so few representations either ask them to do something definite or anticipate and preempt the pressure on MPs to act as mailboxes for Whitehall by, for example, proposing intelligent letters that they can send to Ministers in their own right or asking for assistance in contacting Ministers.

Many of the letters sent by an MP may in fact be written by his secretary and simply signed by him. Either may call on the resources of the Commons library or their party research department but in the main they are flying blind.

Against this background, it is unfair for outsiders to complain that MPs do not understand their industry or its concerns. You should take the attitude that inaccurate Select Committee reports or broader misconceptions held by backbenchers are the product more of your failure to comprehend the politician's psyche and to explain your case clearly than of prejudice or stupidity. If the role and limitations of MPs are understood and they are handled personally and with sensitivity to their needs, they can be of great assistance in facilitating access to Ministers and advising on the handling of local problems. If ignored, they can develop misconceptions on issues of concern to you, leading to high profile criticism that is avoidable if time is spent on educating them and assisting them with an arduous and often thankless job.

because it believes that the issue should more correctly be dealt with by Government. In other cases, unless the Bill is non-contentious it may either be whipped against; it may not attract enough support (these Bills have their Commons Second Reading debate on Fridays, when many MPs are in their constituencies, and 100 votes are required if a Bill is to proceed to Committee - promoters must be prepared to lobby their colleagues strenuously); or it may run out of time if Private Members Bills ahead of it in the queue are still being debated when business closes at 2.30pm on Fridays. If that happens, it is placed at the back of the line and there may not be room in the schedule for it to come up again (seven Fridays from the middle of December are set aside for Private Members Bills, which are debated in order of their position in the ballot). The promoters of those Bills for which there is no time for debate must either try to force a vote without debate at the end of Friday's business - but just one MP shouting "object" halts proceedings - or hope that time may be available later.

Private Members' Bills are therefore best regarded as a device to demonstrate the strength of parliamentary feeling on an issue in the hope that Government may adopt the Bill or to give a higher priority to your lobbying. However, if an issue is non-contentious an MP placed outside even the top 10 in the ballot may be able to leapfrog over colleagues whose Bills stimulate concern and are delayed (on average, some 15-16 Private Members' Bills are passed every year).

A tactic increasingly used by interest groups is "double tracking", meaning introducing similar Bills into the Commons and Lords at the same time in order to increase the opportunities for debate. Bear in mind that Bills introduced in the Lords go to the back of the queue when they reach the Commons and are therefore unlikely to make progress.

While the promoter of a Private Members' Bill is not obliged to produce a Regulatory Impact Assessment, officials are required to do so to back their advice to Ministers on the line to take. Whether the Bill is antagonistic or advantageous, interested parties should contact those officials to discuss their view on impacts since they may not have had sufficient notification of the Bill to undertake a normal consultation exercise. If the Bill is hostile to your interests, you should brief MPs and officials to press the Bill's promoters to produce an RIA. If the promoters refuse, you may seek both to exploit that publicly or to challenge them to rebut your own impact assessment. Alternatively, you may seek more quietly to persuade officials and Ministers to oppose the Bill or to seek amendments to it on the basis of your assessed impacts (unless it appears that the Department's own RIA is likely to support your views, in which case leave the work to them). The corollary of this is that if you seek to promote a Private Members' Bill, you will increasingly come under pressure to publish an assessment of business impacts. Better to get your retaliation in first.

In Scotland, individual MSPs may not introduce more than two "Member's Bills" in the same session. Members lodge a notice of a proposal for a Bill with the Clerk, which sets out the name of the Member and the proposed short title of the Bill. Other Members may notify the Clerk of their support and this, in addition to the original short title will be printed in the Business Bulletin. The Bill may only be introduced if it gains the support of at least 11 other MSPs within one month of it being printed. If the proposed Bill falls, it may not be reintroduced for six months. Alternatively, a MSP may submit to the Parliamentary Bureau a draft proposal for the Bill which is then referred to the appropriate subject committee and the committee then decides whether it should propose the legislation. In this case the Bill becomes a Committee Bill (ie introduced by the committee) but will be clearly recorded as originating from an MSP's draft proposal.

Bills introduced by backbench MSPs follow the same route as for Executive and Committee Bills. However, the sponsor of the Bill can, after the last amendment has been taken at Stage 3, propose a motion that the remaining proceedings at this stage be adjourned until a later day. If agreed, a further debate may take place to clarify uncertainties. A debate on the Bill being passed is then held at which the sponsor may request that no more than half of the clauses of the Bill be referred back to Stage 2 (this can only be done once). The final amendments in Stage 3 must only be as a consequence of amendments made at Stage 2 or those which were referred back to committee.

Welsh AMs can introduce secondary legislation through a ballot. The details of the proposed legislation and its financial implications are set out within two working days of the Assembly voting on a resolution on whether or not it will instruct the Assembly Secretary to make the draft Order (see p 120 for details of Welsh secondary legislation procedure).

• Deregulation Act Orders, which enable unnecessary regulatory burdens to be removed without the need for primary legislation. Organisations seeking elimination of a statutory requirement or restriction need to follow these steps:

The Deregulation Act requires that proposals should satisfy three criteria: the Act to be amended must have been passed before 1994; the amendment must remove a burden on business; and it must not remove any "necessary protection" (this is deliberately not defined in the Act: discretion lies with Whitehall).

Application should be made to the Department with lead responsibility for the legislation it is proposed to amend. It then decides whether to propose that an Order be agreed to, although the Regulatory Impact Unit in the Cabinet Office may give guidance. The Unit also acts as coordinator if other Departments are interested.

A Cabinet Committee on deregulation then assesses the proposal.

If the three criteria are satisfied, the normal consultation process for secondary legislation takes place and a draft Order is then sent to the Deregulation Select Committees (one in each House) which examine it. They can recommend changes and may decide to hold a hearing if they feel there is enough public interest.

This does not mean that it is easy to obtain an Order. The lead Department may not want to act, and lobbyists may have to bring other Departments, No 10, groups of MPs or the media to bear. Or the Cabinet Committee may not wish to approve too many applications from one Department since, as with primary legislation, there is competition for space on the Select Committees' agendas (they are required to consider draft Orders within 60 days and Whitehall therefore carefully controls the flow of proposals to avoid bottlenecks).

At the time of writing, legislation is to be introduced to allow the Dregulation Act's procedure to be used to repeal or amend parts of existing measures rather than the entire Bill or Order which may be unnecessary and cause difficulties.

Local Government decision-making

For those familiar with central government's processes, the mechanics of local government should not cause great difficulties. There are only a few key principles to remember:

- The bulk of your focus should be initially be at Chief Officer level in the Department of relevance to you. They will decide whether your issue should be referred to their Directors or handled at a lower level.
- Officers are authorised to deal with some issues on their own initiative – for example expenditure up to a prescribed level, issuing particular kinds of permits and initial discussion with prospective contractors as well as mundane activities such as road repairs.
- The balance between officer and Member contact will depend on whether the issue of interest to you is largely administrative or, on the other hand, is one where the council has a distinct policy, where a fair degree of public interest is evident, or where national policy considerations will weigh significantly. For example, permission to build a car port will be processed by officers and rubber stamped by the committee handling planning. An application to build an orimulsion-burning power station is likely to be debated vigorously in committee and in full council meetings, and there would probably be some liaison between officers and DTI/DETR

and between Members and the local MPs and county councillors representing the area.

• It will also be governed by the political stability of the council. You should broadly assume three cultures:

CONTACTING COUNCILLORS AND OFFICERS

Councillors: call the Town Hall and ask for Member Services, the office that services councillors. It will give you home/work telephone numbers and addresses (the latter are listed in the Municipal Yearbook (see p. 278). It will also tell you about committee memberships.

Officers: call the Town Hall (numbers listed in the Municipal Yearbook) and ask for the officer who either services the committee you need or who heads the section responsible for the issue of concern to you.

Where one party has a solid majority and has had one for some time, the council may either be virtually run by the officers, who may develop policy and refer to Members relatively infrequently, or it may be controlled by strong leading figures (sometimes associated with a forceful, ideologically driven approach).

Marginal councils may, because ward by-elections are frequent, change control on more than one occasion during an electoral cycle. Individual Members are more important and officers need to have regard to possible changes in council policy. Unlike central government, opposition councillors see and deal with officers on a regular basis and have the right to receive papers which at Westminster would only be available to the Government.

Hung councils, where there is no overall control, may be run by a coalition of parties or committee chairmanships may be assigned at each meeting. In this situation the officers are likely to come into their own but decisions requiring political sanction are obviously precarious.

In each case, officers will usually give you a reliable guide to power balances, key members and policy/political dimensions to your problem.

- The key members are the Leader, the appropriate committee chairmen (and possibly their deputies), the majority party Chief Whip, relevant ward councillors (whether controlling or opposition, any noted dissidents in the controlling group, the Leader of the Opposition, chief opposition speakers on appropriate committees, and (unless the council has unitary status) relevant ward councillors from other tiers - for example, the county councillor for the area where the issue is handled by districts.

- Districts and counties do not operate in separate worlds. Where development issues are involved, districts must operate within County Structure Plans, which cover housing, Green Belts and conservation areas, the rural economy, major employment-generating development, main transport facilities, mineral workings, waste disposal and land reclamation, tourism, leisure and recreation. They are produced following local consultation and the Secretary of State for Environment, Transport and the Regions can either direct the council not to approve the plan until specified modifications have been made or he can "call in" the plan. Districts produce local plans within this framework, although these are not approved by Whitehall; nor are the Unitary Development Plans produced by London and other metropolitan councils. Wherever possible, organisations with development objectives should seek to influence the drafting of these plans, both by submitting formal representations and by lobbying officers, the key members listed above and ward councillors whose area may benefit from your proposals.

- Structure and local plans, DETR Circulars and Planning Policy Guidance notes (which clarify legislation relating to planning and the local environment) will dictate officers' recommendations. They need good reasons to overturn established policy. Members usually accept those recommendations and the chairman and other senior members of the committee on the majority side will have discussed them with officers before the committee meets.

- Do not judge party discipline by Westminster standards. Emotions of local residents may run high, forcing local councillors to oppose their own party's policy or to ignore the advice of their officers. The pressure which can be exerted on ward councillors by local residents (and the loyalty they may feel towards the area they represent and in which they are likely to live) is considerable.

• On planning issues, follow this checklist:

Initial research: who controls the council; stability of the majority; when are the next elections due; in which ward (district and county) is the site located; if near a boundary, which other wards could be affected (travel to work radius, lorry routes, residents affected by emissions etc); who are the ward councillors and do they sit on relevant committees or play a leading role in the council; council decision-making record on this type of application?

Next level: local press search for comments about the area/site; check the news sheets put out by the main parties in most council areas; assess key players and local factors (officers may help if you are prepared to approach them in confidence; otherwise it may be best to use consultants with links to the council and to local political party organisers). Identify residents associations or local action groups. Identify local businesses likely to be impacted/benefited by the development.

Discuss the potential application with the Director/Assistant Director of Planning (depending on the scale of the proposal) on a 'without commitment' basis.

Put your case to ward councillors at an early stage. Leave it too late and local pressure may have forced them to make promises they cannot break.

Do not just write to them: arrange to meet them (possibly after work, although some are full-time councillors). Give them arguments they can use in response to representations from constituents.

If necessary, pre-brief the local press. Once your application is published, opponents may be quick off the mark in raising the profile of their concerns.

If there is a strongly established body of local opposition, it may call a public meeting to which you, a planning officer, the ward councillors, local MP and planning chairman may be invited. It is unwise to refuse to attend but assume that feelings will run high and that no-one will change the public's views. You are there to be shouted at.

It goes without saying, but ensure that your application and associated representations stress conformity with council policies, and in particular the local plan; or that there are exceptionally powerful reasons for setting policy aside.

Planning Gain may be relevant. If there is any chance of difficulty, explore with officers at the outset whether associated funding (which might range from direct mitigation such as landscaping to priority council projects that may only be tenuously linked to the development) could be a pivotal factor. Landowners can make a unilateral undertaking as a form of planning obligation which may moderate the council's demands since if it refuses permission, the undertaking may be taken into account by the Secretary of State in considering any appeal. Handle Planning Gain offers sensitively: they must not look like inducements.

If the controlling group is likely to be split on your issue, Opposition votes could make the difference. However, Opposition parties tend to side with residents, particularly if the ward is marginal.

Remember that while only the Planning Committee may approve your application, others (eg Transport/ Highways/ Environment - titles vary from council to council) with an interest will receive a paper for information. Make sure the councillors on those committees are briefed before their meeting.

Some projects require production of an Environmental Assessment. There may be considerable benefit in preparing one before the planning authority rules that one is necessary or even, in controversial cases, if it rules against having one. If there is any doubt, you would be well advised to seek a preliminary ruling to avoid a public squabble later when the plans are clearer and an application is imminent or already published. You may also, in the case of large scale projects, have to consider an approach to the

European Commission to ensure that it is satisfied with the way an EA is produced – opponents could attack it on methodological or procedural grounds as happened, for example, when an organisation sought to build a railway line from the Midlands to the Channel Tunnel.

PREEMPTING PLANNING OPPOSITION

When BP sought to develop the inland oilfield at Wytch Farm in Dorset, it gave two people responsibility for contacting local organisations and individual opinion formers to persuade them to support (or not to oppose) its plans. The list included not only the county, district and parish councils but also Chambers of Commerce, unions, residents associations and local branches of environmental groups. BP arranged public exhibitions and spokesmen were available to visit schools, WI branches, church groups and other local organisations.

BP was able to identify and defuse potential controversies in advance. Plans were amended while still on the drawing board to take account of environmental interests. BP was given planning permission with much less public opposition than was first expected.

- In parallel with Structure and Local Plans, local authorities also have environmental policies, both because of the profile given to this area (which can lead to councils vying with each other to be "greenest", for example in setting noise limits for local airports) and because of their statutory duties to authorise industrial processes and produce Waste Disposal Development Plans and to police environmental claims. You should find out what investment the authority has made in developing a policy and who at Member and officer level is in charge of it. In particular, you need to know whether the policy specifically comments on the role of business in setting and meeting environmental targets. Some questions to ask the council are
- Has it conducted an internal environmental audit? Has it prepared a report on the state of the local environment? Does it address the role of industry?

If the answer is No, is the council intending to produce one and how will local industry be consulted?

How is environmental policy coordinated at Member and officer level?

Does every council department have an officer responsible for implementation of the environmental strategy? If so, what level of seniority do they have?

Is local business represented on any council bodies dealing with environmental issues? Are pressure groups represented?

POLLING CAN BE IMPORTANT

In the campaign to prevent proposals for the Channel Tunnel Rail Link from being overturned by local protest, the promoters commissioned opinion research throughout constituencies and local authority areas through which the line would run in order to show MPs and councillors that local opposition around the line was balanced by support or disinterest among the majority of voters on a constituency or council-wide basis.

- Armed with answers to these questions, you can then consider whether to brief officers and Members on your own environmental performance with the aim of establishing your record and procedures as Best Practice. You may wish to offer assistance in preparing the council's environmental audit; with input into educational projects or with sponsorship of recycling or disposal campaigns or facilities.
- Environmental policy is not the only area in which partnership may benefit your organisation. Sponsorship or other assistance to a local Environmental Health Officer's campaign on alcohol misuse or a Social Services Department programme to educate on sensible heating use in winter may offer advantages for your relationship with the local authority or the general public.
- Local authorities have for some years been required to subject core services to competitive tendering. This regime is now being replaced by a "Best Value" requirement, which differs in concept from Compulsory Competitive Tendering in that it applies to all

CHALLENGING LEGISLATION
THE ROLE OF JUDICIAL REVIEW AND
REGULATORY IMPACT ASSESSMENT

You may need to stop Government from regulating or making policy decisions. Under such circumstances, there are two key devices for ensuring accountability:

Judicial Review applications, *contending that Ministers have exceeded or failed to exercise their statutory powers or have made a decision without fully considering the evidence. A large number of these are now made every year and few are granted by the courts, but they can be heard much faster than other legal actions and Government must observe them if upheld. However, if you have a range of weapons to choose from, use judicial review or recourse to EU law as a last resort. Departments and DGs will clam up, preempting negotiation or the gathering of information about their case, if they believe that legal action is likely; and they are likely to be less obliging in their future dealings with you.*

Regulatory Impact Assessment, *a set of Cabinet Office, Scottish Parliament and European Commission guidelines (the process is known as Business Impact Assessment in Brussels) which state that before deciding to introduce new regulatory proposals, officials must calculate the cost to a typically affected organisation of complying with the measure's requirements; produce a risk assessment, in which the risk to be avoided (eg motor accidents) is given a value; consider the extent to which regulation is likely to reduce the risk; and set against that the financial and other costs of achieving the reduction. Consultation is required and the UK requires publication of these appraisals. UK Regulatory Impact Assessments (known as Financial Memoranda in Scotland and Regulatory Appraisal in Wales) are required both for domestic and EU proposals and again when EU measures are translated into national legislation. Ministers must sign a certificate to show they have read the Appraisal and that the balance has been fairly struck between benefit and burden. All proposals to Cabinet or Cabinet sub-committee should have one of these; they should be produced by Whitehall early in the EU legislative process; and proposals should not go to full Commission meetings without one.*

These rules/guidelines (available from the Regulatory Impact Unit in the Cabinet Office; Brussels guidelines are unpublished but the Enterprise or Internal Market DGs should give you a copy) offer considerable opportunities to lobbyists. While they are not legally enforceable (although failure to follow the requirements could give rise to a complaint to the UK or EU Ombudsman (Parliamentary Commissioner for Administration, House of Commons, SW1A OAA; European Ombudsman, 1 Ave du President Robert Schumann, BP403, 67001 Strasbourg) on grounds of maladministration), they give outsiders the ability:

- to press officials and Ministers to make sure that consultation is representative and timely
- to check that the methodology used is acceptable and, if not, to challenge it (for example, was all the relevant evidence considered or are there flaws in the evidence they have?)
- to press the system (particularly in Brussels, where a relaxed attitude prevails) to produce assessments before regulating; and to embarrass it through the media, the UK Opposition and the European Parliament Rules of Procedure Committee if it omits or refuses to act. Failure to observe the guidelines can be reported to the UK or EU Ombudsmen, whose reports can be embarrassing for Whitehall and the Commission.
- to continue to monitor burdens and benefits post-implementation in case the assessment is invalidated by experience; and
- to produce their own Assessments, following the rules precisely, in order to influence or second-guess the system's approach or to make the case for their own proposals.

This can be highly effective: as an example, an EU tax proposal was challenged for lack of a Business Impact Assessment even though the Council had reached Common Position. Embarrassment at the omission was such that the draft Directive was withdrawn. Seven years later, it has not reappeared.

council services, need not involve contracting out, is based on quality as well as cost, and compares performance between councils.

Although the interests of counties, districts and metropolitan authorities do not always coincide, they are represented by a single body, the Local Government Association, which produces a wide range of guidance notes for local authorities on issues such as Best Practice and proposals for Government on generic issues such as out of town development. It has very good access to most Ministers and is an essential target both for lobbying and for obtaining information on policy (26 Chapter Street, London SW1P 3BJ, 0171 834 2222).

EU Decision Making and Legislation

Whether you are seeking to respond to EU proposals or promote Europe-wide legislation, start by looking at the key pressure points:

- Commission officials between A3-6/7 grades, the former being responsible for formulation; the later for drafting and day-to-day

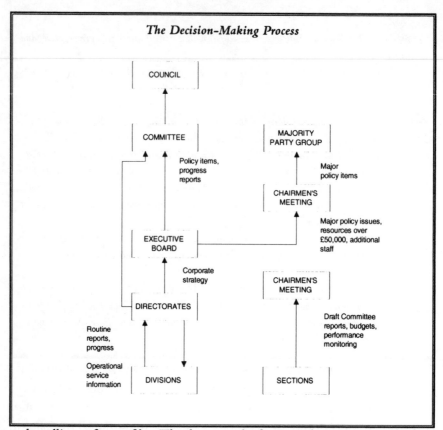

The Decision-Making Process

handling of case files. The best grade for initial contact is Head of Unit, the equivalent of Whitehall grade G5/Assistant Secretary.

- Member State administrations. Proposals need their votes, both indirectly at an early stage (the Commission is unlikely to act if it feels it cannot carry a proportion of Member States with it) and directly in Council, where Member States have weighted voting power and on many issues the rules allow a minority to block agreement. Similarly, in the European Parliament the national groupings of MEPs will liaise with their domestic parents. EU lobbying therefore cannot just concentrate on Brussels: it must work on mobilising and canalising national Government and political party views.

- The Commission's advisory committees, divided into Committees of Experts (usually national officials and technical specialists) and

Consultative Committees (representatives of sectional interests, usually nominated by umbrella groups). The former, which discuss Commission legislative proposals or regulatory casework (eg competition complaints) at an early stage or which may have a licensing (eg applications for authorisation of Novel Foods) or budget management function, are more important.

HOW THE VOTES STACK UP

The legal base chosen will also affect the way the Council is required to vote

Unanimity, *mainly for issues not precisely defined in the Treaty: indirect tax, industry, financial regulation, environmental taxation, planning, culture, energy sources/supply and some R&D issues. Also where the Council wants to amend a Commission proposal against the Commission's wishes. Abstentions do not count as votes against a proposal.*

Qualified *Majority Vote. There must be 62 votes for a proposal to be adopted. A Blocking Minority exists if there are 26 votes against or abstentions. Voting power varies:*

Austria	4	Germany	10	Netherlands	5
Belgium	5	Greece	5	Portugal	5
Denmark	3	Ireland	3	Spain	8
France	10	Italy	10	Sweden	4
Finland	3	Luxembourg	2	UK	10

- Council working groups, which negotiate on the fine detail of proposals once the Commission has completed its drafting.
- The legal base selected for a proposal. This is vitally important: legislative proposals whose scope is not covered by the Treaty cannot proceed; choice of an inappropriate legal basis (for example, using a Treaty article covering removal of barriers to trade when the measure proposes banning a trading activity) can be challenged in the European Court by Member States or affected parties; and EU legislative structures vary depending on the legal basis chosen. In summary, the three main procedures are

Consultation, mainly applying to agriculture, indirect taxation, competition, state aids rules, fiscal measures applying to the environment, planning, energy sources/supply measures, financial regulation, some EMU issues, adopting R&D programmes, industry, international agreements, or procedure under Article 235, which allows the EU to act where no specific Treaty provision applies. There is a single European Parliament stage and Council need take no account of EP views.

Cooperation, mainly used for health and safety, common transport policy, implementing Trans-European Network (eg railways, pipelines) decisions, implementing R&D and environment action programmes, some EMU issues, implementing European Social Regional Development Fund decisions and worker consultation and information. The EP produces two Opinions, once when the Commission has completed its drafting and a second time when the Council reaches agreement (known as Common Position). If it wants to amend or reject the Council position, it must do so by absolute majority. Outright rejection can only be overturned by a unanimous vote in Council (even if the legal base allowed the Common Position to be reached by a weighted vote - known as a Qualified Majority Vote or QMV). This means that only one Member State can overturn a Common Position reached by the Council by a qualified majority if it works with the Parliament and the Commission. If amended by the EP, the draft must within a month be reconsidered by the Commission and reported to the Council, which has three months to adopt the re-examined proposal (the Commission may ignore all the EP amendments) by QMV or amend it - including reverting to its original Common Position - by unanimity.

Co-decision, used for measures covering free movement of workers and freedom of establishment, Single Market issues, education, culture, health and consumer protection, Trans-European Network guidelines and adopting environmental action programmes. It gives the EP the right to veto legislation: the procedure is broadly similar to Cooperation, except that the EP has a defined period (three months) in which to act after the Council has reached Common Position. If it rejects the Common Position the proposal is lost. If it makes amendments which are not accepted by the Council within three to four months, a Conciliation Committee, on which every Council member, an equal number of MEPs, and Commission representatives, is convened with six weeks (plus another two if both sides agree) to reach a compromise. The Council (by QMV) and EP (by absolute majority) then have a further six weeks to adopt the joint text. If agreement cannot be reached, the Council again votes on its own proposal, which the EP can finally reject by absolute majority.

EP committees and the views of the rapporteur on draft legislation. Committees vary in influence depending on the subject they cover (in terms of EU priorities, agriculture is considered more important than women's rights), the reputation of their chairman and his effectiveness in securing harmony within his committee, and the level of expertise of his members – the Legal Affairs Committee is full of lawyers. Rapporteurs, who are selected by agreement among the party groupings (each committee has group "coordinators") have (at least under the Cooperation and Co-Decision procedures) two opportunities to develop understanding of an issue since they produce reports after the Commission submits its draft to the EP and then after Common Position is reached in Council. They may rely on their research assistant, the Secretariat of the EP or of their own political group, the Commission, or outsiders. It is always worth approaching them or their assistant to ask what form of briefing they want and to offer views as soon as they are appointed. While their recommendations may be amended by their committee (in the case of proposals which overlap more than one committee, up to three may be asked for views but one will be named as the lead committee and only it will report to the plenary session; it is often worthwhile producing a less detailed version of your rapporteur's brief for the committee(s) as a whole) or by plenary itself, they set the framework for debate

THE FIGHT TO SAVE DUTY FREE
THE IMPORTANCE OF LUCK

Manufacturers and retailers of Duty Free goods around Europe, having successfully lobbied in 1992 for an extension of the system to June 1999, sought a further lease of life. The odds were against them: because it was a fiscal matter, the 1992 decision could only be overturned by a unanimous vote in the Council of Economic and Finance Ministers, and most Member States claimed that Duty Free was an anomaly that should go after 1999. Furthermore, the Commission, having been defeated in 1992, was adamant that the decision must stand. Although its second campaign had moved a number of Member States from opposition to benign neutrality, it looked as though time was running out. 1998 was reaching a close and the issue had still not been decisively raised in Ecofin. However, fortune can swing...

- *The Germans were due to go to the polls in the Autumn of 1998. The main challenger to Chancellor Kohl represented a constituency heavily dependent on ferry trade. It was easy for him to see the populist appeal of support for Duty Free. His espousal of the case forced Kohl to follow suit, delivering to the industry a major Member State which had opposed extension in 1992.*

- *The Germans were also due to hold the Council presidency in the first half of 1999. Schroder's win in the elections guaranteed that Duty Free would be placed on the Council agenda at a critical time.*

- *The new German Finance Minister raised eurosceptic alarms around Europe when he was reported as calling for the EU to harmonise income tax. Other national Ministers (in particular Tony Blair, who had been lobbied by his French and Irish counterparts at two of the bilateral meetings which traditionally take place before the heads of government summits that close each EU presidency) suddenly found it convenient to make a stand on behalf of Duty Free as a means of waving their flag against Brussels centralism. Oscar Lafontaine's timely remarks unexpectedly pushed the Duty Free issue to centre stage at the summit which closed the Austrian presidency in December 1998. Once the major Member States declared their support for the campaign, a number of smaller (and hitherto opposed) states declared that they had no objection to the issue being re-examined.*

- *Although Commissioner Monti, who had charge of this portfolio, had implacably opposed Duty Free, Commission President Santer, nearing the end of his term and seeking renomination, was keen to court Member State support. He therefore did not argue strongly against the summit's compromise proposal that the Commission should assess the economic impact of abolition - an assessment that would almost certainly show that the cost would be considerable and the benefits largely theoretical.*

Well though the industry lobbied, it had to acknowledge that events undoubtedly turned in its favour at just the right time.

It thought. In the end, the Danes, who were expected to give way if all other Members States supported an extension, continued to exercise their veto at the June 1999 Cologne Summit that represented the last chance to do a deal. But their reason for frustrating the Duty Free campaign had little to do with the issue in hand. The French, who had coordinated the lobbying of Prime Ministers to maintain Duty Free, opposed the nomination of a Dane to coordinate the EU's common external and security policy in favour of its own candidate and the maintenance of the Danes' blocking vote was their retaliation. There was little that the Duty Free lobby could have done.

To take the process from start to finish, let us take a hypothetical example:

FIGHTING FOR THE DISABLED

The European Federation of Disability Organisations has for several years been lobbying the Commission, alongside the efforts of its counterparts within Member States, to secure legislation to require international transport services to improve facilities for access by the disabled. They have targeted the Transport and Employment and Social Affairs DGs and are aware that they should plan to at least a five year timescale, since the EU decision-making process can be very slow.

Despite securing support from members of the two parallel EP Committees (one of the members of which has been persuaded to produce an "Own Initiative Report" - largely drafted by EFDO - with the aim of securing a debate at a plenary session and a possible EP Resolution on the subject) and from the Intergroup on Disability, which the Federation established as a lobbying vehicle, for some time it is met by

The international aspect of this is important. The Commission can only set EU-wide standards where failure to do so would distort trade between Member States and where national action alone will not be enough. A purely national problem would be one for national legislatures.

It is possible for two DGs to work on parallel proposals at the same time. From the Federation's point of view, this gives them a greater chance of success and a shot at two Commissioners rather than one, although if both want to take the credit the issue could get enmeshed in rivalries. Conversely, one way to delay action is to play DGs off against each other.

EFDO's national members will have lobbied their MEPs, who will have been able to take the case to their political grouping, to colleagues on the relevant committees and to the

sympathy and excuses about other priorities. It then finds that the key official at A6 grade in the Employment DG is replaced by someone more sympathetic to the disabled. EFDO prepares a brief setting out

- statistics on the extent of under-provision of facilities and evidence of the extent of difficulties in cross-border travel being faced by disabled people as a result
- a table showing the wide divergence in regulatory requirements and disability provision between Member States and their international transport providers
- an assessment of policy options. EFDO knows that the Commission often finds it easier to adopt an action programme, which may offer money to Member States to remedy problems but which is more likely to major on largely worthless exhortation, so it needs to show that only legislation will do
- suggested outline text of a Directive, together with a commentary on the right hand side of the page to

Commission (unlike MPs, MEPs can contact officials direct). Intergroups can be established relatively easily if enough MEPs are prepared to sign up.

To show them that there is a prima facie case to answer and to avoid the Commission feeling it must engage its own consultants to quantify the problem. This could lose EFDO not only the nine months taken in tendering and report production but also a slot in next year's Commission work programme.

The Commission would otherwise have to do this research itself.

This is unlikely to be accepted complete as the Commission's legal service takes the same view as Parliamentary Counsel about

explain why that wording was selected. EFDO proposes that Articles 49 (free movement of workers) and 129d (guidelines on Trans-European Networks) be the legal base as they would involve QMV rather than unanimity and give greater power to the EP

- an assessment of the likely views of Member States and transport providers.

The official agrees to take the matter forward and drafts a paper for her Head of Unit. He agrees that a proposal should be prepared for endorsement by the cabinet, with the aim of finding space within the Commission's next annual work programme, and the Head of Division is briefed; he informs the cabinet and the matter is discussed with the Commissioner. The DG may at this stage convene an "expert group", which will usually be comprised of Member State officials but may occasionally include representatives of outside bodies, or it may proceed direct to distribution of the proposal to other DGs and cabinets for views: this is known as inter-service consultation. The result

drafting, but it does make it easier for officials to envisage the shape of legislation.

The system needs to know how much hostility or support it is likely to encounter.

Commissioners think just like national Ministers when presented with a proposal:

- *What is this about?*
- *Why should we do anything about this?*
- *What will it cost?*
- *What do other Commissioners and the Member States think?*
- *Who will back me?*

In some cases, however, Governments only find out because sectional interests tell them or because their Permanent Representations chance upon the information. Not unlikely, bearing in mind that transport providers will wish to lobby their own officials.

171

may be inter-DG strife, agreement subject to amendments, or a conclusion that further external views should be sought and a Green Paper should be produced.

If the proposal is ready, it will be discussed by the cabinet specialists at one of their weekly meetings to agree the agenda for the next plenary meeting of Commissioners (always held on Wednesday). If there are no problems with the proposal, it is put on the agenda for next Wednesday, but if one or more cabinets has reservations the issue is either sent back to officials for further work, deferred, or re-tabled at the separate weekly Chefs de Cabinet meeting before being sent to the Wednesday Commission meeting for approval. The text is then sent to the Council Secretariat, which copies it to the EP.

If they have not done so already, Member States will start to consult domestically. Both sides to the debate will seek to influence officials and Ministers, parliamentarians and the media. UK Departments increasingly establish small consultative groups,

Brussels usually consults widely and openly before producing consultation papers.

All proposals likely to have a significant impact on business, particularly small business, should have a Fiche d'Impact, or Business Impact Assessment (see pp 162 and 252-263). Lobbyists should either keep nagging the Commission to produce one - it usually ignores the requirement - and to get the methodology right or they should draft one themselves. EFDO's plans could be flawed because of the cost of adapting facilities relative to the proportion of passengers or potential passengers that would benefit. This also applies to the UK. Whitehall is meant to produce a Regulatory Impact Assessment to guide its negotiating position on EU proposals, and another when legislation has been agreed and has to be transposed into UK law.

If you have a significant interest, contact the lead official and ask to be included in the group; or, if you are not a major player, work through possible allies on the group. Avoid meetings close to Councils for which those officials have to prepare: they will be

with members drawn from the relevant sectors, to guide the official in day-to-day control of the negotiating file (usually at Grade 7 level) on the implications of technical provisions and amendments.

The Commission will brief the EP committees responsible for the draft as well as the next meeting of the relevant Council (there is usually no debate; the issue only becomes a live one when a Presidency decides to take it up, and that could take some time). The EP committee rapporteur produces a first report, which is debated in committee. A few weakening amendments are recommended following evidence from manufacturers about technical difficulties in adapting some aircraft types and they are voted through in "First Reading" by the plenary session.

The EP Opinion is sent to the Council and to the Commission, which takes a view on whether the amendments should be accepted. If it does not reject them it must produce an amended proposal.

A working group of officials from each Member State,

under pressure and unlikely to give your issue full consideration.

If EFDO has really done its work, the EP Committee may be sufficiently interested to have appointed its rapporteur before the Commission has even adopted the proposal (however, following lobbying from the transport providers the EP's Conference of Committee Chairmen has decided that the less supportive Regional Policy, Transport ad Tourism Committee will lead, with input from the Employment and Social Affairs Committee). Each Committee will also meet and question the chairman of the relevant Council at the start of every Presidency and EFDO will have briefed its allies on the Regional Policy, Transport and Tourism Committee to highlight this proposal. Issues sent to committees are divided up between the political groups, each of which is allocated proposals in proportion to their size, and their MEPs lobbyfor the right to handle certain dossiers.

EFDO may want to propose amendments to any of the institutions. The standard form for this is to set out the original text on the left hand side of

serviced by the Council Secretariat and chaired by the current Presidency, which will be advised by the Commission, will then meet, often for months on end, to seek agreement. Impasse may be reached on more than one occasion and Coreper may several times have the draft referred to it to see whether some way forward can be found.

The draft is ready to be discussed in Council. Although the legal base allows for QMV, if the Council seeks to make amendments to which the Commission is opposed it can only do so by unanimity. In fact, both institutions have accepted that concerns expressed by airlines and some rail operators are valid and Common Position is reached with a number of new derogations and exemptions.

The draft goes back to the same EP committees, which have three months to report to a plenary session. Lobbyists for the disabled are now thick on the ground in Brussels and in every Member State, where the media has been stimulated to put MEPs on the spot, and the PSE, Green and many in the EPP groups have been persuaded to vote at

the page and new text, with changes underlined and omissions marked [...] alongside it on the right hand side.

EFDO keeps in close touch with the Commission and with supportive national officials to gain intelligence on changes in Member State and Commission positions during this stage.

Not all problems are resolved in working groups or in Coreper. Officials may decide that some issues can only be settled by political negotiation and may agree to brief their Ministers to cover them in closed session. These meetings can take many hours and some items on the Council agenda may be lost as a result. Organisations seeking debates on policy issues must accept this as a hazard of the system.

Whenever EFDO briefs an MEP for the first time, it has a 1-2 page note summarising its case and proposed amendments ready to hand over. Note that only amendments adopted at First Reading can be considered at Second Reading unless the Common Position differs significantly from the Commission's original proposal.

MEPs are given voting lists by their political groups. These consist of

"Second Reading" in plenary for reinstatement of most of the EP's original demands.

The draft goes back to the Council, which has between three and four months to accept by QMV the EP amendments approved by the Commission. In this case, the Commission has softened on some but not on most of the changes, and since there is no chance of these being accepted by unanimity the Conciliation Committee will be convened. It is still possible, if the Council accepts some but not all of the amendments proposed in Conciliation, that the EP may decide to vote the measure down, but in this case that is unlikely.

a long list of amendment numbers with voting instructions ("FOR, AGAINST, ABSTAIN") for each one. To avoid confusion, it is sensible shortly before plenary to send a brief to your supporters with a list enumerating your favoured amendments.

This could be a problem for EFDO since a fundamental disagreement between Council and EP on costs, timescales or technical feasibility could lead to the proposal being lost. MEPs' fervour may develop its own momentum unless EFDO can show them that accepting compromise proposals would not be seen as a sell-out by its more militant supporters.

This is only one example of the way the EU machine works but it shows, albeit in rather abbreviated form (we have not, for example, mentioned other institutions which must formally be consulted but which carry little influence), how Brussels makes up its mind. It also demonstrates the key success factors:

• If you want to stop Brussels from acting, do so early. The transport operators could not raise their profile to match EFDO for fear of appearing churlish to the disabled but they should brief national officials and other parts of the Commission, produce their own cost/benefit analysis and demand that the Commission followed suit, and mobilise supporters of their technical case as soon as they learn of the Employment DG's plans. It is not easy to influence positions once Council working groups have been convened.

- As with Whitehall, the trick is to make yourself useful to the Commission or to MEPs even if you do not represent an entire sector or industry. While Brussels officials give preference to the views of umbrella bodies, they will usually be happy to meet you and if they feel you are a reasonably objective source of information they may give your subsequent representations greater weight. Do not skimp on the external research or internal number-crunching you may need in order to prove to them that your case holds water.

TARGETING THE RIGHT OFFICIALS AND MEPS

The **European Public Affairs Directory** lists the names, addresses, numbers and responsibilities of most officials and of all MEPs. Vachers European Companion, which is revised quarterly, contains a useful summary and lists Ministries in all the Member States. Whitehall officials handling the brief will also help you. If, after using Vachers or contacting other officials, you know which DG and Unit you need to approach, the universal Commission switchboard number is 00 322 299 1111. The EP's "grey list", available from national EP offices, contains constituency office addresses.

Vachers lists all MEPs and the membership of committees. If they support your case, your constituency MEPs or their researchers should be able to advise on others to approach or avoid. Intergroup membership can usually only be ascertained by inspecting the register of MEPs' interests held at the Parliament itself - a friendly research assistant may help. Write to MEPs either at their constituency address (available from the EP office, 2 Queen Anne's Gate, London SW1H 9AA, 0171 227 4300) or at the European Parliament, rue Wiertz, 1047 Brussels.

- Think laterally in dealing with Whitehall on EU issues. If the Department holding the brief is unsympathetic to your case, is there an angle which might appeal to another Department? Does the EU proposal affect Scotland, Wales, Northern Ireland, the Channel Islands, Isle of Man, or Gibraltar? If so, try to involve the territorial Departments and the Foreign Office.
- While the transport operators might be able to block domestic action through logical case-making behind the scenes, fearing that

contact with MPs would draw them into an emotive battle they could not win, the greater power of the EP requires them at least to attempt to brief MEPs or carefully to examine procedural devices for stymieing EP agreement. For example, is there room for dispute over the legal base? Has the Commission failed to produce a Fiche d'Impact? If so, the Rules of Procedure and Legal Affairs Committees might enjoy the opportunity of summoning the Commissioner before them – and the transport operators might finish the job by arranging for the media to be ready to interview him outside the committee room.

WORKING THE BRUSSELS SYSTEM

Shippers were concerned that a revised Liner Convention promoted by shipowners would significantly raise their freight costs. The Convention was about to be approved by the Transport Council when the shippers' adviser spotted that it was the Commission, not the Council, that had competence on that issue.

He immediately contacted members of the European Parliament's Legal Affairs Committee and persuaded them to summon the Commissioner for questioning. And, in case that was not enough to put the Commission on the spot, he made sure that a Financial Times journalist was outside the room to interview the Commissioner.

Result: the Commission accepted that it had to take over the matter, including listening again to the shippers' case.

• If you cannot stop a proposal at an early stage or secure a Blocking Minority in Council through national lobbying, consider whether amendments – for example, changing definitions or introducing transitional periods or derogations – might mitigate or eliminate your problem. This is particularly sensible if you can only start lobbying late in the process: you are unlikely to secure the cooperation between EP political groups needed to reject a proposal in plenary, and remember that while Member States may have a host of concerns about a draft, by the time it gets to working group their broad support for its objectives may be irreversible.
• The Whitehall official handling the negotiating brief (usually G7) will often convene a consultative group of the major UK players

on the issue (ie those Whitehall has heard of). At the outset, you should ask if one is being established and make your case for inclusion. Consider whether any of its members could help your lobby.

- The main weakness of MEPs lies in their limited interference in the legislative process. The rules make it difficult to amend a draft at Second Reading, and the fate of amendments passed at First Reading is largely in the hands of the Commission. At the end of the day, European Parliament amendments are only effective if they are endorsed by the Commission (or failing this, if they are reinstated by a unanimous vote in the Council).

Another limitation when addressing issues to the European Parliament is that only a few MEPs are committed to EU issues (UK MEPs are an exception to this rule due to the constituency/regional election systems). Lobbying therefore tends to target a restricted number of key MEPs, who are therefore swamped with letters and faxes.

- Wherever possible, make your problem or lobby a transnational one by showing either that action would facilitate cross-border flows or remove inter-state distortions or - preferably in consortium with other national or pan-European bodies - that the undesirable impact of a proposal will cover a number (if not all) of the Member States. If you cannot do this (because, for example, a Commission proposal would particularly affect apples grown only in one part of the UK) you have to consider four questions:
- Most obviously, leaving emotion aside can we show the Commission that its proposals are technically flawed?
- Can we persuade the Commission and the UK that this is an issue that should be handled by subsidiarity, with Whitehall addressing the problem (if any)?
- Can we challenge the Commission's jurisdiction on the basis that the proposal falls outside the Treaty? For example, if those apples are not exported, there is no impact on inter-state trade.
- Can we generate enough trade/public/MP support in the UK to make Government agree to go to the wall for us? This may mean

USING THE PARLIAMENT TO PRESS THE COMMISSION

*Every month, all Commissioners face questioning by MEPs during the Parliament's ple-
nary session. The political groups select a number of oral questions, to which they may
attach a draft Resolution if they feel that the issue would command cross-group support.
The groups tend to prefer Orals on issues topical to that month, but others may be selected if they are likely to strike home - Commissioners do take note of well-drafted oral
questions, whereas written PQs generally receive peremptory or bureaucratic answers.*

*Suggestions for Orals should be made to a MEP or to a Group's secretariat. They
must be tabled at least two weeks before the relevant plenary week and they should follow a particular style. As an example, consider an Oral and draft resolution that was produced in order to draw attention to the Commission's failure to observe Council requirements on assessment of regulatory costs:*

Subject: Business Impact Assessment

*Council Resolutions of 27 May 1991, 13 July 1992, 3 December 1992 and 30 June
1998 and Council Decision of 9 December 1996 require the Commission to undertake
Business Impact Assessment in respect of proposals that may have an impact on enterprises. However, there is widespread concern among enterprises that assessments are rarely
carried out and that the Commission's original unpublished proposal for procedural rules
has been replaced by a requirement that gives little guidance to the services and is consequently frequently ignored. As a result, it is possible that non-legislative options may be
given insufficient consideration; and legislative requirements may impose unnecessary costs
affecting business competitiveness.*

*1. Does the Commission agree that it is important that Business Impact Assessment is
undertaken in respect of any proposal that could impose costs on enterprises?*

*2. Does the CCE share the view that effective legislation requires adhesion of those who
will have to implement it and early and transparent discussion is the best way to prevent lobbying ?*

*3. What steps is the Commission taking to fulfil the requirement set out in its January
1999 Guidelines on Legislative Policy to produce detailed Business Impact
Assessment guidelines?*

*4. Will the Commission, in fulfilling the requirement set out in its January 1999
Guidelines on Legislative Policy to produce detailed Business Impact Assessment
guidelines, work closely with Business organisations and Member States to ensure that
its guidelines reflect Business needs and national best practice?*

*5. Will the Commission ensure that the production of Business Impact Assessments is
mandatory, not discretionary?*

6. The Commission is proposing to establish a unit within the Enterprise Directorate General to administer the Business Impact Assessment system. How will it ensure that the Unit will be able to take effective action against other services, both in terms of complying with the Business Impact Assessment requirement and in having regard to the conclusions of Business Impact Assessments?

Draft motion for a resolution
calling for an accurate and reliable business impact assessment to be implemented when proposing EU initiatives

The European Parliament,

- Having regard to rule 40(5) of the rules of procedure;
- Having regard to the Amsterdam Treaty and notably the Declaration No 18 on estimated costs under Commisson proposals;
- Having regard to Council Resolution of 3 December 1992 on administrative simplification for enterprises, especially SMEs, which strongly supports the improvement of Business Impact Assessments;
- Having regard to the Council Resolution of 13 July 1992 on future priorities for the development of consumer protection policy, and more particularly its annex which calls for drawing up an adequate impact assessment concerning proposals particularly sensitive to consumers
- Having regard to the Commission Recommendation of 22 April 1997 on improving and simplifying the business environment for business start-ups which recommends that the effects of regulation and administrative procedures should be assessed and calls on Member States "to introduce a systematic evaluation procedure to assess the impact on business of regulatory proposals"

Having regard to Article 109 of the Treaty of Amsterdam;

A. Whereas consultation mechanisms by EU institutions are mostly limited to general policy guidelines such as Communications and Green or White Papers, whereas in most cases the Commission does not divulge its proposals before they are formally adopted by the College;

B. Whereas the Commission has highlighted in its 1997 report on the Business Impact Assessment System that many Business Impact Assessments were not good enough and did not provide an accurate assessment of regulatory impact; whereas the overall impact of legislation should be assessed on the basis of the cost benefit analysis that will derive to those who have to implement it and the benefit for the general good;

C. Whereas at a time of high unemployment in much of the European Union, BusinessImpact Assessments would provide a useful indication of the effect of regulation on employment, especially since pursuant to Article 109 of the Amsterdam Treaty

*'the objectives of high level of employment shall be taken into consideration in the for-
mulation and implementation of community policies and activities';*

D. *Whereas it is necessary to understand the cost and benefit of any proposal for legislation in order to assess the need to adopt legislation; whereas, moreover, an accurate
impact assessment will contribute to reinforcing adherence by those who are primarily
concerned with it;*

E. *Whereas accurate impact assessments would provide the tools for EU legislators to put
in perspective alleged impacts put forward by lobbies; whereas several recent lobbying
campaigns were fuelled by the absence of business impact assessments*

1. *Calls on the Commission to integrate Business Impact Assessment into its internal procedures and ensure that it will be effectively implemented by its services and that
decisions to conduct impact assessments are not discretionary*

2. *Invites the Commission to attach a Business Impact Assessment to any legislative proposal expected to have a significant impact on business, as part of the
Explanatory Memorandum;*

3. *Requires that the Business Impact Assessment requirement is extended to any
amended proposals that the Commission adopts in the course of the legislative process.*

4. *Requests its President to forward this Resolution to the Commission and
Governments of the Member States.*

Ministers conceding a position on another issue as a trade-off for
securing agreement to drop or modify the proposal affecting you.

- Are there less burdensome solutions that might meet policymakers'
objectives?
- Do not ignore the cross-border links of the unions. If they are likely to support your case, use their network, either through union-
union contact or via European TUC.
- Does the media influence Brussels? Nothing like as much as it does
nationally, but coverage in the publications read by Brussels insiders (The Bulletin, European Voice and the FT) can embarrass
Commissioners and officials if they have failed to act or to take
account of your case.

MEPs are at their most accessible during Plenary Sessions. They
like to be contacted in Strasbourg, where they are likely to be less
pressed than during the week in every month when committees meet
in Brussels. However, Strasbourg is not served by frequent flights and

is expensive once one gets there. If you need to telephone them during Plenary, call before 9.00 and between 2.30–3pm (between lunch and resumption of Plenary). Do not go to Strasbourg to buttonhole them, however. They prefer an appointment to be made in advance.

MEETING COMMISSIONERS

The procedure for seeking meetings with Commissioners is broadly similar to that in Whitehall or the devolved administrations. However, there are some differences:

- *Always start with the Chef de Cabinet who, unlike a Principal Private Secretary, will also control the Commissioner's diary. The Special Chef responsible for the issue in question may be able to help.*
- *Officials in the relevant DG may make a favourable recommendation if you approach them but they are not normally asked for views by the Cabinet except in cases where a competition inquiry is pending.*
- *Unlike MPs, MEPs are rarely approached to seek such meetings and they have little influence over the process.*

How pressure groups can influence the system

In the final part of this section, we look at ways in which organisations, be they action groups or commercial competitors, can work the system against you. We have now reached a point where lobbying issues, involving the influencing of policy, legislation or regulation, merge with "public affairs" issues, essentially public relations problems with a governmental dimension. We will again take the example of ComCo, which finds itself under attack on several fronts.

Local residents have for some time been sending letters to their councillors, MPs and local papers to complain about the siting of relay masts. They have now enlisted the support of the Council for the Protection of Rural England, which is calling on DETR to tighten Planning Policy Guidance. ComCo has not yet had any planning applications refused but it is facing difficulties with two local authorities which have repeatedly remitted the papers and called for further study on environmental impacts.

MPs have tabled written and oral Parliamentary Questions about this and four have tabled an Early Day Motion which mentions

ComCo and backs the need for stricter planning controls.

What does this mean? To take these items in turn,

Parliamentary Questions: for reply in writing, at the daily 30 minute ministerial Question Times (a Whitehall Department will every three to four weeks answer questions at the start of Commons business; all Scottish departments are questioned during a 45 minute session on Thursday afternoons and two Welsh Departments are questioned for 15 minutes each on Wednesday afternoons) or at the start of Lords business (four questions are selected by ballot irrespective of Department) can only be tabled by an MP, MSP, AM or Peer, but most are asked on behalf of outsiders.

They are usually happy to table PQs if it can be shown that they are needed to obtain information - they can be useful sources of statistical statements - or statements on the record (all answers are

---

SELLING IDEAS TO THE SYSTEM

You would not dream of retailing a new product without detailed market research; take the same approach to dealing with UK and EU institutions

- *What is our target market?*
- *What does it want?*
- *How will it react to our product?*
- *How must we adapt our product to secure maximum market acceptance?*

Detailed market research is by far the most significant element in lobbying success. Ask yourself

- *Who really makes the decisions; who influences them?*
- *What are their views on the issue in question? What are the policy/legal/cost/administrative/time constraints on action? How are they likely to react to your case? What flaws will they find?*
- *How do your targets want the case made? By whom? Which points do they want you to address?*
- *Who do your targets respect? Who will they consult for views on your arguments; what are they likely to say? Are your allies respected by your targets?*
- *Who will lobby against you; what are they likely to say and do?*

---

published in Hansard and the other assemblies' official records) but it helps them if you can do the drafting. If you want to seek PQs, follow these steps:

- Be clear that the information you need would not be more readily available from another source. PQs are expensive to answer and there is no point in wasting taxpayers' money unnecessarily (see p. 189 on ethics).
- Consider whether you will gain any benefit from the answers. You may want to be able to quote Government's own words back at it, to have the benefit of data collated in a particular form for the first time, or an MP may agree to publicise the fact that he is asking questions on a matter of concern. But bear in mind that officials are trained to say as little as possible in Parliamentary Answers and to exploit any drafting flaw that might give them the excuse not to provide data; and that nothing is achieved at Question Times unless a Minister faces several questions on the same issue and he perceives a genuine mood of the House on the point. In all other cases he reads from a file and gives a political answer to the supplementary points that the questioner (and a limited number of others – Privy Councillors and Opposition spokesmen are given preference) is allowed to make as a rejoinder.
- In most cases, therefore, a letter (either from you or, if officials are likely to have to work hard to produce statistics, from an MP/Peer) to the relevant Department is likely to elicit more detail. Scotland and Wales are hardly more forthcoming with information than is Whitehall, but questions tabled in the Scottish Parliament and Welsh Assembly could offer additional details that might be used to assist an English campaign.
- If you still want to proceed, write to an MP, MSP, AM (selected because of relevant subject or constituency interest) or Peer or call their researcher (you will still need to write to confirm) setting out who you are; the information you need or the problem you have faced in getting it direct from Whitehall; and a request that the attached PQs might be tabled as a result. If you seek oral questions,

explain why and offer to meet the MP/Peer to brief them further. There is of course no point in approaching Government loyalists to table PQs designed to embarrass Ministers.

• The Commons Order Paper (see p 278) lists the date for answer for written questions. There is no set deadline, but most are answered within seven to 14 days. It is possible to specify that a question be treated as a priority (answer within three days or even, if pressed, next day) but the subject matter for these should be chosen with care – if detailed statistical or other research is requested it is likely that only a holding answer will be given. The Lords Order Paper lists written questions without an answer date, and the oral questions selected for up to a month ahead. In the Scottish Parliament, questions will normally be answered within 14 days. They must be tabled at the Chamber Office by 4.30pm if they are to appear in the Business Bulletin for the next day. Welsh Assembly questions

---

PQs RARELY KICKSTART THE SYSTEM

On page 95, we mentioned a medical equipment manufacturer which had developed a new test kit that could have saved the NHS considerable treatment costs. However, such items have to be subjected to a testing process before the Department of Health will allow GPs to be reimbursed for using them, and for reasons unknown to the manufacturer it could not get the system to review the kit. Out of frustration, it persuaded an MP to table a PQ asking why such products could not be given reimbursable status; it hoped that this would bring the problem to the attention of Ministers who might then unblock the logjam.

Of course, the officials who drafted the answer, which told the company nothing, understood the process. Had the company sought a meeting with the Minister, they would have been able to give him a clear brief explaining why there was a long testing queue: they did not tell the manufacturer because no-one was prepared to admit to responsibility for handling this issue and the company was unwilling to persevere in trying to find an official prepared to educate it about the procedure and to advise on the correct course of action.

The lesson here is that there are rarely any shortcuts: if you do not know what is going to be in the Minister's briefing note or have not tried to influence its content, do not try to get to him. The odds that he will accept your word (or a friendly MP's) over the advice of his officials are around three to one - against.

can be tabled for answer on a named day and in any event are answered within one week.

LOBBYING BY TELEPHONE

Political parties now use professional agencies to target and contact potential supporters. You can use the same firms to stimulate calls to a dedicated line in support of your cause. It is the easiest way to show that you have several thousand people behind you and is a technique that can be used alongside or independent of opinion polling.

Similarly, although politicians place some weight on personally written letters about an issue (simply signing a mass-produced card is not regarded as a sign of commitment) it is hard nowadays to persuade people to write on most issues. But the same agencies can encourage people to ring and leave a message with key MPs' or MEPs' constituency or parliamentary offices. It only takes around 20 different calls for the profile of a lobby to be raised significantly

---

You will need to follow a number of rules in drafting PQs: each question should be typed on a separate unheaded sheet; they should always begin with "To ask the [Chancellor of the Exchequer/Secretary of State for XXX, or in Wales, to The Assembly Secretary for XXX] as Commons questions are always tabled to the head of a Department. However, the Lords wording is "To ask Her Majesty's Government" and in Scotland, all questions are directed to "the Scottish Executive"; questions covering more than one Department must be individually tabled to each Department; they should be only one sentence long; they must not ask Ministers whether they agree with a statement or to state an opinion; they must not be rhetorical; they must relate to the work of that Department or to the bodies for which it has responsibility – questions about the private sector must relate to the Department; separate unconnected points must be made in separate PQs, but information about connected points (for example, details of (a) capital and (b) maintenance expenditure by a Department on PCs) can be requested in a single question; questions which the department has previously refused to answer can only be re-tabled after an interval of three months; and commercially sensitive matters cannot be covered. As an example,

PQs about ComCo's masts could look like this:

To ask the Secretary of State for Environment, Transport and the Regions, how many planning applications for TV and radio relay masts were approved in England; how many were rejected; and how many were called in by his Department, for the last year for which statistics are available; and whether he will make a statement.

This should receive a precise answer. Had it specified a year without knowing whether data had yet been assembled for that period, the reply might have been "no information is available for the period in question". The request for a statement is designed to prompt a paragraph on departmental policy; in most cases, it elicits a stonewall answer such as "planning policy in relation to radio and TV relay masts is set out in Planning Policy Guidance 8. The Department regularly monitors such applications." Remember that officials are trained to give away as little as possible. You must ensure that your drafting leaves them with no option but to answer the question.

- House of Commons Oral PQs must be tabled no earlier than ten days before the relevant departmental question time (the Commons Information Office will give you dates or you can obtain a printed schedule from the Parliamentary Bookshop – see p. 277) but in practice they are tabled exactly ten days beforehand. MPs can only table one oral question at any one time to any one department, with a maximum of two per day. In Scotland, Oral Questions must be lodged between the eighth (until 2pm) or ninth day before the session in question. Of those lodged, up to three questions will then be selected randomly by the Presiding Officer as 'Open Questions', on which there is general debate for a total of fifteen minutes after the main oral questions. There is also scope for asking an emergency oral question which must be tabled by 10am on the day. Welsh Orals must be tabled five to ten days in advance and presented in the normal Westminster format.
- Oral questions enable the tabler (plus, if they want to, an Opposition spokesman and possibly another backbencher) to ask a

supplementary question and they are therefore of greatest use: where agreement has been reached with Ministers that they will make a helpful statement on an issue, usually a constituency matter and the questioner wants to respond; where it is hoped to embarrass Ministers by tabling a broad and anodyne question ("To ask the Secretary of State for Trade and Industry, what is his policy on the Foresight Programme") and then asking an unanticipated and detailed supplementary ("Will he therefore explain why ComCo, a company in my constituency, has been refused Foresight funding despite having been told by his Department that it satisfies all the Programme criteria? Is he aware that, in an area with 17 per cent unemployment, ComCo had planned to create some 600 jobs if it had received Foresight funding?"); where it is intended to place important information before the House.

• If it is decided that an oral PQ would be useful (local papers could be alerted to it), do not proceed unless you can be reasonably certain of the answer the Department will give. If the motive behind the question is not self-explanatory (eg "To ask the Secretary of State for Trade and Industry, what is his policy on trade with Mexico") because you want to ambush the Government, the MPs or Peers you approach will be depending on you to give them a strong supplementary question (eg "Is the Minister aware that a constituency company, ComCo, has repeatedly been refused assistance by our commercial counsellor in Mexico City"...etc) and if they are on the Government side they may be approached by the Minister's PPS for information.

•Note that oral questions must not express a point of view and Scottish Orals must not ask for information which has been provided to a similar question in the previous six months. In the Lords, an oral PQ is effectively a seven minute debate. Others join in and you should speak to your tabling Peer about two or three more who could be approached to drive home different aspects of the same point. Peers can put down questions at shorter notice than MPs; but if the issue is urgent, an MP can table a priority question for answer within 12 sitting days, although the answer will be correspondingly shorter.

- Bear in mind that question times are short and only around half of the oral questions in the Commons Order Paper will be answered on the day. The rest receive written answers.

ComCo sees the questions in the Order Paper. Its defensive options are:

- to ignore them, on the basis that most PQs are unnoticed by the outside world and make no waves within Whitehall

---

DEALING WITH THE OPPOSITION

Consider briefing the Opposition

- *If Government is on (genuinely) weak ground and public embarrassment might force it to rethink.*
- *If Government needs to be reassured that your proposal is likely to attract broad political support.*
- *If you are a public body, with a duty to inform Parliament on a non-partisan basis.*
- *Because Oppositions eventually become governments and value those who remembered them on the way down as well as up.*

But remember

- *Opposition parties will usually seek to make political capital of information you give them even if that would not be in your best interests.*
- *Government must resist virtually everything proposed by the Opposition. Attacking the Government will usually make it clam up.*

Attacking people (even non-attributably) is not the best way to win their support. As we have said, only consider it if Government is on weak ground and if there is no scope for negotiation.

Conservative MPs have two official sources of briefing other than their research assistants: Conservative Research Department, based in Party HQ (0171 222 9000) and the Parliamentary Resources Unit, which is in the House (219 1549). If you want to make input to papers for parliamentary debates these are the access points.

- to use third parties to contact the MPs or Peers and find out why they have tabled the questions. If the nature of the concern is revealed, ComCo could offer to brief them on the planning regime; on the problems of siting relay masts; and on what will happen without them

---

DO WE NEED TO ATTEND PARTY CONFERENCES?

Organisations spend many millions of pounds a year on stands, fringe meetings, receptions and other entertainment, not to mention staff time, at the political parties' main and local government conferences. Most of it is wasted.

- *Go to keep an eye on your competitors and to pick up political gossip.*
- *Go if you are seeking to sell products or services to local authorities (many delegates are councillors).*
- *Go if you will derive value from meeting and briefing the political grass roots. Party conferences can be useful occasions for Lottery distributors, for example, to demonstrate public accountability.*

But otherwise, accept that you will only emerge poor and tired from a week in Blackpool. Not only is there intense competition for attention, with at least a dozen meetings (at which politicians, separated from their officials, usually speak off the cuff and rarely say anything worth noting) being held at any one time throughout the day but also, in truth, very little that is discussed at meetings during party conferences ever sinks in: MPs feel like fish in a barrel and Ministers have no staff with them to keep track of the conversations they have (nonetheless, it is possible to have informal discussions with Ministers without their official minders being present). In most cases, by lunchtime they have forgotten what happened at the breakfast meeting and by dinner they have forgotten about their lunchtime discussion. Those who claim that the conferences are valuable networking opportunities are usually politicos who like talking to their mates about matters of little relevance to the world outside.

Parties always welcome sponsorship, but at major conferences it has to be substantial to stand out from the crowd, and lead sponsors of large events can fall foul of the media.

All the party headquarters have conference offices which issue passes and handle stands, fringe meeting bookings and sponsorship.

- to contact the officials who will have to draft the answers and, if relevant, offer information. They should be asked whether Ministers have received representations about this issue and whether it is regarded as a matter of concern at this time. Unless the reply is unequivocal, ComCo should assume that this could become a matter of concern if Ministers are put under enough pressure by their backbenchers, by well-connected councillors or by the Local Government Association. It should therefore produce a three page note covering the headings offered to MPs prefaced by "You may have been made aware of concerns being expressed in some parts of the country about the siting of radio and TV relay masts. The attached note explains the problems of siting them and the implications of restricting planning guidance. Should this issue raise any problems, we would be happy to brief you in person"

- to ensure that it is in a position rapidly to pick up and respond to any local or national media coverage. If an oral PQ is tabled referring to a particular part of the country, the local media should be briefed on the morning the question is due to be asked
- to approach the relevant committee of the LGA with a view to heading off further action by setting out the problems faced by relay services and planning authorities and securing recognition that masts are necessary

Early Day Motions (also called Motions in Scotland and Statements of Opinion in Wales) are tabled by the sackload every Session and have been devalued by overuse – Whitehall takes little notice of them. However, if they appear with a large number of respected Government party signatories and if the media notices them the Whips and PPSs will on occasion pay attention.

They can also be indicators to Ministers of the strength of political support for the parties to a contentious bid or government tender – when HSBC and Lloyds were bidding for Midland Bank some years ago, HSBC was able to secure over a hundred signatories; Lloyds had to follow suit but only gathered a handful. Government was able to infer that a decision in favour of HSBC would not face a mass of orchestrated parliamentary noise. The trick is to secure a number (up to six) of respected founder signatories who will be prepared both to back your letters urging other MPs to sign by corralling their colleagues and to publicise the Motion.

An organisation personally criticised in an EDM will find it difficult not to respond. However, ComCo should resist the temptation to seek to table a counter-motion as this will certainly be ignored. If the EDM is covered in the papers (the broadcast media does not bother with them), ComCo should deal direct with the Lobby correspondents. It may also write to each signatory (new ones are published in the Commons Order Paper) if it believes they may have been misinformed. In the end, it should accept that most MPs sign EDMs to do a favour to a colleague and, if pressed by the Whips or PPSs, have forgotten that they signed them or show no strong commitment.

Now let us assume that a further threat emerges. Brussels has drafted legislation about safety clothing to be worn for certain processes. Since this is likely to be uncontroversial, the Health and Safety Executive has already started work with DfEE to draft the Regulations required to implement the measure when it is adopted by the Council. ComCo has for some time been negotiating special provisions with the Employment DG and HSE to cover the unique equipment requirements of mast maintenance. Just then, World In Action features a report by an environmental pressure group that TV masts emit dangerous levels of radiation and interviews two former ComCo employees who claim to have resigned because the risks were known by the company but ignored.

The programme triggers a series of consequences. The unions for ComCo and other mast operators express concerns to MPs and a raft of questions emerges. One MP obtains an Adjournment Debate, a Peer puts his name in the ballot for a short debate and the Education and Employment Select Committee decides to hold an inquiry into the subject. MEPs seek a debate at the next plenary session and the EP Social Affairs and Employment Committee requests the Commissioner to halt work on the legislation until a full study has been carried out into the effect of emissions from masts on workers, the local population, wildlife and the natural environment. This might seem bad enough, but the media has not yet decided to highlight the scare, ComCo's sources suggest that the pressure group is intending to place large signs by main roads near relay masts and to hold a series of media events across Europe to call for a moratorium on further planning approvals (threatening both the UK business and the planned Eastern European expansion), and there is a danger that ComCo's other dealings with the system could be prejudiced if its business is regarded as unsafe – this would be an ideal opportunity for its regulator to intervene.

We will again take these episodes in turn:

Adjournment Debates are held on Tuesday and Wednesday mornings and at the close of the day's Commons business (usually late at night) and slots are awarded by ballot. They give MPs the opportunity to raise (normally local) subjects and to obtain a response on the record to show his constituents and local media. The sponsoring MP speaks for 15 minutes (the time can be shared with other MPs) and a Minister replies. And that is about all: the House is always empty and, unless the MP can extract a concession beforehand, the Minister's response (they are often the only two speakers) will be lengthy (15 minutes as well) but sterile. However, the debate's promoter may persuade journalists that it has more significance than it merits and the coverage (which is usually on the lines of "Ambridge MP Henry Crun will tonight call on Ministers to apply tougher controls to ComCo") can damage an organisation's reputation. While ComCo should not consider seeking such a debate for lobbying purposes, nor even briefing another MP to be present to raise its arguments, it should ensure that the Department is fully briefed beforehand and should attempt to give the sponsoring MP the true facts. Scottish Adjournment Debates are called "Members Business" and are held in the half hour following Decision Time on plenary days. Subjects must be non-controversial and preferably of a constituency nature. In Wales, there is a weekly ballot for short debates which follow the Westminster pattern in length and structure.

Lords debates are also balloted for but are more substantial affairs, usually lasting 90 minutes in mid-late afternoon or early evening and attracting up to 18 speakers. The sponsoring Peer speaks for ten minutes, often followed by Conservative and LibDem spokesmen, and when other Peers have had their say the Government spokesman responds with a statement of current policy. Once again, these only work if they are seen by the Government Whips as a genuine expression of the mood of the House, which involves highly respected speakers and a fair number of participants on the Government benches. ComCo should nonetheless ensure that the Department is briefed; it should try to persuade at least two or three Peers to speak on its side to balance the debate; and through those Peers or others it should obtain a copy of the list of speakers (available to Peers some days beforehand and regularly revised) so that it can send all of them a single page factual rebuttal of the scare stories.

Select Committee Inquiries will be announced by press release, although the Committee may already have decided to invite key witnesses and they will have been written to beforehand. The announcement will usually set out the terms of reference or the issues on which the Committee would welcome written submissions. There is no set pattern to inquiries: they may last a day and call only two sets of witnesses, or several months with a large number of oral evidence sessions. Reports may range from half a page to a hundred pages with three volumes of evidence. There are, however, common principles for ComCo to observe whether it is seeking to stimulate or respond to an inquiry; and while we predominantly refer to Westminster committees there is little procedural difference between them and their counterparts in Scotland and Wales:

- Anyone can ask to be added to Select Committee mailing lists (call the relevant Select Committee office via the main Commons number, 0171 219 3000) or they can find out about forthcoming inquiries through the internet (see p 280).
- Inquiry subjects are suggested by the committee members, in most cases as a result of lobbying by outsiders; by the specialist advisers appointed by some to help them with technical issues; but mostly by the chairman and clerk, who have a dominant role in deciding what should be covered and who should be invited. Suggestions for inquiries should usually be made in writing unless an opportunity presents itself for a meeting with the chairman, but bear in mind that (unless they know you well or your cause is unimpeachable) Select Committee members do not generally like being lobbied on subjects being covered by their committee: inquiries are not quasi-

judicial but committees like to create an atmosphere of slight detachment.

- If you want to give oral evidence, either because you are a closely interested party, because you have expertise that might assist the inquiry or because you want to raise your profile, you should write to the clerk as soon as the inquiry is announced to explain why you are keen to be called. Slots (of around 45 minutes but they may be

---

BALANCE IS ESSENTIAL

While you may have to encapsulate your case in summary brief form, highlights which emphasise only the favourable aspects of your case will be spotted and will count against you. A major UK industry lobbied hard in alleging dumping by other EU exporters some years ago: it was only when MPs were persuaded to see Ministers that they discovered the industry was itself operating a cartel. It is still regarded with scepticism in Westminster and Whitehall.

---

longer for major witnesses or shorter if other witnesses overrun or there are a large number of them to be heard) are usually automatically given to the leading players and always to the Department shadowed by the committee, but others are often called if they can show that the inquiry would benefit from more than just a written submission.

- Committees may appoint advisers with expertise covering only that inquiry. ComCo should ask the committee office in the House if the committee is intending to do so (in which case ComCo might suggest specialists who will give a fair picture) or has already approached someone, since they will propose questions to the committee and will be turned to for a view on the quality of the evidence.
- Whether giving oral evidence or not, all participants must produce submissions. These should be no more than ten pages long; should stick closely to the terms of reference; should make it clear at the outset which issues they will be covering within those headings; should provide hard information and workable solutions, rather than vague criticisms; and should preferably be formatted like a

committee report, with numbered single spaced paragraphs and emboldened recommendations. As with Whitehall submissions, they should avoid emotion and should not contain a single unreferenced fact or statement. A useful guide to structure would be

Education and Employment Select Committee Inquiry into radiation risks from relay masts

ComCo is the UK's largest provider of radio and TV relay services through a network of 270 masts (map attached at Annex 1). We will respond to the Committee's terms of reference in turn:

Radiation emitted by relay masts
1. XXXXXXXXXXXXXXX
2. XXXXXXXXX

Relative risk
3. XXXXXXXXX

Safeguards for workers, the public and the environment
4. XXXXXXXXXXXXXXX

etc

- Submissions, which can be submitted in hard copy or on disc (In Scotland, the committees prefer submission by EMail or disc, accompanied by a single hard copy) are regarded as the property of the committee, although summaries can be released to the press and copies of witnesses' papers are made available in the committee room when they give evidence (there are not usually enough copies to go round and it pays to be near the front of the queue).

ComCo should seek through a friendly MP to obtain the submissions produced by the Department and by those opposing its case. Commercially confidential material can be withheld from public copies by agreement with the clerk and closed sessions preceding public evidence are allowed.

WORKING WITH CANDIDATES

Time spent working with parliamentary candidates - or at least those expected to win - is rarely wasted. They are more receptive to arguments since they are keen to please and they often have more time to visit constituency organisations. There is also less competition for their attention than they will experience once they are elected.

In the six months leading up to a likely election, national campaigns can seek the support of candidates, either directly or by using the local paper - coverage in which is enormously important to candidates - to canvass views from all the main contenders (for example, on whether books should be taxed). In solid seats, the main candidate will usually seek a line from party headquarters, but in a marginal constituency he may find himself under pressure to support the newspaper's line.

One point: many organisations send questionnaires to candidates in order to establish their views on issues. Don't - they hate them and will again invariably refer them to HQ. You have little option but to use a reputable polling organisation unless you have a string of constituency representatives prepared to write personally or to meet them.

• Some committees like to be tough with their witnesses but most only want information. They respect responses that are short and which answer the question. They do not like witnesses who do not know their facts (if you are caught out by a question, say you do not have the information to hand and offer to send it by return); are long-winded; interrupt (they can interrupt you, however); bring along lots of people who either contradict each other or are largely silent (two is ideal); and do not treat them with respect (by being offhand or by fielding junior executives). In general, while they will offer witnesses the opportunity of making an opening statement, they prefer not to hear perorations: the promised 120 second introduction usually stretches to seven minutes and in most cases the points it makes could be covered in response to questions. In some instances - and this is a matter of fine judgement - the committee's approach to the witness can be influenced by opening remarks, but only if they are directly relevant to the evidence session, effectively proposing the agenda to be followed; and if the text is given to the clerk at least 48 hours beforehand, he must be seized of the fact that it is more than just rhetoric.

- Witnesses should hold a rehearsal beforehand, preferably at an unfamiliar venue, where they should run through committee procedure and etiquette; have a video of the Committee - most sessions are filmed by the Parliamentary Recording Unit in the House 0171 219 5512 (the cost is, however, very high) to familiarise themselves with faces and questioning styles; background details on the members, including stance taken during similar past inquiries and speeches/questions in the chamber; an assessment of the written evidence and of the inquiry's oral sessions to date to gain pointers to the committee's thinking (it is sensible to attend them); and the outline questions they will face - the clerk will be largely responsible for drafting these and will be happy to discuss them a day or two beforehand (but there is nothing in advance of that to stop witnesses from suggesting lines of questioning that will elicit useful information from them). However, if the rehearsal cannot be held that close to the session there will be a need to produce mock questions, which should be tougher than might be expected, followed by analysis of answers. It is often easier for these sessions to be run by outsiders, since employees of an organisation may feel constrained from pressing their senior executives to the extent necessary in a thorough rehearsal.

- Although the clerk will give pointers to the likely questioning areas, witnesses should not assume that committee members will follow them rigidly: expect a few "man in the street" points or leading questions designed to elicit a confession.

- Committee sessions are often televised but rarely make the news programmes unless major issues are involved. The profile of an inquiry will be determined by the chairman, who will decide whether to press the Department to act on his committee's conclusions, which may in some cases be announced at a press conference. In most cases, the committee just moves on to the next subject and Whitehall issues a cursory response.

- Following evidence sessions, a transcript will be sent to witnesses for correction. They will also be entitled to an advance copy, which will be made available between one and 24 hours before formal publication in order to allow them to prepare media responses. Leaking advance copies is a breach of parliamentary privilege but most reports seem to appear in the Sunday papers before even the advance copies are out.

ComCo's strategy must be to establish the credibility of its own information by producing a strong submission and by stimulating supportive experts to submit evidence and offer themselves as witnesses. Unless the oral evidence slots have been decided at the outset, a further aim must be to persuade the committee that there is effectively no case to answer and that there is no point in scheduling new sessions. If the pressure group is called, ComCo will offer questions to the clerk and to one or two receptive members (who may prefer not to be contacted) in the hope that the group's research will be discredited on TV. It will also have its media specialist present at each session to debrief any reporters, who sit in a separate section at the side of the room.

Responding to parliamentary concern and direct pressure group activity. At the outset, ComCo will have had to decide who could make the decisions that might damage it. In this case, it is Whitehall and the Commission, the two parliaments, HSE and the Radiocommunications Agency, the Commission's advisory committee on safety equipment, planning authorities, and its customers. The second stage is to assess whether these targets believe the scare or whether they have a sufficient body of countervailing information to dismiss it; and at the same time to consider what or who will influence them. In most cases, official-run bodies will not take a view until they have assessed the evidence, and we will assume that in this case the radiation risk is well known by scientists, who accept that the levels emitted from relay masts are no greater than those experienced by people living in Aberdeen. ComCo's customers are similarly unlikely to bother provided they are not tainted by association. However, politicians often respond to perceived public concern which may be born of ignorance. Even if ComCo believes that most of the main players have a balanced picture of the risk factors involved, it should

- immediately (or as soon as it has been possible to analyse the programme and the report) produce a brief outlining the allegation and setting out the evidence against it. There should be two versions: a detailed one, which would be sent to officials in DTI, DfEE, DETR (natural environment), the Employment DG, HSE, all members of the EU advisory committee, the Agency and the National Radiological Protection Board, plus the Departmental Special Advisers, the employment and industry advisers in the No 10 Policy Unit, the Employment Commissioner's cabinet and the clerk and secretariat to the Select and EP committees, all of whom should also receive a two page bullet point summary; and a second, simpler document of two pages which concentrates less on the complex science and more on comparative risk factors, exposure of flaws in the TV programme and pressure group report, ComCo's health and safety code and a short list of acknowledged experts who could be contacted to endorse the statement that relay masts represent no risk to anyone. This should go to members of the Select and EP Committees (the covering letter would tell them that a full report could be obtained from their committee office), EDM signatories, the MEPs calling for an EP debate, and PQ tablers. It would be discussed with the unions and explained to every member of the workforce at site briefings. ComCo's head of PR should be involved from the outset to ensure that this second document is in a form suitable for use by the media if necessary (however, if it is too visually interesting politicians will regard it as a slick attempt at PR).
- at the same time, ComCo's technical specialists should be contacting every expert they know on the subject across Europe to see

whether they would be prepared publicly to endorse the company's view on risk. If they agree to help, a view will have to be taken on whether to take informal soundings from environment

---

CONVEYING COMPLEX INFORMATION

Rail Link Engineering, the company responsible for building the Channel Tunnel railway, had to brief MPs along the length of Kent on construction details, such as road closures and spoil disposal, that would affect their constituents. RLE realised that while it had to send maps and project briefs, most MPs would not have the time to study them. It therefore offered each MP the chance to be driven along their section of the route on days when they might not have to be in the House (Wednesday morning or Friday) allowing them to be briefed in context at greater length than would have been possible at Westminster, and to be photographed on the ground by their local newspapers .

---

correspondents on the main broadsheets, tabloids, news programmes and agencies (this could include EU-wide media if the EP's activities have started to attract attention or if the pressure group is taking action against other European relay companies, in which case the industry's evidence must be coordinated between them to avoid inconsistent data being made public) about their view of the issue: if they are aware of it, they can be referred to the list of experts; if not, they can be briefed into a state of boredom and offered the list in case the story re-emerges. There will always be some scientists prepared to take an opposing view and ComCo needs to ensure that the debate is not just balanced but seen overwhelmingly to support its case - hence the emphasis on lots of experts. It regards the NRPB as an essential ally because the Board established strong public and media credibility following the Chernobyl incident.

• learn from the Brent Spar case, where reliance on behind the scenes agreement between experts was countered by a stronger emotive campaign. ComCo should therefore invite NRPB (after first establishing that the Board has few concerns) to visit masts in some of the constituencies represented by concerned MPs. The

CHANGING THE SYSTEM'S MISCONCEPTIONS.
HOW CHARTER AIRLINES DID IT

Britain's charter airlines were concerned over actual and potential discrimination against them at UK airports. Ministers and their adviser, the Civil Aviation Authority, believed that scheduled operators were more important than, and occupied a separate market from, charter carriers. Charter flights were banned from Heathrow and Ministers threatened to move charter traffic away from Gatwick.

Charter airlines had up to then distrusted Government. They had traditionally shouted at Ministers and complained that Whitehall did not understand them. That changed. This is how one operator ("Bird Aviation") lobbied successfully under the last Government - but the principles are still valid:

1. It produced a series of papers and presentations to the CAA, G2-G7 officials and Ministers which explained, with detailed corroboration, that

- Charter was important politically and economically: most people fly for leisure purposes and charter dominated that sector; and that
- Charter and scheduled were in fact in close and substantial competition.

2. One problem was that Ministers and officials do not travel on charter flights. They thought charter operators tawdry, run down and small. So charter's image had to be improved, but a more important element in Bird's strategy was to ally a perception of size and efficiency to the clear point that competition would suffer and the largest aviation industry in the EU would be harmed if discrimination persisted.

3. The Conservative Backbench Aviation Committee was not well respected by Ministers; indeed, no backbenchers were regarded as aviation experts. This was not, in any event, judged to be an issue on which Ministers would yield to pressure. Bird briefed MPs and secured their support, but only as a token: absence of opposition was a more important consideration in a case that would be won on the facts.
LESSON: consider the realities of decision-making.

4. All the time, the targets were changing. The Secretary of State with whom the industry had started had quickly been replaced by two others, and with a change of people came a change in attitude. (Unsolicited) publicity over-egging BA's lobbying successes irritated Government. The new Secretary of State told his advisers that no favours should be given to any one operator and the Department of Transport's attitude was transformed.
LESSON: campaigns cannot be planned scientifically; luck can be a major element.

5. There was one lever that Governments fear more than delegations of MPs or most media coverage. Bird obtained an Opinion from a leading QC suggesting that discrimination would breach EU law and that the UK's allocation of traffic between airports was, *in effect, illegal. Legal challenges are well respected by Ministers and officials and put Departments on their mettle. The operators made sure the Opinion was sent to the Department and secured the tabling of a number of PQs designed to obtain confirmation that the document had been received, read and understood.*

LESSON: understand the system's sensitivities; use the EU angle.

***6.** Ministers come and go but officials stay. So Bird concentrated on developing support from officials such that they would brief new Ministers on their arrival. By developing a close relationship with officials (through establishing itself as a source of uncoloured information and advice) Bird found Whitehall more susceptible to requests to put the issue near the top of its agenda. It finally secured a commitment that plans for displacement from Gatwick would not be implemented and were wrongly conceived.*

LESSON: establish credibility. Professionalism often counts for more than weight.

***7.** That still left Heathrow. Once again, Bird assembled its case first and foremost to hit the Government's sensitivities - what it wanted to say was almost irrelevant. Taking counsel from officials and the Department's Special Adviser, Bird learnt that Ministers most wanted reassurance that opening Heathrow to new entrants would not disrupt the capacity allocation system. Bird was helped by the campaign fought by Heathrow incumbents which, in its exaggerated contentions, was exactly what Ministers expected: any change would be ruinous to British airlines and Heathrow would imminently burst. Bird made a clear submission to the CAA and, through the Special Adviser, explained the reality:*

- *Heathrow was full already. Few would be able to get in even if they wanted to.*
- *Incumbents' rights meant that those already at Heathrow could not be displaced.·*
  Many airlines would try to get in but most would have to go elsewhere, boosting Gatwick and Stansted contrary to fears aroused by BAA and others.
- *And that excluded airlines only sought the right to seek capacity, not automatic entry.*

LESSON: the system will guide you on the points it wants you to address.

***8.** Bird's case was low key and reasoned; but it was also sent to airport MPs and the Conservative Aviation Committee to allay concerns generated by the Heathrow incumbents. Bird explained that there was no longer any administrative or economic reason for maintaining discrimination.*

LESSON: appeal to Ministers' philosophy, but do not forget minutiae.

When the Transport Secretary announced that restrictions on access to Heathrow would be dropped, his statement echoed Bird's submission almost word for word.

LESSON: Bird ensured its arguments could not be faulted.

visits, scheduled for a Monday morning (ie before many politicians travel to Westminster), would allow ComCo to invite all concerned MPs and MEPs, members of the Select and EP committees (which often make site visits), officers from the local authorities where there may be planning concerns, the unions and the media. ComCo's letter to the politicians and officers (which could be faxed, given the short notice) acknowledges that most of them will probably not be able to come and promises to fax the results of the tests to them as soon as they are announced (there are many agencies offering rapid multifax facilities), effectively persuading them to hold their fire until they hear from the experts. The aim is to show politicians and public that the scare is a non-event.

• additionally, or alternatively, ComCo may want to absorb another lesson from Brent Spar - that many pressure groups can only be effective if they remain outside the Establishment and resist being drawn into reasoned debate. ComCo could therefore propose the establishment of a study group on which known experts, HSE, members of the Commission's advisory committee, Whitehall officials, the unions, and the LGA would be represented and an invitation would be publicly issues to the pressure group, which then has the option of accepting and being wrapped around with likely opponents or of publicly refusing.

Special Issues

Budget formulation. The preparation that is put into the Budget is similar to that for any White Paper or Bill but with two differences: the Budget is an annual event and its procedures are firmly institutionalised; and it is prepared in conditions of greater secrecy, with consultation taking place only on a limited range of items.

The Budget is in effect one continuing process, not an annual set piece. It exists to maintain the course of a Government's medium term financial strategy and its formulation starts almost as soon as the previous Budget is announced with discussions within the Treasury about the shape of the following year's public spending and the outlook for the economy. A broad decision is taken about the amount Government needs to raise and on the Chancellor's freedom of manoevre in providing fiscal concessions, although there are usually frequent revisions geared to the price of Sterling or North Sea oil, major industrial disputes and other unexpected circumstances. The decision is taken on the advice of Treasury economists and statisticians, who have access to a computerised model of the economy with some 700 options in its program. They are able to ask the model "What if...?" and receive a projection about the effect of changing tax rates, duties and allowances.

Within the limits of the first decision – how much does Government need and what can be given back to taxpayers – a series of detailed option papers are then prepared by the Treasury, Inland Revenue and Customs & Excise to list alternative combinations of measures that would achieve the objective, which will always have to take account of the Government's political commitment to particular forms of taxation or concessions. There are also pet ideas that officials may press on Ministers year after year.

At this stage, around September, lobbying by outsiders begins in earnest on two levels, with organisations seeking changes in the Government's broad financial strategy or, more specifically, to obtain relief from taxation or an increase in allowances or welfare benefits. The CBI would fall into the first category; the Child Poverty Action Group or Scotch Whisky Association into the latter. The very largest permanent lobbies, such as the TUC, meet Treasury officials and Ministers throughout the year to put their case for change or maintenance of the status quo.

In any Budget year the Treasury will receive thousands of representations. A light year, with few organised lobbies, might generate 2000 letters and briefs; in a more contentious year, 12,000 might have to be processed. Many may be stimulated by traditional hints given by Ministers who want to assess likely reactions to their policy options. Others may be generated by the November Pre-Budget Report, in which the Chancellor gives an assessment of the economy, announces a number of consultations on policy options – for example, in the 1998 Report views were invited on reform of Vehicle Excise Duty and energy taxation – and makes tax adjustments that cannot be held over to the March Budget (for example, in November 1998 it was announced that the threshold for employers' NIC contributions would be aligned with the Income Tax personal allowance). During the course of the year the Inland Revenue and Customs & Excise may publish consultation draft clauses which may or may not be incorporated into the next Finance Bill. All representations are summarised and put to Ministers. In general, they and their officials are more likely to take account of those covering specific rather than macroeconomic areas.

There are, however, certain announcements that cannot be floated in advance for any of three reasons:

• The Chancellor wants maximum media impact on the day
• They are market-sensitive
• Advance notice would generate inconvenient lobbying

A MODEL BUDGET LOBBY

The campaign to gain tax relief for provision of workplace nurseries was spearheaded not by professional advisers or well-funded companies but by a group of dedicated working mothers. Having made all the usual submissions assessing the cost and the social and economic impact of their proposal, the group ran a concentrated programme of parliamentary and media briefings, culminating over the month leading to the Budget with promotion of the line that tax relief was now regarded as a "hot item" and was likely to be granted. Other Ministers such as the Social Security Secretary were lobbied and found it difficult not to express support when questioned on TV. By Budget day, the fait accompli angle had been repeated by the media so often that it would have looked churlish for the then Chancellor John Major not to have given in.

The workplace nurseries case was more newsworthy than some, and while the skilful campaigning of the group could not have succeeded if the figures had not stacked up it offers an object lesson in supporting Budget representations with real pressure exerted through the media.

The climate of Budget secrecy within Treasury is deeply ingrained. Enquiries of officials on the status of possible Budget items are always met by "we cannot comment in advance of the Budget". The absence of early warning adds a degree of risk to the process of Budget lobbying, since there is virtually no chance of successfully opposing a Budget item once it has been announced despite the lack of consultation on the principle of the proposal or on its impact.

Amendments can be made, but once the Budget speech is made the Government is committed.

As the content of the Budget crystallises, two lists are produced under the headings of "minor starts" or inexpensive measures, and "major things for the Budget" - items affecting the whole economy. There are always too many proposals on the two lists and a sifting process takes place to assess the effect of each measure on the economy and to consider the political implications. More than in most policy formulation processes, the Budget is a genuine partnership between officials and Ministers since the planning involved is intensive and expert, and the implications to a Chancellor of a Budget poorly received by his own Party can be serious.

From the turn of the year, policies become firmer, although items are dropped and possibly reinstated even at the last minute. Eight weeks before any Budget, The Chancellor, other Treasury Ministers and Special Advisers and some senior officials hold a lengthy planning session and then enter what is known as the Purdah period, in which they have no meetings with outsiders and concentrate on finalising items and preparing the Budget speech. In that period a series of meetings take place as the culmination of hundreds of hours of liaison between officials and Ministers. They may include the Chancellor and Chief Secretary to the Treasury, the Financial Secretary and Paymaster General, the five Permanent Secretaries, the Chief Economic Adviser, the Chairmen of the Board of Inland Revenue and Customs and Excise and economic or statistical officials. While Ministers may have had to consider representations on behalf of interested parties from their sponsoring Department throughout the stages of Budget planning, most Departments produce a list of their recommendations for the Treasury a few weeks before Budget Day. Although other Ministers are not told of the content of the Budget until a few hours beforehand, these recommendations summarise Departments' views on the effects that likely measures would have on the sectors for which they are responsible.

The burden on the Treasury, Inland Revenue and Customs & Excise increases as Budget Day approaches since they have to prepare explanatory memoranda for public consumption on every measure. Other Departments such as DSS or DTI are involved if, for example, maternity benefits or industrial grants are affected. As soon as the Chancellor's speech – which is given on a Tuesday in mid-March and lasts around 80 minutes – is delivered the memoranda are released with a "Red Book" of forecasts for the economy. The Budget Pack can be ordered in advance from the Central Office of Information (Hercules House, Hercules Rd., London SE1 7DU) or read on the Treasury's website, although it can be difficult to read tables in that format.

The Budget is, in effect, an oral White Paper on which the five succeeding days are given to debate, except that a White Paper often leaves room for views to be taken on uncertain policy areas whereas the Budget is an unchangeable statement of fiscal policy for the current year and also, less definitely, for the future since the speech may announce forthcoming consultations or taxation reviews. The draftsmen turn the Treasury's proposals into the Finance Bill which, being a Money Bill, is not debated by the Lords. It is usual for the Treasury to produce redrafts of clauses during the passage of the Bill if officials

---

POINTERS FOR BUDGET LOBBYING

Start early - *get submissions in by the end of November to leave time for mobilising support and for negotiation with the Budget departments - Treasury, Customs & Excise and the Inland Revenue - before their options have crystallised.*

Your representations may be tagged as "Special Pleading" unless you can **demonstrate third party support**. *For example, publishers and booksellers may have spearheaded a number of campaigns to avoid VAT being imposed on their books but they were also able to secure backing from business leaders concerned about industrial literacy and from education and library bodies.*

Budget lobbying is easiest if it seeks to **address an anomaly**. *US investment banks found that unlike UK clearers they could not reclaim withholding tax on swaps deals because, while tax relief was available to "banks", they were still defined as licensed deposit takers because legislation had not caught up with Big Bang. The US houses explained the problem, showed that considerable new business would be transacted in the City, and secured a redrafting of the provision.*

Your gain is someone else's loss. You must **calculate the cost of your proposal and the realistic economic benefit (meaning benefit to UK plc) it would create.** *And consider carefully the administrative and legal implications: will legislation other than the Finance and Taxes Acts have to be amended?*

Many lobbyists seeking tax concessions claim that their industry is suffering for all sorts of reasons. They may well be right, but the **Budget departments are hard hearted and only deal in proven facts.** *They ignore assessments of the profit that might have been made or growth that might have been expected had it not been for (whatever). You must demonstrate actual loss, or alternatively the damage that tax changes would bring, beyond reasonable doubt. A campaign to rescind Air Passenger Duty could not make any initial impact because airlines and tour operators absorbed the tax and it could not therefore be shown that it had affected demand. When APD was passed on to passengers, Customs & Excise was able to point to healthy increases in demand even though it might have been greater in the absence of APD.*

Be persistent. *Even if your case is a good one, competition is fierce and it may take several years before you make headway.*

Most Budget lobbies are settled not through high profile announcements by the Chancellor but through compromises *quietly negotiated between officials and organisations, their accountants and tax lawyers and confirmed in correspondence or Extra Statutory Concessions.*

Wherever possible, **seek support from other Government departments.** *They may be reluctant to take up your case with Treasury; if so, bring in more MPs or third party endorsers.*

Because most Budget announcements are made without notice, the Regulatory Impact Assessments produced by officials are likely to be flimsy since affected parties cannot be consulted beforehand. While it is improbable that a Budget measure will be dropped because Government's maths or understanding of impacts is incorrect, you could secure Year 1 revisions to the scale of a change or more substantial action in subsequent years if you **produce a comprehensive RIA,** *challenge Budget departments to fault it and persuade the serious business media to support you.*

Unless the issue is highly technical or the anomaly you identify is obvious and can be addressed at official level, **it is always worth trying to meet Treasury Ministers** *(usually the Financial Secretary, who is responsible for Inland Revenue matters, or the Minister without Portfolio, who handles Customs & Excise) to make your case. They will of course be heavily guided by officials, so brief the Revenue or Customs first. Individual organisations are likely to find it difficult to get a slot, so try to work within sector coalitions or trade bodies.*

or outsiders have spotted loopholes or imprecisions; the most important of these clauses are debated on the floor of the House while the rest are examined in a larger than normal Standing Committee. Some of the provisions of the Budget, such as changes to Excise Duties, do not have to be endorsed by the House and can come into force within hours of the Chancellor's speech.

Procurement lobbying.

Officials administer all Government contractual tendering subject to initial political guidance – on buying British, for example, where EU rules allow – or occasional strong parliamentary or direct pressure on Ministers once the purely commercial aspects of the tender have been settled. A full description of every aspect of procurement procedure, rules and negotiating techniques requires a book to itself, but an example of the interface between the commercial role of Civil Servants and the political considerations that may influence their work can be seen in the case of a fictional contract for the replacement of helicopters for the Navy.

The Navy Helicopter Contract – a case study. *The Royal Navy has decided that one of its current types of helicopter is reaching the end of its service life and that a more modern replacement is needed. A series of papers detailing requirements and cost options are prepared for discussion by an MoD Integrated Project Team (IPT), which includes representatives from the Defence Procurement Agency, the Chief of Defence Logistics and Operational Requirements staff, and may include personnel from industry, before a coordinated proposal is prepared for the MoD Equipment Approval Committee which may need authority from the Minister for Defence Procurement. At this stage, only two considerations are important: are the new helicopters needs; and can the defence budget afford them? Although the defence estimates of expenditure are presented to Parliament each year in the form of a White Paper for debate, requirements need to be assessed many years in advance in view of the long R&D, construction and testing period involved in producing new warships, aircraft or armaments. In this case, it may be years from tendering to supply.*

The helicopter contract is relatively small - £400 million - in MoD terms and non-controversial compared to nuclear submarines or missiles, so there is unlikely to be any interdepartmental discussion, other than with the Treasury, at this stage. If the Navy's request is agreed, it will be written into future defence estimates after very detailed drafting of construction and performance parameters by the IPT and others, and an assessment of the total cost ceiling within which tenderers would have to operate. At this stage, DTI's Aerospace and Defence Industries Division (within which a Branch, EID1d, specialises in helicopters and defence procurement) would be contacted for its views about the state of the British helicopter industry. It may advise that the domestic industry is not healthy and that departmental policy is to give every possible assistance to British manufacturers since it is considered important for the UK to retain a strong presence in this field. It might also provide an outline assessment of the likely competitors for the contract and the extent to which each company would be likely to receive subsidies from their governments.

While the basic rule of government contracts is value for money, other considerations might apply:

- Even if it is decided not to subsidise British manufacturers or restrict the competition to British suppliers only, principles of public procurement such as the Smart Procurement Initiative (which, among other things, allows for Government to insist that prime contractors should use particular British subcontractors in order to develop the size and experience necessary for British companies to become independently competitive) may be embodied in the tendering rules, or the tenderers may take the initiative and aim to achieve as high a UK content as possible.
- MoD will be aware that, since it is seeking a new design of helicopter, this contract may give the lead to other countries to procure the machine it chooses. The nationality of the winner is therefore important.
- All the potential tenderers are aware that policy requirements may override specification and have therefore entered into joint ventures with British companies who will assemble their helicopters in the UK as a means of persuading MoD that employment will be generated at home.

There are four responses to the call for tenders - from the USA, France, Brazil and the UK. All match the performance criteria set by the Ministry:

two contenders comfortably exceed them. Two of the helicopters have been sold successfully in different specifications to other armed forces around the world; the British model has achieved a few sales but the company has essentially been established to pitch for, and grow on the basis of, this contract. The US competitor is still on the drawing board and is regarded as an outsider.

Initially, the three foreign contenders, through their UK partners, and the UK manufacturer, deal with the Ministry's technical experts only. The helicopters in production are subjected to rigorous testing and "drawing board" offers are carefully analysed by the Defence Evaluation and Research Agency (probably in conjunction with the operational user), which makes up its mind on the model it prefers on a pure speed/handling/weapons capability basis. However, this is but one recommendation considered by the IPT in determining the optimum combination of operational effectiveness and financial investment. Questions of programme risk and future enhanceability are also weighed in the balance.

Nevertheless, it is then that an essentially administrative and practical decision might begin to be tempered by political considerations, assuming that few restrictions were imposed in the call for tenders. All four companies start to lobby the Minister for Defence Procurement, the Secretary of State for Defence (both of whom will have to see all or none of the contenders in case excluded competitors make Judicial Review applications on the grounds that Ministers have given undue weight to other tenderers' cases), and the DTI Minister of State responsible for the aerospace industry. A second set of considerations begin to emerge alongside cost and specification:

- *British banks have lent considerable sums to Brazil, a major debtor nation. Strengthening the export prospects of its aerospace industry would improve Brazil's ability to repay those debts.*
- *The three British partners of foreign manufacturers all claim potential trade-offs of their own aircraft for US, Brazilian and French defence orders if they win the British contract.*
- *One of the British partners is based in a high unemployment area that is a marginal Government seat and which has been designated for preferment wherever possible.*
- *All four companies make different claims for UK job creation and invest-*

ment that would be generated if they were awarded the contract.

• *The sole British manufacturer organises a publicity campaign to impress MoD of the sense of supporting a domestic product.*

With constituency MPs and defence-related Peers also being mobilised by each of the contenders to debate the issue, question and write to the Defence Procurement Minister, it is decided that the Navy's Brazilian favourite should not be selected yet. It must enter a final review with the French contender: both British partners will be asked to resubmit prices to see whether economies could be made.

In the end, the judgement is decided by two issues that overturn the Navy's practical judgement and bring the Prime Minister and Secretary of State for Trade and Industry into the argument on the side of the French helicopter. Firstly, French Government subsidies enable the price to undercut the Brazilians; and it is decided to change the engine to a more powerful version manufactured by a DTI Foresight-funded British company which adds its own lobbying resources in the form of direct representations to the two Ministers, both of whom are firm supporters of the company. The French win.

Lobbying on competition issues

Organisations need to deal with UK and EU competition authorities for three principal reasons: they want clearance for, or to resist, a merger; they become subject to an industry or sector inquiry in connection with anti-competitive practices; or they are the target of a complaint about their company's activities.

Lawyers have cornered the bulk of competition work, quite rightly in most cases because much of the procedure is defined by law and it can be complex (for that reason, this section is somewhat more detailed than many of the others in this book). However, once it is understood, dealings with the Office of Fair Trading and Competition Commission in the UK and with the Competition DG and the Merger Task Force in Brussels are essentially a matter of sound assembly of evidence, professional advocacy and negotiation and the harnessing of third party support.

The role of lobbying in competition cases is misunderstood because lobbying has always been misunderstood. As is already clear, lobbying does not just involve politicians and it is rarely about pressure. Competition authorities are parts of the system and lobbying, to repeat the definition at the start of this book, is any action designed to influence the actions of the institutions of government. Competition issues do not therefore have to involve extensive ministerial interest for lobbying techniques to be involved in their resolution.

We will start by covering M&A work, where most of the procedural subtleties lie. First of all, the balance of power in merger cases between the UK and Brussels should be understood. The thresholds above which mergers fall automatically to Brussels under the Merger Regulation have a combined worldwide turnover of 5bn Euro and EC turnover of 250m Euro. Above that level, only in transactions where each of the parties to a merger has more than two thirds of its turnover in the same Member State does jurisdiction remain with the national authorities. The Commission also acquired jurisdiction in 1998 over certain mergers which fall beneath the thresholds but have an impact in several Member States.

The Commission has the discretion to refer part or all of a merger transaction which affects competition on a distinct market within a Member State to the competition authority of the relevant Member State (so long as that distinct market does not constitute a substantial part of the Common Market). It is no longer necessary to demonstrate that the transaction threatens to create or strengthen a dominant position in that distinct market. The convention is that Member States must request (and justify) repatriation and the Commission can grant or deny it, but in an attempt to deflect concern over centralised power, the Competition Commissioner has in at least one case offered to cede jurisdiction (the Member State in that instance refused it) .

The Office of Fair Trading advises on cases where it may be appropriate for the UK to seek repatriation. Its concern will generally be with effective and consistent competition assessment rather than with policy issues; but it is the DTI Secretary of State who decides whether to approach the Commission. The UK has made little use of this facility but others (notably Germany) are more keen to repatriate mergers with a significant national interest and may take advantage now that the criteria have been slightly relaxed.

Of more significance for "policy" concerns are:

- the limited circumstances in which the Member States can exercise parallel jurisdiction with the Commission: and
- defence-related cases where the Member States can deny the Commission jurisdiction.

The first of these options is available when the Member State can show that it has a legitimate interest in judging an "EC merger" against its own regulatory criteria, particularly in the fields of public security, media plurality, or prudential financial or fiscal rules. The UK has used this facility to investigate the acquisition of The Independent under its newspaper merger control regime and to refer to the former Monopolies Commission the acquisition of Northumbrian Water by Lyonnaise des Eaux (water mergers being subject to an automatic reference requirement under UK law). In each, the Commission gave clearance under the EC Merger Regulation while the Secretary of State determined the basis for clearance under UK rules.

Such cases of parallel control may remain significant in regulated sectors. The UK retains the right to block a merger on regulatory grounds even if it gains merger clearance from the Commission. Lobbying may help the UK to conclude that it should exercise its right of national assessment. However, bear in mind that the UK's desire to press for recall may also be influenced by OFT's workload and the view taken by officials and Ministers on the likelihood of a rebuff by Brussels (a view that will be influenced by intelligence gathered by UKRep). Concern over media coverage of rejection may lead to a conclusion that recall would be desirable but is not essential..

The defence sector is particularly tricky. The UK asserts its right under Article 223 of the Treaty of Rome to deny the Commission jurisdiction over defence-related activities, including mergers affecting military capability. The companies involved are instructed not to notify the military aspects of a transaction to Brussels and national merger control procedures are then applied. This technique was applied in the case of the bids for VSEL (see p.241) and also to the 1998 joint venture in defence electronics between GEC-Marconi and Finmeccanica of Italy. The Commission, however, is no soft touch. It will not yield jurisdiction over the civil component of defence mergers (even in the VSEL cases there were some non-military elements to the deal which were cleared under the Merger Regulation). And where dual-use products are involved, the Commission may assert that it has exclusive jurisdiction.

Merger control systems in individual Member States generally provide for strict competition criteria to be overridden by "national interest" considerations in some cases. The desire of Ministers to intervene in the Brussels process is triggered when factors (such as regional employment or industrial policy needs) arise which might well lead in a national context to clearance of a merger on national interest grounds. The first step may well be to seek repatriation of the merger decision. If the Commission will not agree to this, then the political lobbying begins.

From a lobbying point of view, the decision makers, and those who influence them, are

The Office of Fair Trading, which vets merger proposals and makes recommendations to the DTI Secretary of State on all bids qualifying under the Fair Trading Act (25% share of the "relevant market" in goods or services; £70m or more of assets acquired). It can recommend that a merger should be cleared, that it should be referred to the Competition Commission or that enforceable undertakings be given in lieu of a reference. OFT also has a role after a Competition Commission reference is completed. The Director General gives the Secretary of State his views on the Commission findings and on any remedies proposed by the Commission. OFT also negotiates any undertakings required post-reference.

OFT seeks information from parties to a merger; and from customers, suppliers and competitors. The definition of the relevant market is the key to establishing whether the merged entity will have much-enhanced market power. The OFT will also want evidence of the dynamics of the market and the extent of barriers to entry. Although its overall competition manpower has been significantly increased, OFT has a small mergers staff and much of this information has to come from the parties themselves and from other market participants.

It is rare for the Secretary of State to refer a merger when OFT recommends clearance (only around three per cent of qualifying mergers are referred). It is slightly less rare, although by no means common, for the Secretary of State to wish to clear a merger (with or without conditions) when OFT has recommended a reference. OFT has a well-developed "nose" for the policy instincts of the Secretary of State of the day and, within certain limits, will adapt its advice to avoid being overturned by its political masters. As a result, Ministers overturned or significantly differed from OFT's advice only eleven times between 1995 and 1999.

OFT operates a system of Confidential Guidance which allows a predator, or parties to an agreed bid, to seek a view on the likelihood of a reference. OFT will consult interested Departments, whose strong influence thus extends over both the decision to bid and consideration of bids in progress. If necessary, the Mergers Panel is convened to consider a Confidential Guidance request and in some cases Ministers may be consulted (on two occasions between 1995 and 1999 they disagreed with the OFT's guidance recommendation). OFT may conclude that it cannot give an authoritative view without consulting third parties outside Whitehall - and in this case there may be no guidance. Equally, Confidential Guidance is not a conclusive green light to a bid: new facts may come to light at the public stage once third parties are consulted, and there is a tendency for the parties to emphasise the positive in assembling their Confidential Guidance submissions. However, of 800 Confidential Guidances given between 1995 and 1999, only five cases were subsequently sent to the Monopolies Commission and of those two were blocked.

Other regulators. The utility regulators play a significant role in the assessment of mergers involving companies subject to their regulatory regimes. The licence under which a utility operates may need to be amended in the event of a change of ownership and it is essential to establish what new terms the regulator wishes to impose. In the water industry, where mergers are automatically referred to the Competition Commission, the regulator has insisted on price reductions as a condition of issuing revised licences. In electricity, licence conditions have been amended to ensure that new owners provide proper financial backing for the regulated activities of the acquired company.

In utility merger cases, much of the consultation with third parties and competitors is conducted by the regulator. A public request for comments is issued and the regulator then makes his recommendation to OFT. But the advice to the Secretary of State as to whether the merger should be referred to the Competition Commission still comes from OFT.

There are other examples of parallel regulation. For instance, the Bank of England, the financial and rail regulators and the Independent Television Commission exercise their own controls alongside the Fair Trading Act regime. Each has its own consultation procedure and will feed views to OFT in preparation for action under the Fair Trading Act.

Whitehall Departments and Agencies, the most effective lobbying force for two reasons:

- Whitehall, like everyone else, respects and believes those who it knows and trusts. Bodies inside the system lobby better than those outside it.
- All Departments with an interest in a bid will sit on the Mergers Panel, an OFT-chaired group which debates departmental views on a particular merger. Armed with knowledge of these views, the OFT then prepares the reference advice to the Secretary of State. The Panel considers the more important cases, including all those that OFT thinks should be referred to the Competition

Commission. Other Departments may call a meeting of the Panel if they are particularly concerned about a bid. Around one deal in ten has to clear this hurdle, with another 10-15 per cent being the subject of what OFT calls a "long paper" sent to relevant officials around Whitehall.

What sort of points will worry a Whitehall Department? The merger may be relevant (or even inimical) to a Government policy for which that Department is responsible (healthcare provision, rail/road transport, defence industry consolidation, gambling, research and development etc.). There may be implications for employment blackspots or for industrial strategy. Departments submit memoranda to OFT and follow this up with arguments at the Mergers Panel. A little detective work can often establish which officials from sponsoring or territorial departments are likely to attend the Panel meeting. They may welcome briefing and material (particularly statistics) to buttress their case.

The regulatory and industry Special Advisers at DTI and in the Prime Minister's Policy Unit have been influential in advising on utility mergers, where they have been keen to have the merger control process seen as one of the ways to push forward overall Government objectives for utility regulation.

Trade bodies, suppliers, customers and other companies in the target sector can be important targets. Arguments from these sources regarding the effect of a bid on competition or product availability and quality are weighed carefully by OFT and utility regulators. Under the 1997 Labour Government, consumer interests have been given more weight in decisions to refer issues to OFT and the Competition Commission.

Members of the public will also carry weight if the concerns they express to competition bodies are regarded as genuine and well-articulated. But they must be expressed in sufficient numbers without any suggestion of manipulation (e.g. identical pre-paid postcards) by interested parties.

DTI Ministers have sole responsibility for merger decisions. They are always advised by officials to decline meetings with parties to a bid or merger. As the decision-taker, the Minister must not "fetter his/her discretion" by appearing to give preferential access to those who happen to catch his ear or by prejudging the issue in any way. Requests for meetings with parties to bids are therefore declined. The risk of Judicial Review is simply too great.

In August 1999, DTI published a consultation document proposing that Ministers should withdraw from involvement in mergers other than those involving newspapers and the defence industry but that they should be able to add further special interest criteria for intervention by SI. In fact, as we have shown, Ministers rarely disagree with OFT and only reversed the conclusions of the former Monopolies Commission on ten occasions in the decade after 1987. However, political concerns do exist in some cases and the harmony between Ministers and OFT is as much a tribute to the latter's ability to anticipate political sensitivities as anything else. Withdrawal from a formal decision-making role will not, however, mean that merger decisions will only be made on objective grounds: liaison between DTI and regulatory bodies will simply move from being a formal process to an informal one.

Ministers in other Departments can express views to DTI counterparts (either direct or through their officials) on public policy grounds. Such grounds usually spring from the policies for which an individual Minister is responsible. But both the Treasury and the No. 10 Policy Unit may seek to intervene when some general tenet of Government policy is involved. However, the extent of political infighting over mergers should not be over-estimated. The number of cases which throw up policy issues is very limited. As already noted, the larger mergers (which tend to be the most contentious in public interest terms) are now handled mainly by Brussels. Ministerial interventions are more likely to take the form of submissions to the Competition DG or to other Member States.

The role of Parliament, and in particular MPs, is much misunderstood. While Select Committee criticism can in rare cases generate genuine pressure to mount a Competition Commission industry inquiry (e.g. into the compact disc market), committee investigations often take place after policy decisions have been taken and cannot be mounted with sufficient speed to match the Takeover Panel's timetables in merger cases.

Individual MPs, MSPs, AMs, MLAs and MEPs may help a case by giving OFT information (perhaps sent to them by companies in their constituencies) of which it may be unaware, or they may very occasionally express detailed and expert views that may reinforce OFT's thinking or weaken its convictions. But the DTI Secretary of State will be no more disposed to "fetter his/her discretion" through discussion with parliamentarians than through discussion with the parties. PQs will elicit the bland response that the Secretary of State cannot comment because of the functions falling to him/her under the Fair Trading Act.

There is no need for organisations to lobby OFT, the Competition DG and sector regulators indirectly if they can effectively do so directly. A letter from a parliamentarian attaching representations from constituency companies supplied by a bid target will carry no more weight than the same representations sent straight from those companies to the Mergers Secretariat of OFT.

The Media, like Parliament, is another example of an apparent pressure point that in practice carries little influence with OFT and the other key power centres, provided both bidder and defender make their representations professionally to those power centres. Where this condition is not satisfied, media comment may be influential. A little-known bidder that fails to discuss its intentions with Whitehall Departments, for example, may find that officials believe adverse publicity generated by the other side in the absence of any other information. Even if the important regulatory work is taken care of, the media is a powerful weapon in communicating with staff, shareholders and the City. Its lobbying power therefore lies mainly on the commercial, rather than the regulatory, side of bids.

The Competition DG is the EC's competition authority. Decisions in the most significant cases are taken collectively at their Wednesday meetings by the College of Commissioners, to whom the Competition Commissioner presents his recommendations. Individual Commissioners may have strong views reflecting their policy responsibilities or national affiliation; but a strong-minded Competition Commissioner backed by Competition DG staff can almost always push through decisions based on a consistent set of competition principles. On very rare occasions, he is outvoted. However, most competition decisions are cleared by a written procedure or delegated to the Competition Commissioner, whose judgements are not subject to review or oversight by the Council of Ministers. The only appeal route is to the European Court of Justice, which can strike down decisions or to send cases back to the Commission if the latter's analysis is found to be faulty or misconceived. Appeals can take many years. Note that in contrast to the DTI Secretary of State, the Competition Commissioner is not constrained from meeting parties to a merger.

The Mergers Task Force regards itself as the cream of the Competition DG and is proud of the high reputation it enjoys with business and Member State governments. Its procedures follow a well-grooved track and because mergers falling to EC jurisdiction have to be notified for regulatory approval (with supporting information), the process in Brussels gets under way rather quicker than in the UK. The two-stage procedure (Stage 1 - 4-6 weeks, which may end with clearance, negotiation of undertakings/divestments or reference to a Second Stage - four months, which can be compared with clearance, negotiation of undertakings/divestments or total blockage) the separate stages of investigation by OFT and the Competition Commission but the analogy is not exact. In particular, the same Commission case officers stay with the case until the end of the process (although note that recent pressure of work has led to some qualifying mergers being farmed out by the MTF to the Competition DG units responsible for the relevant sectors.) Mergers subjected to the second stage of investigation simply undergo a more profound analysis (with extra third party input and hearings etc.) by essentially the same team.

The Commission does not operate a formal Confidential Guidance system but it is always happy to discuss possible competition concerns on a Commercial In Confidence basis. Such discussions can help to diminish problems that might arise if the contact with the Task Force is not made before submission of the merger notification form.

Other DGs vary in power and influence. Apart from the Competition Directorate, the strongest are probably External Relations, Trade, Economic and Financial Affairs, Enterprise and Agriculture. The Information Society DG works closely with Competition to a broadly similar agenda. But Transport often finds itself at odds with competition officials and usually loses out to them.

All DGs with an interest in a merger are consulted by the Competition DG, normally through three inter-service meetings during Stage 1. Does the merger affect an EC policy (e.g. the liberalisation of telecommunications or of air services) for which particular DGs are responsible? They can argue for a preferred outcome in bilateral discussions with the Competition Commissioner or Competition DG officials. If they do not win the day in these discussions, the relevant Commissioners can raise their concerns when the College considers the case. They are a natural target for lobbying. It can be helpful to send a brief to the relevant Chef de Cabinet in order to suggest concerns that might be raised with the Competition DG. DGs will impose a deadline (around four or five days before the last date on which a Stage 1 decision can be announced) beyond which they will not formally consider written submissions, but they will pass on views to the Task Force after that cutoff if they support them.

National Ministers, in particular Industry or Economics Ministers, often exert the strongest pressure on the Competition DG. This can be accompanied by representations to the President of the Commission from Heads of Government in the most sensitive cases.

The Advisory Committee on Concentrations is the forum for formal consultation with Member State authorities and parallels the Merger Panel. The Member States themselves determine who should attend. The UK is represented by OFT and DTI's Competition Policy officials. This pattern (competition authority plus Ministry) is also adopted by a number of other Member States. The Ministry representative will tend to take the lead where the Member State has a policy interest to assert.

Meetings are chaired by a senior Member of the Merger Task Force. Officials from other DGs (notably Enterprise) may also attend. The main role of the Committee is to comment on draft decisions which the Commission proposes to make (usually at the end of Stage 2). The Commission is free to ignore or follow the advice. Because it meets late in the regulatory process (when the four month deadline may be approaching), it is unusual for the Commission to be persuaded by the Committee to change tack entirely. At best, the Competition DG thinks again about points such as the form of undertakings to be sought as a condition of clearance. It is only on the rarest of occasions that Member State opposition in the Committee causes the Competition DG to retreat. Those Member States who play the Brussels process to best effect will have made their case to the Commission long before the draft of a decision is prepared.

European Parliament influence is steadily growing. MEPs can make representations to the Competition DG on issues falling within the scope of a merger inquiry and they can make a certain amount of noise. As more of the larger mergers are referred to Brussels, increasing attempts will be made to persuade delegations of MEPs to lobby Commissioners to advance a particular viewpoint. But competition law enforcement by the Competition DG is not one of the areas in which the Parliament has any formal power of co-decision.

Why, you will ask, have we not included the **Competition Commission?** Simply because it is not lobbyable. However, the techniques set out below, particularly those relating to managing trade and departmental views, apply equally to the Competition Commission and to OFT. Furthermore, the giving of evidence, whether behind closed doors or in public hearings, provides an opportunity for non-attributable media briefing by the main parties or direct briefing by other interested bodies (such as consumer organisations), all of which can condition the approach taken by DTI Ministers to CC recommendations.

The arguments considered by regulatory authorities fall into two groups:

• Economic, involving definition of the relevant product and geographical market, calculation of market share; analysis of the extent of restrictions on competition/diversity of supply, and consideration of the effect of the bid on product/market pricing and quality and on R&D etc.
• Public interest, which could include (for example) problems caused by foreign ownership of a strategically important UK company (particularly in the defence industry); lack of reciprocity in the bidder's host regime; gearing of the bid (important these days in utilities where the acquiring company must show it can give adequate long term support to guarantee continuity of supply); regional implications; effect of a takeover on employment, product supply or treatment of sub-contractors etc.

The process is not always objective. A Minister may have had a bad day and may feel that a "just in case" decision to refer against the advice of OFT may be preferable to media criticism if the case has become controversial. This does not mean that pressure can turn a data-based case into a political one. Unless the parties have on their hands a case like Westland involving the future of a unique UK asset (and the Cabinet seat of Michael Heseltine in 1986), it is pointless for them to seek to confuse the two. Commercial lobbying may sow doubts in the minds of shareholders and push the price up or down, perhaps causing a predator to withdraw. Lobbying aimed at influencing the regulatory decision is a different animal. Pressure from

225

MPs and City editors will not under normal circumstances change the views of OFT, utility regulators or the Competition DG. Given enough pressure, however, any institution will yield. We have seen such overt pressure work on only one occasion, when Knoll International's bid for Sotheby's in 1983 was referred following a flag-waving campaign by MPs. The Sotheby's bid was the first in which lobbying, as we now know it, was used in the UK, but pressure may in exceptional cases force Ministers to move from a passive to a robust position in defending UK interests in Merger Regulation cases.

At EU level, there is never any explicit recognition in decisions that industrial policy considerations have palliated the competition analysis. The Merger Regulation is firmly based on competition criteria and does not make provision for a public interest test. Effective lobbying has therefore to aim at influencing the presentation of the case so that competition criteria are shown to be satisfied. This can be done through achieving a more benign market definition or through negotiation of undertakings to divest part of a merged business. The market definition used by the Commission can also be challenged in the ECJ.

What should *defenders* do to prepare themselves? First, ensure that Departments/DGs and agencies with an interest in the company understand it and are familiar with the level of competition in its sector. This is critically important: as the box on p.242 shows, in the BAe/GEC case it emerged that BAe's "own" officials in DTI had a misleading view of its financial performance because the annual reports in their files were three years out of date. Had BAe not corrected this, DTI could have assumed that VSEL would not be well-managed under BAe's ownership. It may be that only DTI is relevant, but it pays to think about others that might be consulted by (or persuaded to make their views known to) OFT: MoD and DoH if the company has contracts with the services or the NHS; it may have major supply contracts with any Department; it may operate key research projects funded through MAFF or DfEE; it may have a strong Scottish, Welsh or Northern Ireland investment record or may be a substantial recipient of grant aid from Regional Development

Agencies; it may, like an air or shipping line, be heavily regulated by, or it may co-sponsor environment-friendly schemes with, DETR. If in doubt, consult officials with responsibility for your industry or interests at around Director or Assistant Director/A5-7 level..

Since none of the parties can gain access to the Secretary of State, they must find others to make their case. Once the targets in Government have been identified, defenders should ensure that Section, Branch or, exceptionally, Directorate heads in sponsor or regulatory Departments have full details of the bid plus the information needed to judge its implications. Defenders should stress points such as export and research record and future development plans which may be frustrated by the takeover. As a rule of thumb, treat sponsoring officials as if they were City analysts; briefings produced for the latter are perfect for Whitehall and the Commission too. All discussions will be treated as confidential. In each case, it is preferable that the subsidiary(ies) whose work would be relevant to the Department, not the parent, should make contact unless there is a particular reason – which should be explained to officials – for doing otherwise. That contact may take a number of direct or indirect forms:

- An invitation to visit your company for a presentation on it and on its sector/industry given by you or by a reputable research organisation commissioned to assess the sector. The assessment may include an attempt to define the "relevant market" – defenders naturally seek to persuade regulators that the market it should be examining is one in which the predator or potential predator would have an unacceptably high market share – although such exercises can only be academic in the absence of a bidder.
- An invitation to a similar presentation near Whitehall.
- Selective media leaking of research or educated comment designed to show, as would the presentations, that market share in your industry is already critical (this may, however, be a two-edged sword: you could seek to make a takeover yourself in the future) or that the nature of the company's work or relationship with Government is such that a bid by any one of a number of

organisations, named or generic, should be critically considered by Government.

- You may also seek to commission or fund research into the industrial and economic effect of hostile bids or the practice of growth by acquisition. Much recent academic research has been sceptical of the efficiency benefits claimed to flow from mergers. The instinctive Labour suspicion that many hostile takeovers are a manifestation of inefficient short-termism has not totally evaporated and could prove helpful. In the utility sector, in particular, Labour may still wish to relate merger proposals to its own vision of the future regulatory regime for the utility sector, Make sure your Whitehall contacts are aware of any articles that result from research you commission.

Ideally, Whitehall should be able to use the defender's statistics and arguments wholesale in its submissions to OFT. The chances of achieving this are considerably increased if prime consideration is given by organisations not to the arguments they want to advance but to the considerations of those regulators they seek to influence. The company's case, consistent with the system's needs, is what must be advocated.

Turning to EC mergers considered in Brussels, much of the UK-related advice above also applies. Guidance should be taken from the Task Force and you should brief DGs other than Competition if you believe that a bid could lead to scrutiny by Brussels. Approach officials in the relevant DGs at A3-A4 grades - usually the Head of Section, the equivalent of the old Assistant Secretary grade (Grade 5) in Whitehall, or one of the administrators below him. Arrange to meet them in Brussels (site visits are possible although, for obvious reasons, they are less likely in practice) and present to them in similar manner to Whitehall officials. Your research will, however, have to cover EU-wide market shares and potential competition. The presentation should in each case be given by the most senior affected level in your company or group: it may be the European parent company but could include subsidiary representatives. You will seek to demonstrate that any bid for your company is likely to fall within Brussels' jurisdiction (this will be self-evident in some cases), that competition is finely balanced in one or more sectors of your business, and that your company has a good record of innovation and is considered efficient.

Bear in mind that your research could be used against you if you turn from target to predator.

UK parliamentarians and MEPs may have greater value in bids in scaring the City than in influencing the regulatory process but they should not be ignored. Approach them in this way:

- Local Members should be invited to meet your company (or relevant subsidiary) in their constituency. For bid purposes, it is important that they should know what you do and feel that you do it well; that you have a record of involvement in local affairs, for example through educational sponsorship, and that your presence in the constituency is valued. Monday morning or Friday (and, for home counties MPs, Wednesday morning) is a good day for briefing in situ, although Labour MPs are encouraged to spend a full week a month in their constituencies and may therefore be available on other days. Alternatively, parliamentarians could be briefed by local management at Westminster, in Edinburgh, Cardiff or Belfast or in Brussels at any time. Firms without links with their Members should write explaining what they do, how many they employ and how much they contribute to the local economy, and setting out reasons why they want to meet the MP, MSP, AM or MEP. There is nothing wrong in simply inviting him/her to come and see what you do; alternatively, and preferably, you may have specific national or local problems that will provide a more legitimate pretext for contact. Keep your letter to one page.
- While such advance meetings may be arranged for courtesy reasons only, a parliamentarian must feel that there is a point to them. A company will be important to him if it is a substantial employer, if it is the only provider of a service in the constituency, or if its activity is objectively interesting or strategically important. Be realistic

229

about this: a new die-casting process that will not create a significant number of jobs does not warrant a parliamentary visit; a major new skills training programme does. Try to find such pegs as the opportunity to make the key points listed above. But remember - while it helps to leave parliamentarians with the impression that a company is well managed and does not need to be taken over, that is essentially the company's affair, they feel. The company's value to the constituency, gauged both by employment and corporate responsibility programmes, is theirs. Ultimately, nothing wins support more than helping a parliamentarian, for example through assisting with favoured local charitable schemes, giving him information that he can use before debates or committee proceedings in which he will be involved, or providing him with facilities that help him do his job better.

- MEPs should be targeted both at local and legislative committee levels; some may overlap. While local MEPs can be treated like constituency MPs, others should be met in Brussels during their committee meetings or in Strasbourg during plenary sessions. Remember that the Commission has little scope for consideration of public interest arguments, and a bid qualifying for apparently exclusive consideration in Brussels may be snatched back by OFT, for example if issues of defence or media control are involved, but where the Competition DG is likely to have jurisdiction, MEPs may help to reinforce arguments, particularly if they seek to show that competition-based concerns expressed by MEPs in committee during consideration of EU legislation may be validated if the structure of the company's market or industry changes through concentration or asset stripping. Watch the progress of EU legislation carefully, therefore.

- While mentioning that last point, do not just target UK MEPs. The largest Merger Regulation bids will be fought in a number of Member States as well as in Brussels and all European subsidiaries should make a point of briefing their national MEPs. An Italian Commissioner for research, for example, will be more susceptible to representations from Italian MEPs of his political persuasion.

- As with the UK, make maximum use of research reports on the state of competition in your EU market. Distribute summaries to MEPs at briefings. If a UK/EU exercise of this sort is commissioned, it should be reviewed annually in order to maintain a company's defences. Annual meetings with MEPs will be sufficient unless the company has to deal with them for other reasons, in which case the above tactics can be combined with any other lobbying the company needs to carry out.

Vulnerable organisations should prepare a crisis management plan to be implemented if a hostile bid is launched. The plan should include an advance lobbying checklist as follows:

Whitehall/Scottish/Welsh/N Ireland Departments
- Names and numbers of current officials (grades 3-7) in relevant positions?
- Briefed on market shares/state of the sector/competitive position/public interest arguments?
- Concerns about competition in your sector or about a bid for you (eg defence contracts)?

Brussels DGs
- List of current officials (grades A3–A4) and Cabinet members prepared
- Fully briefed (as above)/concerns?

UK/Scottish/Welsh/N Ireland Ministers
- Extent of contact with (likely) relevant Ministers?
- If no close contact, can they be accessed through a strong relationship with their Special Advisers?
- How politically important is your sector? Any ministerial concerns about takeovers? Any statements on this to Select Committees/in debate/in other speeches?

MPs/MSPs/AMs/MLAs/MEPs
- Which parliamentarians are respected by relevant Ministers?
- Which parliamentarians may have an interest in us (by career or

political background)?
- Government backbench committees briefed?
- Local Members briefed?
- MEPs briefed?
    Committee members
    Constituency members
    Subject specialists (other than committee membership)
    Cross-border/cross-party spread

Suppliers/trade customers and associations
- Up to date lists kept centrally?
- Are they likely to support us?
- Plan for briefing strongest links with suppliers/customers to mobilise support?

Media
- Heavyweight correspondents fully briefed?

Bidders will of course be concerned about confidentiality. It is therefore more important than with defenders that their advisers take preliminary soundings within Whitehall and Brussels on the system's likely attitude to their plans. Since these must be taken non-attributably, it is important that advisers are respected and trusted by their targets. The scope of their soundings should cover: Third Departments and DGs, UK parliamentary specialists, Relevant European Parliament committees, Relevant journalists, The target's trade bodies, plus major customers and competitors.

This is part of building up a file on the target which will include all known links between Whitehall, Brussels, politicians and the target; statements it may have made to the media or to parliamentary committees on relevant issues in case they could be used against it (ditto with Ministers or officials - departmental press releases, Select Committee submissions, brokers' research or media reports of conference speeches, interviews and suchlike can be fruitful); likely views of key officials, politicians and the media; and details of how competition policy has been applied in the target sector(s) in the past (eg via past Competition/Monopolies Commission reports). Do this even if it is believed the bid will be decided entirely in the markets: an apparently commercial bid may be turned, as happened in the Pembridge Investments/DRG case, into a closely fought regulatory battle. Such dossiers repay the effort involved in compiling them - in one case, it enabled a non-EU bidder to show the UK Government and media that its target and key Ministers had on more than one occasion given evidence to Select Committees in which they opposed protection for the target sector, supported foreign entry into the UK market and denied that any efficiencies resulted from the maintenance of independent status in the area concerned.

The research recommended above will help to identify, even before deciding whether to seek Confidential Guidance (which can take around five weeks to complete), both the likely areas of concern to be addressed and points of weakness to be exploited in the target. Predators can tailor their market and public interest research accordingly. Again, remember that addressing the system's concerns and needs is more important than pressing any particular arguments to which you may be wedded.

Assume that the target has done its pre-emptive homework. Counter its research with other independent studies to indicate that the "Relevant Market" should fall within an area of strong competition and, in the UK, that the public interest would not suffer and in Brussels that technical and economic progress (as defined) would not be impeded or that a dominant position would not be either created, extended or abused. Use them if going through the Confidential Guidance process; otherwise, do not liaise on the possible bid directly with Whitehall or DGs in advance. Bear in mind that OFT or the Competition DG, if in any doubt over the Relevant Market, market share figures or the public interest, may be inclined to recommend a reference (or the Brussels equivalent) or restrict the bid.

And think of how a defender could exploit information politically. For example, it is relatively easy for a company with a strong regional base to stimulate MPs to question the motives and stability of a foreign bidder.

Bidders' lobbying checklist should read on the eve of attack as follows:

Whitehall/Scottish/Welsh/N Ireland Departments
- List of relevant officials (grades 3-7) with telephone numbers.
- Likely attitude of officials; past statements.
- Detailed research initiated or completed.

Brussels DGs
- List as above.
- Likely attitude.
- Research initiated or completed.

UK Ministers
- Likely attitude. Are there any political implications?
- Any relevant statements?
- Will they intervene in Brussels?

Customers/suppliers
- Compile list for quick mailing.

Media
- Views of heavyweight correspondents known.
- Outline concerns addressed (within limits of confidentiality).

Parliamentarians
- Influential MPs/MSPs/AMs/MLAs and committees identified.
- Target's political links researched.
- Concerns assessed and defused in outline.

MEPs
- Possible targets identified.
- Any past comment by key committees or individual MEPs on this sector or type of issue (eg reciprocity; non-EU companies expanding in vital EU industry areas)?
- Are relevant MEPs familiar with us; do they regard us as benign?

Brussels Advisory Committee
- Possible targets identified (not only UK members).

- Likely attitude.
- Research initiated or completed.

Permanent Representatives
- As Advisory Committee

Irrespective of whether the bid is hostile or agreed, it pays to establish an Attack Task Force to consider both how the other side (or trade competitors and other third parties) will attack your case and how their arguments can be pre-empted. As we have already said, there is no point in hoping that difficult issues will not be identified by the system or by outsiders - get there first.

Timing. While the state of the target and the markets, availability of finance and a number of other factors may be regarded as more important, a bidder will also wish to consider the possibility of minimising regulatory intervention in deciding upon the timing of its bid. A bid mounted in the last week of July, for example, effectively allows a defender only one week in which to attract attention through UK lobbying, since Parliament rises at the end of July and many Ministers and officials also take their holidays during August.

The Merger Regulation process allows more time to assess bids but the same considerations may apply, albeit to a more limited extent, since almost the entire Commission and the European Parliament are effectively on holiday for six weeks from the middle-end of July (the Competition DG, conscious of this, always keeps the Mergers Task Force adequately manned). It is not accidental that Hoylake launched its bid for BAT Industries at the end of July 1989; where public interest and general PR issues could be turned to the target's advantage by vigorous departmental and political lobbying, the timing of attack may benefit from taking the political and regulatory calendars into account.

The clock is all-important. While on UK bids the OFT is not subject to strict deadlines for submitting advice to the Secretary of State, the Brussels process operates to a rigid timetable. Member States seeking repatriation must notify the Task Force of their intention to claim jurisdiction over the case within 21 days of deemed notification of the merger to that State (usually a day or two after formal notification to Brussels). The Commission must decide on whether to proceed to a second stage within a month of notification, or six weeks if a repatriation request has been made. In many cases, DGs will not take formal account of submissions received less than a week before the Stage 1 deadline. Representations and lobbying must fit within these parameters.

Call key officials immediately the bid is launched. If you are the target, tell them a bid has been launched and give them details of the bidder, including any information about it that you feel is pertinent. Ask them if there are any further details they need, pointing out that you believe the bid falls within either the statutory monopoly limits or the consideration criteria of the Merger Regulation and that you believe there are grounds for public interest concern. Make clear to them the two obvious facts that you are keen to ensure that Whitehall or other DGs make their views known to OFT or the Competition DG and that you will be following the appropriate procedures with the key regulatory authorities. You will not want Whitehall or the Commission to feel you are lobbying Departments as a substitute. However, before citing the grounds that persuade you, ask them to advise you of the points you would need to make in order to attract their legitimate interest. Ask them whether they would wish to meet and question you, and find out how quickly they need any submission you may produce.

Advance briefing of officials, insofar as it is possible for a target to be prescient, obviates some of this explanation, but you will wish to mention factors that are either particularly relevant to the bidder's situation or which bring up to date your most recent submission or presentation to them. For example, when the travel firm Thomson bid for Horizon, the regular liaison between Thomson's airline subsidiary Britannia and the Civil Aviation Division of the (then) Department of Transport paid off. Britannia contacted the Assistant Secretary handling competition issues as soon as the bid was launched, ran through its market share details and those of Orion, Horizon's airline, and reiterated what officials already knew, that competition in the charter/leisure sector was fierce and was unlikely to be affected by the demise of a small carrier. Officials had been well-supplied with information on the market, which inclined them to petition OFT on Britannia's behalf. Although the deal was referred to Monopolies Commission because of concern over the package tour market, the Department's intervention ensured that the aviation element in the bid would be regarded as a formality.

Either side's contact with officials need not be constant. But you should send officials a copy of any response you make to the other side's offer or defence documents if they make points relevant to that Department or DG which you contest. It is also sensible to give officials a copy of your OFT submission and any documentation supporting the Merger Regulation notification form that is relevant to OFT and/or DGs. Make sure that any submission sent to DGs is copied to the Merger Task Force.

Under the Merger Regulation, liaison between OFT and the Competition DG has been strengthened. UK bidders or defenders will wish to gain the support of UK officials on the Advisory Committee. They must also lobby other Member State officials on the Committee. Clearly, defenders will wish to ensure that opportunities for national and Brussels involvement are maximised. They should produce as many different reasons for intervention to as many different bodies as possible - in most instances, the more complex they make the case, the better. Bidders want to make the issue seem as simple as possible and will seek to persuade national authorities (and other DGs) that they have no role.

A strong parliamentary defence (a bidder should primarily seek to rebut the target's parliamentary allegations and, by so doing, silence the defender's lobby rather than expect to build up one of its own) is necessary in cases where a noticeable public interest element is present. Parliamentary expressions of support or concern attract the media, which is itself closely studied by those in the City or other financial centres who influence share prices. The next diagram may be somewhat cynical; but it is also accurate.

THE EFFECT OF PARLIAMENTARY LOBBYING

PARLIAMENTARY CONCERN/SUPPORT	POLITICAL EDITORS	CITY EDITORS
(statements to the the Press, PQs, motions, also letters or delegations to Ministers/Commissioners) →	*(denied access to the regulatory process)* →	*(don't understand regulatory process; denied access)*
	REPORT IT AS "PRESSURE ON ..." ETC	REPEAT THE STORY

CITY ANALYSTS ↙

(who often don't understand the factors shaping regulatory decisions either)

SHARE PRICE MOVES

Bearing that in mind, contact your target parliamentarians for advice on identifying the right targets) as follows:

Local and constituency MPs, MSPs, AMs and MLAs (or MEPs, where relevant): by telephone, backed by a confirming letter, as soon as the bid is launched. The Commons number is 071 219 3000; the European Parliament's Brussels centre is 00 322 284 2111 although each MP/MEP, their secretary and in some cases their research assistant, will have direct lines. If you make contact with parliamentarians in advance, keep note of those numbers. If you do not reach them immediately, the confirming letter should mention that you have left a telephone message. They should as soon as possible be made aware by defenders of the nature of the bidder and the initial company view of the bid's consequences and should ask for a meeting at the earliest opportunity.

The target's local Members should also be contacted at the same time by bidders. Their letters should seek to reassure parliamentarians (if they can) on employment and investment prospects and to offer a meeting to address any concerns they may have. Bidders may receive letters from concerned Members or hostile groups (it is rare for a letter to be received from an MEP). They should always answer them promptly, fully and with courtesy, bearing in mind that anything they say may be leaked to the media. And they should offer to meet any Member who contacts them.

For the sake of speed, letters should be delivered to the Commons by messenger. While a single hand-delivered letter can be unstamped and delivered direct to the Palace, hand deliveries of letters to several MPs or Peers must be channelled via the Post Office in Howick Street, SW1 and all such letters must be stamped. All letters should be addressed and written personally, explaining the possible effect of the bid on them: do not send circulars unless time precludes any other approach, and even then explain in the circular why it is not possible for a personal letter to be sent. Make sure that titles (Privy Councillors or Knighthoods) are up to date. Do not use labels: some parliamentarians will not even open a letter if they suspect that it may be mass-produced.

Letters hand-delivered to MSPs should be channelled via the Scottish Parliament's garage in Victoria Street EH99 1SP. Mass-mailings need not be stamped. Mass-mailings to the Welsh Assembly should be delivered unstamped direct to the Assembly building in Cardiff Bay CF99 1NA.

All MEPs have pigeonholes in both the main Parliament buildings (Palais de L'Europe, 67006 Strasbourg; Rue Belliard 97-113, B-1040, Brussels) but unless a monthly plenary session is taking place or you are aware of their constituency movements, it is safer to deliver or send mail to Brussels. Vachers and the so-called "Grey Book", available from the European Parliament's London office or from HMSO, lists the constituency addresses and numbers of all MEPs.

MPs, MSPs AMs, MLAs (and, to a lesser extent, MEPs) receive many telephone messages each day. Defenders, if they have done their prep, will be familiar with their targets, but in any event they should tell parliamentarians quickly

- who they are
- why they are contacting them (because a bid has been made by X)
- their reaction (including an assessment of what the bid may mean for that Member's constituency)
- the actions they want parliamentarians to take (it may take a few hours to assess the likely implications of the bid and the type of action needed to attack the bidder's plans and reputation. They can be asked to await further contact once decisions have been taken. If they are close to one of the parties, they may ask to be kept informed of any contact made by the other side).

Remembering the role of the UK Parliament in bids, a defender will not only want local Members to intervene with a well-informed delegation to Third Department Ministers, particularly if the defender's local MPs, MSPs, AMs or MLAs are also respected by them, but will need them to give as much external visibility as possible to its case

- By tabling Early Day Motions which the defender should send to other MPs to canvass signatures and to the local and national press – an EDM is only worthwhile if it attracts publicity, especially along the City/investor route of influence outlined in the above box but also as a morale-booster with workforce and customers. It can, exceptionally, give an indication to the Whips of the real level of support for either side: when both Lloyd's Bank and HongKong and Shanghai bid for Midland Bank in 1992, Lloyd's tried the EDM ploy but attracted few signatures; its rival's attempt was well supported and suggested to Ministers that foreign takeover of a High Street bank would not generate political concerns. A critical feature, however, was HKSB's retention of a former Treasury and DTI Minister who was able to emphasise the significance of the EDMs to his former colleagues.
- By tabling large numbers of Parliamentary Questions, both written and oral, remembering that oral PQs are selected at random. Several may therefore have to be tabled by different MPs to give defenders a reasonable chance that one will be called; that it is even

GEC v BRITISH AEROSPACE
THE BENEFIT OF ADVANCE PREPARATION, AND LUCK

In 1994, British Aerospace launched a friendly bid for VSEL, the UK's only nuclear submarine yard. GEC followed suit. The size of the two bidders and the strategic issues involved - BAe's potential entry into the shipbuilding market; the threat this posed to GEC's Yarrow yard, the future of UK naval procurement; and the possible vulnerability of BAe to a bid from GEC if it did not capture VSEL - meant that policy factors would play a central part in the battle.

GEC's plan was to secure acceptance by the Ministry of Defence of the inevitability that the naval shipbuilding market will decline and that managed rationalisation of the two largest UK yards under a single owner would be better than the consequences of shrinking by competition. Only when it was sure that MoD had bought this idea did GEC launch its bid.

Although BAe gained support from a number of Departments, many MPs and, apparently critically, from OFT, it was not able to counter one exceptional point which made GEC's advance preparation pay off. The then President of the Board of Trade, Michael Heseltine, had been Defence Secretary and had a close personal interest in the subject. He also had a deep respect for the Ministry's expertise in assessing its needs. As a result, not only was the bid given more careful personal consideration by him than might normally have been the case, but he was predisposed to assume that MoD's view should be paramount. Although OFT recommended referral only of GEC's bid, he sent both to MMC, before which MoD maintained its ground. But most of the evidence to MMC supported BAe and the report recommended significant restrictions on GEC's right to proceed. Nonetheless, the President remained steadfast and cleared both parties to bid.

This case has two lessons for bidders and defenders:

- *proper preparation inevitably involves over-preparation. Like the old adage about advertising, only half of it may work, but you will not always be sure which half*
- *luck can play a great part in bid battles involving major policy issues. Statistically, the chances are that a different President would have upheld OFT's and MMC's advice. GEC gambled everything on the axis between Heseltine and MoD fending off all other pressures and did little lobbying in the system; this time, it paid off.*

more the case in bids, when the way to grab attention is to show considerable concern - a defender's ideal is therefore to monopolise an oral question time or to be able to tell the media that, say "20 MPs have tabled no fewer than 90 PQs on the X bid"; and that a Department answers oral PQs less than once every three weeks.

- By writing detailed letters to Ministers, OFT and regulators on different aspects of the bid and leaking them to the media.
- By holding regular press conferences featuring supportive MPs, trade bodies, major suppliers and customers.

MEPs, although to date a largely unused resource in bids, can help in three ways:

- By seeking meetings with Commissioners and their Cabinets, either informally during plenary sessions in Strasbourg or in Brussels.
- By raising points with DGs: MEPs' links with officials are generally far stronger than MPs' relations with Whitehall.
- By raising issues of concern with the bidder.

Bidders may share local MPs with the defender and should expect to be given a hearing even if they have a much smaller constituency presence.

Bids of major interest (remember that only one in a hundred becomes truly political) may attract the interest of Westminster, Edinburgh, Cardiff and Belfast backbench committees. Defenders will often seek to present their arguments to those groups, both to provoke statements to the media by committee chairmen and possibly to secure expressions of concern to Third Department Ministers. In anticipation of this, bidders should write to the relevant chairmen and secretaries (details are available either from the Public Information Office in the Palace of Westminster or from the Scottish, Welsh and Northern Irish information offices - see pp 48-53 for details) and request from them the opportunity of equal time if their groups intend to meet and question the defender.

Most of the value in higher profile or peripheral lobbying work falls to defenders. Bidders should regard the rallying of political, media and commercial support, at least in their regulatory work, as secondary to correcting misconceptions and defusing emotional opposition. While they may prefer to mobilise parliamentarians, their workforce and others, it is often as effective, and far less burdensome, to ensure that regulators are aware of quiet briefings of potential trouble-makers and that the media is persuaded that OFT, regulators, the Competition DG and other Departments/DGs/Ministers are looking sceptically on the target's scaremongering.

Dealing direct with Ministers or Commissioners will be harder for non-UK bidders for UK companies, or any organisation dealing with Brussels (even though, in the latter case, all Competition DG Merger Regulation cases are referred to Commissioners once officials have completed their work: do not, therefore, neglect direct or indirect contact with a range of Commissioners for example, by MEPs or trade bodies). Seek a meeting through friendly MPs and Special Advisers in the UK or through Commissioners' Cabinets (and, possibly, requests from UK or other Member State Ministers) in Brussels. In the present Commission, a delegation from UK Conservative MPs and MEPs, particularly those who were close to him while he was a UK Minister, may have influence with Chris Patten; similarly, Labour MPs and Socialist MEPs may be deployed to lobby Neil Kinnock, although the responsibilities of both of the UK's Commissioners are unlikely to touch upon any competition-related issues. The principle applies across the Commission: when Sky announced its merger with BSB in November 1990, pressure was mounted equally on the Competition DG and on the then technology Commissioner Pandolfi. Pressure from French and Italian Ministers in the De Havilland case led to strong support for the deal from a number of Commissioners in the face of the then Commissioner Sir Leon's Brittan's decision to block the bid; the Competition DG only won on a split vote and it is clear that the parties had made maximum use of political channels.

Whether meeting Ministers or Commissioners, bear in mind that they need a good reason (such as the impact of a bid on key marginal constituencies) for listening to your arguments.

Bidders may seek to complain about the defender's alleged exaggerations, manipulation of customers, MPs and so on, or simply to dispute the need for national governments or third Departments and

DGs to be involved. In either case, the objective will usually be to ensure that defender-orchestrated pressure is regarded as being more apparent than real. There will be instances, however, when a bidder will wish to persuade Ministers to fight for the deal, both with DTI and, in Merger Regulation cases, with their EU counterparts or Commissioners if there are good reasons to believe

- that the UK sector of the EU industry(ies) concerned could benefit (this could cover anything from the fact that you are simply a more successful company with a better market/export/ financial record of performance than the target, to more specific points such as economies of scale);
- close to that first point, but as an alternative - that the UK sector(s) concerned would become more competitive within the EU/international market;
- that the UK economy, generally or locally could benefit (employment, R&D, infrastructure development);
- that the deal could help to reduce levels of state aid in the sector(s) concerned;
- that, if Competition DG consideration would be to the bidder's disadvantage, Ministers should regard aspects of the bid as "vital national interest" or "distinct market" issues entitling the UK to assess the bid exclusively. There will clearly be room for dispute between Member States and the Competition DG over this point since the Regulation's definitions of national interests and distinct markets are arguably not categorical.

Advance preparation really pays off in lobbying suppliers, customers, and trade bodies. For both sides, an up to date list (insofar as the information is available to the bidder) of those who could be mobilised to influence Whitehall or Brussels' view of the effect of the bid on the market may be very difficult to assemble, even regardless of cost, within the time and manpower pressures imposed by bids. Defenders' fears over investment cuts, price increases, product rationalisation, security or any other aspect that could damage service to individual major customers, demand for suppliers' goods or competition in the market generally should be communicated to targets in this area in three ways:

- by letter, where the targets are too numerous to contact personally. The letter may enclose research extracts or quote from the bidder's past performance and stated or implied intentions. The obvious aim is to show that your targets (in the case of trade associations or representative bodies, the sector or industry as a whole) would be harmed by the bid;
- by telephone contacts from the executive with the closest link to senior management in your target;
- by personal meetings between your executives and key targets.

Defenders will seek four actions from them:

- reasoned submissions to OFT/regulators/Third Departments/ Competition DG/other DGs to express concern over the potential implications of the bid. You may seek to persuade different targets to stress different factors underlying their concern. For example, when Devro International, a Scottish-based manufacturer of sausage casings with a 90% plus UK market share, sought to buy a US manufacturer with around 2% of the UK market, OFT's concerns over reduction in competition and expansion of a dominant position were allayed by directing OFT to Devro's major customers, who had no complaints, and by lobbying the Scottish Office and MAFF, who batted for the only major British manufacturer and a Scottish success story in the Mergers Panel. In some cases, most obviously pharmaceuticals, medical supplies and defence procurement, Government will be a customer and Third Departments can be contacted on both a commercial and a policy basis. In the Pembridge/DRG case, the Department of Health and MoD did not know the bidder and were receptive to DRG's arguments, as a long-standing contractor, to a greater extent than if a familiar and trusted bidder was involved;
- either to send summary copies of their submissions to key parliamentarians (or, in Brussels cases, national officials represented on

the Advisory Committee – who will receive copies from the Competition DG in any event) identified by you; or to request the MPs/MEPs/AMs/MLAs/MEPs/officials to take the matter up with OFT/regulators and/or the Competition DG;

- to express their concerns to the local and national media;
- ideally, to request meetings with MPs, Third Department Ministers, officials or Commissioners. Government prefers, and is more likely to be impressed by collective representations; and the support of a representative body or group of suppliers or customers will carry much more power than individual expressions of concern. Not only that: they are more likely to grant a request for a meeting to one group than to a stream of lone lobbyists, virtually irrespective of their size.

Bidders targeting companies in the same sector may be familiar with the defender's suppliers and customers, and will almost certainly have some link with the relevant representative bodies unless they are foreign and do not have a base in the defender's territory(ies). If they are close to the market, they will be able to exploit their own links with the companies and bodies the defender may seek to mobilise. Whatever the situation, however, they should look to reassure the defender's trade connections, first by informing the leading relevant trade bodies (this should be done in writing at the start of the bid. The letter should state the bidder's view that the bid will benefit the industry or sector and should formally request that, in view of the importance that regulatory authorities – whether in the UK or in Brussels – will attach to the body's view on the bid, it should not take a position without meeting the bidder for discussions, including such assurances that bid rules may permit).

The next step is a letter to the defender's likely individual targets. It should be written to them, not to the industry as a whole, and should again offer such assurances as can be made, not just because of market sensitivity but because the nature of the defender's connection with those companies will most probably be unclear. Historic experience in bids suggests that if trade bodies and other companies in the industry support defenders, it is not just because of loyalty and a perception of good service but because bidders have either ignored them or have failed to deal with them sensitively. Bidders may not be able to influence the first two but they can ensure that the third is not a factor. It only requires the degree of effort that the predator would have to show in any event if it took over its target.

Lobbying consumer organisations, including not only the well-known bodies such as the Consumers Association and National Consumer Council in London and BEUC in Brussels but also, where relevant, industry regulatory bodies such as OFTEL and its consumer committees and smaller watchdogs. In some cases, local authorities may be appropriate targets (for example, where a bid for a bus company may affect regional transport services or where the supplies to schools may be affected). Do not just think in terms of Brussels despite the "consumers' advantage" element in the Merger Regulation's technical and economic progress criterion; consumer organisations may have an influence with OFT similar to, although in most instances less powerful than, suppliers and trade customers.

Where **Third Departments, Regulators or DGs** are lobbied, their possible concerns should be anticipated and addressed. They should receive a separate submission geared primarily to their own area of responsibility. ICI, for example, in defending the 1991 bid from Hanson, will have produced detailed arguments for the Department of Health on the possible impact of a Hanson takeover on pharmaceutical R&D; for DTI and the Department of Employment on regional implications; for the Enterprise, Agriculture and Science and R&D DGs on pharmaceuticals, chemicals, agrochemicals and research, and so on, and its OFT/Competition DG submission would have sought to stimulate consultative liaison between the regulatory body and other "public interest" elements of the system. Remember always to copy Brussels submissions to the Merger Task Force or they may not be formally considered at the inter-service meetings (that does not, however, mean that they will not influence the line taken by other DGs).

Raising possible policy grounds for concern or clearance is not enough, however. You have to be aware not of your priorities but of

247

those of the system you are seeking to influence. While some officials will be defensive, telephone contact prior to submitting any paper will help you gain an understanding of the areas on which information is needed or of the likely reaction to hypothetical arguments. For example, MAFF happily gave Devro's advisers a list of questions it needed to answer. Always attempt to undertake this basic form of market research before constructing your case.

Other tactical points to consider in contested bids:

- With parliamentarians, you are unlikely to be allowed more than one and a half pages in which to attract their attention. Defenders can adopt either a blunt stance, explaining why on policy grounds the bid should be blocked, or a more subtle position in which Government is urged to assess the bid on the basis of criteria favourable to the defender (for example, will the bidder undertake to maintain long-term R&D programmes and expenditure?). ICI, for example, could have taken areas where it was strong but expensive, such as capital investment, and told MPs to make up their own minds on the basis of Hanson's answers to five short questions: "Will they undertake to maintain R&D spending at present and budgeted levels?", and so on. The tactic would have meant that Hanson would most likely be pressed to make commitments on issues not of its choosing. The tenor of such questions could of course be varied according to the target and the result desired (pure media-worthy opposition or public interest-based expressions of concern to OFT etc).

- Bidders' best tactic is also to be pre-emptive, raising likely public interest concerns with officials and politicians before the other side attempts to fight the battle on its own ground. To a great extent, they will already have done so in preparation for the bid but they must assume that the process of addressing official and political sensitivities will have to begin again, this time less privately.

- It is most important that oral or written communication with Government gives the impression that you are forthright and have nothing to hide. Do not be concerned that, by raising matters before they are raised with you, you will alert Government to issues that might not otherwise have concerned it; it is much more important to lead the debate than to be pushed onto the defensive.

• Nonetheless, parliamentarians in particular may seek assurances, particularly on local employment, which it may be impossible to meet to their satisfaction. Usually, however, a prompt and courteous response, including the promise of consultation with local Members following the takeover, will defuse most antagonism.

In agreed bids a short-term PR programme directed at parliamentarians and the press is particularly important if questions of restriction of market diversity are involved.. Similarly, possible conflicts between Government procurement policies and public sector contracts held by both parties should be discussed with officials at the earliest possible stage. This is even more important where foreign bidders are involved, regardless of EU legislation governing public purchasing; they should as a matter of priority ensure that local Members are given assurances on investment, commitment to the UK and standards of service.

Agreed bids are statistically no more likely than contested takeovers to escape reference to the Competition Commission. It is, however, far less likely that the UK will seek jurisdiction over agreed bids that fall under the Merger Regulation since the external pressures on Ministers (provided both sides have done their prep).

The second area in which competition lobbying applies is industry inquiries, which can take the form of investigations into possible anticompetitive practices in a sector or into the activities of a company. Bear four points in mind:

• The system, whether in London or Brussels, is not in the slightest bit interested in the cost and inconvenience that merger or industry inquiries generate. The fact that you may incur a bill for an extra half a million pounds if OFT is uncertain of its ground and decides to play safe by recommending a reference to the Competition Commission (the competition equivalent of a retrial) is neither here nor there to officials or Ministers. In the UK at least, it therefore pays in cases of doubt to keep OFT talking. As an example, when the soap and detergent industry was last investigated, concerns emerged over return on capital and OFT was considering asking the Monopolies Commission (as it then was) for a second opinion. The industry therefore offered to OFT to fund research by a mutually acceptable independent expert on agreed terms of reference. This was agreed and the subsequent study not only cleared the manufacturers but saved them a large legal and administrative bill.

- The need to lobby other Departments/DGs and trade/consumer interests applies in equal part to industry inquiries as to merger cases.
- Irrespective of whether it is a formal inquiry that has been launched by OFT, the Competition Directorate or one of the increasing number of informal OFT research exercises that as often as not are triggered by Ministers seeing media coverage alleging consumer "rip-offs", get in quickly, meaning before OFT has had the chance to consider the sources it will turn to, the content of information-gathering questionnaires and so on. Ring OFT, get through to the case officers and offer to send them an initial brief, which should be copied to your sponsoring department and/or sector regulator. Produce that brief as quickly as possible (within a week) and address head-on the difficult questions. Contact OFT again a few days after you have submitted it, ask whether there are any questions arising from it and offer to meet them. They will probably be guarded on the first point and reluctant on the second, but there is nothing lost by trying.
- MPs, MEPs and Scottish/Welsh/Northern Ireland representatives (not to mention the media) may not wait until the conclusion of an inquiry before pronouncing their views, particularly if a Select or European Parliament Committee has also examined the issue – for example, CD pricing. The announcement of an industry investigation can affect share prices and it is therefore sensible to consider at an early stage which politicians and others might approach or be approached by the media for comment when the inquiry is

announced and then try to brief them. The same applies in advance of publication of findings.

Regulatory Impact Assessment

The UK's Regulatory Impact Assessment system, together with its Brussels counterpart (Business Impact Assessment,) far from being just another bureaucratic requirement, offers business and industry a major opportunity to influence the policy and legislative process. In this section, we explain how it can be done.

RIA and BIA are administrative guidelines, enforced by the Cabinet Office and the Enterprise DG, which require Whitehall and the Commission (a similar system applies in Scotland, Wales and Northern Ireland) to go through five stages before deciding to introduce new regulation (and, in the case of the UK, before agreeing a negotiating line on EC proposals):

- Evaluation of regulatory and non-regulatory options for addressing the problem. The presumption is that regulation is to be preferred only if it is more cost-effective than other options.
- Producing an initial assessment in which the risk or problem to be avoided is given a value and the impact on business, charities and the voluntary sector of various policy options is costed after a first round of informal consultation with likely affected parties on options, followed by a decision in principle on whether to proceed.
- A "robust" assessment is then produced. This is attached to papers for inter-ministerial discussion on the proposal. Ministers cannot take a decision to proceed unless the lead Minister has read the RIA. In Brussels, a second round of consultation should take place before the proposal is put to the College of Commissioners.
- The UK is meant to evaluate EC proposals before they are agreed, and then produce a further RIA for formal consultation when implementing legislation is placed before Parliament. Measures originating in the UK will be subject to further consultation on the draft RIA when they are formally published.
- Apart from considering the impact on a "typical" company/organisation, and also on a "typical" SME, RIA and BIA are meant

251

to assess competitiveness impacts. Post-implementation checking should also take place to ensure that actual burdens and benefits correspond with those projected in the assessments.

Regulatory and Business Impact Assessments can be used

- To oppose or amend policy proposals
- To promote industry's legislative or regulatory proposals
- To challenge Government to review existing regulatory or legislative burdens.

As we have said, the RIA and BIA rules require officials to assess whether an impact assessment is needed; to ensure that it is produced and that it is ready at the right time; to consult properly in producing the assessment; to ensure that the methodological rules are followed; and to continue to monitor compliance cost burdens following implementation of the policy or legislation/regulation. In each of these cases, there are opportunities for companies and trade bodies to call the system to account.

Deciding Whether an Assessment is Necessary

If your Whitehall and Commission intelligence gathering is sound, you should be able to learn of policy plans at an early stage. There will be cases, particularly in Brussels where officials are given discretion to decide whether a proposal is likely to have a "significant" impact, where Business may perceive a relevance that is unappreciated by the system and where you will need to make the case for an RIA or BIA to be produced.

Example: A proposal to introduce motorway tolling might not be considered to be a "business" measure, yet it will have considerable implications for the road haulage industry. While the industry would be consulted, officials might not see the need to produce an RIA and may have to be pressed to do so. In some circumstances it may be necessary to lobby Ministers.

For Brussels regulation, this is easy. The Commission publishes its annual work programme and it is at that stage that companies or representative bodies should remind the DGs responsible for programme items that they will expect a Business Impact Assessment to be produced at the outset.

There will occasionally be cases where Whitehall or the Commission overlook the need to produce an assessment. Under such circumstances, provided the relevance of the measure to business can be proved, you may seek to challenge the right of the proposal to proceed

Example: in 1992, the Commission produced proposals to impose VAT on bar sales on board aircraft and ferries. The draft measure had reached its final stages, gaining political agreement in the Council of Ministers, before the aviation industry noticed that no Fd'I had been produced. Airlines' demand that a full impact assessment should be produced was one of the factors leading to the proposal being sent back to the Commission for reconsideration even at that late stage. Work has still not recommenced.

Ensuring That Assessments are Produced on Time

While the formal requirement is that RIAs must accompany all relevant papers for Cabinet and Cabinet Committees and minutes to No 10 for collective discussions, it is expected that a draft RIA should accompany early drafts circulated for discussion among officials. Such drafts are likely to be sketchy at best and may, through a lack of understanding of industry structures or business practices, fail to take likely impacts into account. Whitehall should be pressed at the earliest possible stage (ie as soon as you learn of outline proposals) to produce an assessment and to consult with industry before completing even its first draft.

A major exception to this is items for the Budget, where confidentiality conventions preclude advance consultation. As a result, the RIAs which have accompanied a number of Budget announcements overlooked a number of serious impacts arising from the imposition of, for example, Insurance Premium Tax or Air Passenger Duty. The lack of detail in both cases has been used as a weapon to secure modifications in the Finance Bill Standing Committee or in the drafting of implementing regulations. Officials have to produce a full RIA before Budget items are brought into force and the opportunity to seek changes to the (details, but not broad principles of the) measure is open up to that point.

The cut-off stage for completion of a BIA is much earlier than for an RIA. They must be finalised before all Commissioners consider a proposal - in other words, before a COM document (to which the BIA should be attached) is prepared for consideration by the Parliament, the Council.

If you produce your own impact assessment (see below), ensure that it is ready in time to place before the relevant European and Scottish Parliament or Northern Ireland Assembly committee or before Parliament at Second Reading Stage in the case of legislation. In the former case, seek to discuss the study with the committee's rapporteur - remember that rapporteurs have little or no specialist assistance and may propose costly amendments without having to follow the procedure required of Departments and DGs.

Consultation

Officials are expected to consult with business in preparing impact assessments. The Commission requires that this be done "at the earliest possible moment"; Whitehall imposes no deadline. In practice, although Whitehall's rules suggest that a preliminary assessment should be prepared for comment, prudent officials will seek advice from industry at the outset. Many, however, will not, and instead of seeking to colour a blank page you may find yourself seeking to disprove a view that has already been taken. It is important to tell Whitehall, the other territorial departments and the Commission that you expect an assessment to be produced for consultation before Ministers or Commissioners take a decision to proceed.

The rules require Whitehall and the Commission to assess a proposal's impact on a "typical" business. However, when officials make up their consultation lists they generally start with the largest or best known companies or representative bodies and they may be unaware of specialist sectors of an industry or of factors which may lead to a measure having an exceptional impact in an unexpected area. Take the opportunity at the earliest possible stage to guide them.

Example: in consultations by DSS on measures to reduce discrimination against disabled people, it would have been natural for officials to turn to British Airways and other scheduled airlines for views. In fact, unknown to them the majority of disabled passengers are carried on charter aircraft, which would bear a quite different cost burden if non–discrimination provisions were introduced. Had the charter sector not responded quickly, officials might have been given a misleading impression of the ability of airlines to adapt their facilities.

Note that Directorates General are required to undertake at least two rounds of consultation if their preliminary analysis leads to development of policy proposals. The Commission requires officials to list the organisations consulted and to summarise their responses. Invariably, given the Commission's culture, pan-European representative bodies will dominate the list and individual companies are unlikely to be contacted. Their representations are, however, unlikely to be ignored if they offer relevant views and data. Whitehall's rules are not as specific but organisations who believe a policy proposal will have a particular impact on them may be able to claim that consultation has failed to cover the most relevant affected sectors and that the RIA has consequently inaccurately estimated the compliance costs involved.

Methodology

Although the Cabinet Office publishes a manual on RIA and the Commission has (unpublished) guidelines that might suggest a standard methodology, experience has shown that no two business impact assessments take the same form. Business should therefore check both preliminary and final RIAs and BIAs carefully to ensure that

- the most relevant industries, sectors or companies have been researched

- all areas facing recurring and non-recurring cost impacts have been covered
- adequate information is provided on the extent of consultation, including the bodies consulted
- the factors used to determine the proposal's impact on international competitiveness are realistic
- the assessment of likely costs is accurate.

It would be prudent, if your intelligence-gathering system is sound and you are able to learn of policy proposals early enough, not to wait for officials to draw up their research plan - approach them and explain how you believe the assessment should be conducted (within, of course, the overall guidelines of the Regulatory Impact Unit/Enterprise DG). There may, for example, be unofficial data sources that are regarded as authoritative by your industry but which are not apparent to officials; there may be accepted industry or sector-wide standards with which Government is not familiar; or, even if officials are following the rules, you may want to recommend a more accurate or representative methodology.

Better still, if your resources allow - and the costs are small relative to the potential impact of a misconceived Government proposal - produce (preferably in consortium with other potentially affected organisations) your own business impact assessment to pre-empt or counter Government's study. This is particularly important in cases where Industry seeks new legislation or regulation - for example, a statutory code to regulate the activities of minicab companies - since it will be for the proposers to prove that their plan will not impose an unreasonable burden on business. If you do produce an RIA or BIA, ensure that it strictly follows the rules but do not miss the opportunity to cover what most Government-written impact studies omit: an assessment, written as objectively as possible, of whether the burdens that your study suggests will be imposed by the policy proposal in question and will be proportionate to the measure's likely benefits. It is this area that will inevitably provide the greatest scope for lobbying the system if you seek to block or amend draft legislation or regulation.

One simple way to ensure your methodology cannot be faulted by Government is to consult officials in advance. Seek their views on the acceptability of the assumptions you intend to use in reaching your conclusions; on the format of your study; and – particularly where you are seeking a concession or some other action from the system – the questions those you are seeking to influence need to have answered.

Example: UK manufacturers and retailers of Duty Free goods had commissioned a number of impact assessments from well-known UK and European economists as a means of persuading Whitehall that the Duty Free system should be retained after the creation of the EU Single Market in 1992. However, while the studies carefully examined the impact of abolition on the industry itself, the lobby was meeting with little success. It then decided to take a different approach. Its advisers, who were former officials, sought to discuss candidly with Customs & Excise the Government's views on the work carried out up to then and on the points that would have to be proven if the Duty Free case was to be made attractive to Ministers. The subsequent meetings revealed that Whitehall was less concerned about the effect of abolition on the industry as on the wider UK economy. Having agreed in advance the questions to be covered in any new research and that the assumptions proposed by the advisers were acceptable, the subsequent business impact study was given the best possible chance of hitting its mark without wasted costs. UK Ministers then saw that it was in their national interest to support an extension of the system and they were instrumental in securing the Council of Ministers' derogation that followed.

If you produce your own impact assessment, take care over presentation of your conclusions. While the RIA and BIA rules concentrate on arriving at a figure, you should seek to add a balanced qualitative analysis provided it can be sustained by evidence.

Example: food manufacturers must cross a minefield of regulatory obstacles in seeking MAFF/DoH approval of new foodstuffs. A preliminary decision as to whether a product should be classified as an additive or as a Novel Food can make the difference between relatively rapid and cheap authorisation and having to follow a process which takes years and can cost millions of pounds. In this case, were the food industry to produce an RIA in response to new regulatory proposals (or even retrospectively - see below) it would be relevant for Government to consider views on the potential of the proposal to inhibit development of new food technologies, with possible international competitiveness implications.

Monitoring compliance costs post-legislation/regulation

This is one area where it is not just desirable but essential that business and industry takes a lead. Both sets of rules require Departments and DGs to compare actual compliance costs against estimates. The Commission also requires DGs to ensure that legislation is drafted to allow for easy amendment. Although significant differences "may imply the need to review the way in which the proposal has been implemented", it should in practice be possible to exploit an unexpectedly greater impact as a lever to trigger a more fundamental reconsideration of the measure itself. The most obvious example of this, although not a business issue, was the Poll Tax.

Reviewing existing regulation

So far, we have outlined ways in which business and industry should both monitor Whitehall and Brussels compliance with the impact assessment rules and exploit the new system to their advantage. However, many organisations are more concerned about the regulatory or statutory burdens they currently face than about the impact of future proposals. Although the rules do not require Government to take retrospective action, in practice it will be difficult for Ministers to resist a strongly-backed call for existing measures to be reviewed in line with the Regulatory Impact Unit's commitment to "make a bonfire of regulation." The strategy to adopt is as follows:

- First, look carefully at the full range of statutory/regulatory requirements under which you must operate. Undertake a broad evaluation of the costs these impose on your business/ sector/industry, ignoring those items (eg the fact, rather than the rate of, Corporation Tax) where it is likely to be politically impractical to consider change.

- Isolate one or more burdens which you believe are disproportionate to the benefits they seek to deliver, either because they are outdated or because their compliance cost is higher than anticipated.
- Assess whether your view on the need for abolition/amendment is likely to be shared by a representative proportion of your industry; if so, then
- Produce a submission to the Department(s) or DG(s) concerned, setting out your parcel of measures; giving your reasons why they are widely believed to be in need of review (you can only outline your case at this stage); and asking whether an impact assessment has been produced to cover them. Almost certainly, the answer will be no. In most cases, it will be sensible to discuss your approach in advance with the Regulatory Impact Unit and with members of the Better Regulation Task Force.
- You then have two options: either to revert to officials or Ministers/ Commissioners, depending on the scale of the problem and the political factors surrounding it, with a request that the burden/benefit balance be assessed; or to produce your own impact assessment for the bonfire and present it to Government with a demand that an urgent review should take place. In both cases it may be necessary to back your submission with some media coverage in order publicly to emphasise the reasonableness of your case, although you will need carefully to consider whether publicity will stimulate concerns among potential opponents, particularly where there may be safety or environmental implications.
- If your representations are handled properly, it should be difficult for Government to suggest that there is no need for a retrospective review.

Private Members' Bills

While the promoter of a Private Members' Bill is not obliged to produce an RIA, officials are required to do so to back their advice to Ministers on the line to take. Whether the Bill is antagonistic or advantageous, you should contact those officials to discuss their view on impacts since they may not have had sufficient notification of the Bill to undertake a normal consultation exercise.

If the Bill is hostile to your interests, you should brief parliamentarians and officials to press the Bill's promoters to produce an RIA. If the promoters refuse, you may seek both to exploit that publicly or to challenge them to rebut your own impact assessment. Alternatively, you may seek more quietly to persuade officials and Ministers to oppose the Bill or to seek amendments to it on the basis of your assessed impacts (unless it appears that the Department's own RIA is likely to support your views, in which case leave the work to them).

The corollary of this is that if you seek to promote a Private Members' Bill you will increasingly come under pressure to publish an assessment of business impacts. Better to get your retaliation in first.

Making the most of impact assessments

An impact assessment is not an end in itself. A lobbying strategy needs to be built around it in order to maximise its effect in questioning Government's calculations or pressing for your own proposals to be considered. While every lobbying programme is different, examples of use of your assessment once it has been sent to the key Department/DG could be as follows:

- If it is being produced unilaterally or by a relatively small grouping of companies, circulate it across your industry if you are seeking to represent a broad view. Look to stimulate supportive representations to officials, Ministers/Commissioners and their cabinets and constituency or subject speciality MPs/MEPs.
- Where relevant, send the assessment to Third Departments or DGs who may support your case. For example, the road haulage sector

should discuss a BIA produced in response to an Environment DG proposal on vehicle emissions with the Transport DG.

- Similarly, a pan-EU lobby on Commission proposals should seek to adapt its BIA to the circumstances of individual Member States in order to secure national Government support within the Council of Ministers.
- Back your submission with publicity. This is appropriate where, for example, you are seeking to prove that your alternative policy option imposes a lower burden on business; it is not where raising the profile of your lobbying may provoke a strong reaction from opponents and where you can achieve your results through quiet negotiation of acceptance of the impact assessment's conclusions.
- As we have said above, it will often be difficult for Government to challenge a case based on a review of existing regulation if it is backed by a strong RIA, by careful media management where advisable, and by UK/EU parliamentary support. The latter will require a bullet point RIA summary of no more than two pages.

In summary, the basic rules for organisations seeking to exploit impact assessment rules are

- If Government is trying to do something to you, make sure it follows the rules; if it does not do so, make sure it is challenged - publicly if necessary.
- Do not wait for Government to produce an assessment: make representations to ensure that it adopts the methodology you believe is accurate; better still, produce your own assessment for Government to challenge if it can
- If you seek to promote legislation or new regulation, always produce the relevant assessments to show the system that the proposal has not only been carefully drafted but also that it complies with Government's cost:benefit requirements

The ethics of lobbying

Given the media's use of terms such as "cash for questions", "lobbygate", and "cronyism", you might assume that lobbying is an unprincipled pastime in which anything goes. In fact, the need to observe proprieties is fundamental. The system usually finds out in the end; and it rarely does anyone any favours: if it did, it would risk flying into the spotlight of a media which appears ever keen to draw the wrong conclusions about a practice largely conducted in private.

The principles to follow are simple and largely self-evident:

- Observe total honesty. Advocacy is about the skill with which the truth is presented. There is therefore a duty on any user of Government to inform policy makers accurately. That duty is paramount in the case of representations to parliamentarians since, as has been explained, few have sufficient resources to corroborate the information on which they may rely to base support for amendments, contact with Ministers and other lobbying matters.

  Officials take pains to check information supplied to them and will try to ensure that the real facts, and the case against the advocate's, are both exposed. The cost of deliberate misinformation is usually the denial of further credibility to those who may have felt they could get away with it. That does not mean that officials, particularly those who may occasionally over-zealously support the interests they sponsor or who are under pressure from Ministers, do not from time to time accept a particular version of the truth.

- There are no undisclosed principals. Whether professional intermediaries or your own resources are employed, disclosure of identity and interest is vital in most work with Government. We say "most" because an appreciable part of any Government relations strategy should be geared to impersonal information gathering, not personal liaison or negotiation.

  It is not normally advisable to present a case to legislators, officials or Ministers without providing the honest and full reasons behind its presentation as well as strong arguments for its acceptance. As we have said, it is occasionally possible to deceive Government, but those who attempt to do so must expect to approach the system once, since attempts to mislead are usually discovered and either result in the opposite action being favoured by

---

GIVING MPs FULL INFORMATION

Study this letter as an example of the way to request the use of MPs' facilities in an ethical manner:

```
Geoffrey Smith Esq MP
House of Commons
London SW1A OAA
```

```
Dear Mr Smith
```

```
Consolidated Escalators is a UK-based firm with subsidiaries in
12 countries. One of our factories, which manufactures handrails,
is situated in your constituency and employs 120.
    For some time we have been trying to obtain information about
total expenditure by Government Departments on rubber escalator
handrails. Unfortunately, it appears that the figures have not
been coordinated in most Departments' procurement records. This
data would be most helpful not only to us and to our industry in
general but also to the many MPs interested in escalators and it
would seem that the only way to secure it would be by PQ. Since
it is our final alternative, would it be possible for you to table
the attached drafts to the 12 major departmental users of esca-
lators?
    We apologise for burdening you in this way but hope you will
understand our need to approach you. We completely appreciate that
our request may be unacceptable, in which case please inform us.
    Etc
```

If the principles on drafting of PQs (see p. 134) are followed, it should be possible to attach 12 questions, each typed on a separate sheet, which could be tabled by the MP without retyping. The letter tells him what you want, why it is needed and why he is the most appropriate person to table the PQ. He need ask no further questions of you.

decision makers or in the Whitehall telegraph creating an unofficial blacklist.

Example: International Services plc has bought a disused oil rig in the North Sea and has designated it an independent state, Maritimia. International Services' intention is to establish Maritimia as the largest "University of the Air" in Europe, with programmes being transmitted to France, Denmark, Belgium,

Holland and the UK. Since the rig is outside territorial waters, IS also intends to turn it into a tax haven, but this strategy is known only to its directors.

LOBBYING BY LISTENING

When Shell UK sought to brief MPs and Peers about petrol retailing during a Monopolies Commission inquiry into the industry, it could have committed the usual error of giving them a presentation. Instead, it recognised that parliamentarians tend to come to briefings with their own questions and do not want lengthy perorations from lobbyists. Shell therefore spoke for only three minutes and then invited views, in response to which it was able to make all of its key points. The audience felt it had been treated sensitively and Shell was able not only to convey its case but also to gain respect.

In another case, a financial services group advocated its views on pension reform to MPs (more to raise its profile among parliamentarians than in expectation that they could influence Government on this issue) by holding a series of dinners on the basis that the Chief Executive wished to consult MPs about the acceptability of its stance on the issue. Once again, this approach made the group's targets feel involved in a way that a conventional briefing would not.

The UK Government has created an Economic Resource Zone to extend its sovereignty rights to cover oil reserves beyond its normal territorial limits, but there is some doubt as to whether this still applies to exhausted fields and decommissioned rigs. IS, in order to attract shareholders for its broadcasting project, needs to obtain the UK Government's recognition of the sovereign status of Maritimia as a safeguard of its inviolability for taxation, social security, defence and other purposes. It approaches the Foreign Office without raising its ulterior, tax haven motive. Not only would the Foreign Office's legal advisers be very cautious about creating precedent where doing so could open the door to a number of potential activities (even if they are not envisaged by IS) that could be unfavourable to UK interests, but the deliberate concealment of IS's true intentions would, even if other factors were promising, militate against the granting of recognition, since bad faith can never provide a basis for negotiations with Government.

This rule also applies to professional intermediaries, who in some cases have a practice of not identifying their clients. All institutions of government react badly to this. Another area where the disclosure is essential is the employment of parliamentarians as advisers to organisations, who must insist that politicians' commercial links to them are declared in the Westminster and other national registers of interests.

The requirement under the ethical code to disclose interests in dealings with Government does not, however, mean that lobbyists need make public declarations of their commercial or policy intentions in this area. Disclosure of the object of any negotiation is still consistent with confidentiality. The demands you make on Government are strictly your business. The only requirement is that you make those demands in a transparent manner.

- Do not abuse the institutions of government. This ethical principle does not concern the inadvisability of flooding parliamentarians with letters or staging demonstrations - such tactics may or may not be suitable depending on the problem and nature of the lobbyist - as much as the opportunities that our generally open system of access to the institutions of government allow to the unscrupulous. For example, any MP can book the five private dining rooms in the Commons on behalf of outsiders if he is amenable, and that facility has been widely used by companies seeking to impress their customers in a grand setting. A passing acquaintance with the same MP can gain an outsider access to the Commons and Lords Vote Offices, where free copies of legislation, Hansard and all other published official documents can be obtained in his name. Thousands of Parliamentary Questions are tabled each year by MPs on behalf of outsiders. They cost over £90 each to answer. Anyone may apply to an MP or Peer to become a researcher; if accepted, their new status will allow them (or most of them - there are two grades of research assistant) access to the resources of the Commons and Lords libraries, the Vote Office and other facilities.

Only the second of the above four examples is illegal: it amounts to theft. But all of them indicate the fine line between necessity and unethical abuse in the strategies open to outsiders in dealing with Government. Do not be tempted by such opportunities to use the benefits afforded to a parliamentarian as may be offered to you.

If it is necessary to approach an MP, MSP or AM to table a question because information is otherwise unforthcoming or because an official response on the record is required, the Member - no matter how willing he is to accede to outsiders' requests - should have the reasons explained to him since the question will have his name against it and, if he is on the Government side, he may be approached for an explanation by a Minister's PPS or, in the case of an Oral Question, the departmental Whip if the question is sensitive or calculated to criticise Government policy. He must therefore be aware of the potential consequences of his actions.

Many issues are considered immoral or unjustified by the majority of the population. They may still be advocated under the above code of ethics provided the truth is told and no attempt is made to suborn decision makers. Parliament is lenient - perhaps too lenient - with those who try to interfere with the processes of representative decision making. In recent years two examples stand out. Firstly, the successful attempt made by supporters of hunting to use sympathetic Members to block a Private Member's Bill aimed at banning their sport. They did this by tabling dozens of amendments to the Bill and effectively "talking it out", ensuring that it ran out of debating time.

Secondly, it was reported that the Law Society, in opposing another Private Member's Bill, this time to remove solicitors' monopoly over conveyancing, had allegedly considered advice that its members should invite MPs supporting the Bill to meetings away from Westminster on the day of the crucial Second Reading debate in order to keep them from voting against the Law Society's lobby. Thankfully, the alleged thought was not converted into deed, but the opinion of many is that even conspiracy to pervert democracy should be the subject of at least a strong reprimand by the Speaker.

RUNNING AN IN-HOUSE OPERATION

- *Skills and resources needed*
- *Monitoring the system*
- *Using help*
- *Sleaze? Sponsorship and other commercial links with the system*
- *Training*

In this section, we will cover the principles and logistics of organising corporate resources to deal with Government. In doing so, we recognise that no two organisations have the same needs and you will therefore have to adapt the advice that follows to match your own circumstances.

Skills and Resources Needed

The staff who deal with Government in your organisation should be regarded not as an overhead but as a profit centre. Their task is to ensure that Government's actions are as consistent as possible with your corporate strategy, and averting or softening damaging proposals or securing the policy direction or procurement decision you need can save, or make you, a fortune.

First, who should be primarily responsible for lobbying? The broad attitude of UK and Brussels politicians can be summarised in two statements:

- "We want to deal with people who make things happen, not with apologists. We PR you; don't you try to PR us."
- "We appreciate people and organisations who deal with us personally; who understand that politicians and officials see themselves as working in a distinct environment with its own rules and

sensitivities. We don't like being regarded as a by-product of some other activity."

That means that unless you are well known to them, your job title matters. You may find that they do not mind, but it is better to play safe:

- For dealings with parliamentarians, give someone the title of Parliamentary/Government/regulatory liaison/affairs manager or director. They want to feel they are being handled by someone dedicated to them. Organisations with head offices and constituency outlets should wherever possible deal with Members on local issues through local office or plant managers.
- For dealings with Ministers, field your top executive. Ministers have an acute sense of status and expect to deal with people whom they see as being on their level.
- With officials, the title is less important, although they tend to be suspicious of PR tags; what they want is someone whom they believe is in command of detail. Senior officials (G3/A3 and above) are also status conscious and want to speak to someone of senior management rank.

Remember their amour propre: if you create a special title for people who handle marketing, advertising, legal affairs, finance and dealing with the public and media, make the system feel you have designated people specially to work with it.

The ideal profile of an in-house specialist depends, as we have said, on the needs and resources of the organisation. If the bulk of your needs are regulatory or can be resolved in negotiation with policy officials, a former Civil Servant or line manager with knowledge in-depth may be best. Political liaison ideally demands someone regarded as a political insider (for example, a former Special Adviser or well respected front bench researcher) but this inevitably associates the executive with one Party. Large organisations, or those which have to work with MPs across the board, solve this problem by recruiting two or more people to operate with equal facility on both sides of the House.

In the end, what you are after is someone who understands the way the system works and is acceptable to it. Those who have worked within the Civil Service or the various parliaments and assemblies tend to have a head start, but there are many examples of very proficient and highly respected operators without that background. Generally, though, they share advantages not enjoyed by everyone: working for an organisation whose name guarantees them easy access at every level; being able to learn from a well-established in-house record of dealing with Government; and being left in post for some years, since there is no fast track to acquiring experience in this area.

The number of people you deploy will of course depend on the extent of your dealings with the system, but even the largest UK organisation will rarely have more than three people centrally handling political and official liaison, with a typical structure being either two politicians (covering the two main parties) and a researcher who may also maintain the contact database; or a political specialist, a Whitehall (or Scottish etc) expert and an assistant (there are exceptions: companies having to report to regulators may have dozens of people working with Offer, Ofwat etc). Many large companies and trade associations also have a parallel office in Brussels rather than employing a Brussels-watcher in London.

A final point about role. The normal rule is that the organisation should make its own representations. This is fair, particularly for public bodies who should not be seen to be using outside assistance. However, if your advisers (whether they are lawyers, accountants, lobbyists or economists) are well respected by the system and understand your case inside out, it may be possible for them to discuss matters more candidly with politicians and officials. A lobbyist who is crass will damage your case and reputation; but if they are good they should have not just a superior understanding of the process but - in some cases - greater credibility because of their perceived balance (officials in particular assume that no outside organisation can ever be objective but that former colleagues can present them with an uncoloured view) and their knowledge of the issue.

In accepting this, some companies and trade bodies take it even

---

ENTERTAINING POLITICIANS AND OFFICIALS

If an issue can be discussed in 20 minutes, arrange a 20 minute meeting. However, entertainment is useful for developing rapport or for lobbying several targets at a time. If you invite politicians or officials, remember

- *politicians only have a maximum of two weeks' notice of parliamentary business. The agenda can change at short notice and party games can mean "running Whips" (constant votes) which are automatic appointment-breakers. No shows are inevitable and there is nothing you can do about it*
- *not to mix politicians and officials or, unless the issue is non-controversial, politicians of different parties*
- *to arrange ministerial invitations through the Diary Secretary. Assume that Ministers will have to bring a Private Secretary with them*
- *not to entertain officials until a working relationship has been established*
- *not to invite MPs, MSPs or WAs on a Monday or Friday. Accept that dinners may be disrupted by parliamentary business, which is only announced the Thursday before. Entertain MEPs in Strasbourg during plenary; otherwise in Brussels (the best time being when Committees are sitting). Thursday evenings are also unwise. Whipping at Westminster is often light to allow MPs to get back to their constituencies and the House ends business at 7pm*
- *to hold lunches and dinners close to their offices and to provide transport for them unless the venue is within 200 yards.*
- *to end lunch by 2.20 and have a taxi ready to take them back. Dinners should start by 7.30 and end by 9.30*
- *always to write and thank them afterwards*

---

further by regarding their advisers essentially as contract members of staff, a seamless extension of their organisation. This avoids the disadvantage of competent advisers having to tell officials or politicians that they are "Mr Brown from ABC Ltd calling on behalf of ComCo plc".

It is essential to coordinate these job functions across an organisation. If there is one fundamental to dealing with Government, it is to look at it as a system in which most decisions are taken through a complex interplay of linked institutions. There is no logic in putting dealings with Whitehall into one side of your organisation and dealings with politicians into another. It is true that some liaison with Ministers, and parliamentarians (and even officials) is pure PR, and the PR department should handle that, but there is nothing worse than "experts" putting arguments together and negotiating with regulators and policy officials and then telling their PR/government relations colleagues to "communicate" them to politicians. Dealings with the system are not usually single-faceted and unless everything really will be settled at official/parliamentarian etc level, it is essential to plan representations and assemble your case as a team. The situation has often arisen where PR people try to send a press pack to Civil Servants in lieu of the detailed brief they need, or executives responsible for dealing with Parliament are given a 100 page regulatory study and told to send it to MPs and others. The answer is

---

IT'S A 24 HOUR JOB

Just as an organisation's press office must be available whenever the media needs to contact it, so the staff responsible for handling Government must be both alert and contactable outside normal working hours.

- *The first weekend of August 1999 saw a widely reported story about the Royal Brompton Hospital's record of heart treatment deaths. The start of the "silly season" promoted the story to the top of the batting order and Ministers were being asked to comment. Although the news broke early on a Saturday, the hospital immediately contacted the Department of Health Press Office (they all have out of hours numbers) and produced a briefing for Ministers which explained that its mortality record was affected by the fact that many of the most complex cases were referred to it by other hospitals. Within two hours, the news broadcasts were featuring a statement from the Health Secretary which reflected the hospital's information.*

- *The panel members for Any Questions, broadcast on Friday night and Saturday lunchtime, are announced at the end of the previous week's programmes. You can try sending a short brief to them or to their Special Adviser/researcher/Party research department specialist (no later than a day beforehand) if your concerns are part of the week's topical agenda. And don't be shy about ringing in to Any Answers if it sounds as though the audience is sympathetic to ill-informed statements that damage your position.*

These are only two examples of a general point. Misconceptions can trigger undesirable policy changes if you let them run. Don't assume that your relationship with officials and Ministers will see you through - they have to be sensitive to perceived public opinion and the media will often shape views when you would rather be at dinner or in the garden.

usually "I wouldn't start from here".

If your organisation is part of a group of companies, you will understand the difference between one company and another; but to Government, and particularly to politicians, the distinction may be less clear. When, for example, the same Member receives separate representations on successive days from an oil company's upstream and downstream companies, it may assume a failure in internal communication even though, as far as the group is concerned, the two companies operate in different areas and with a substantial degree of autonomy.

There is also the problem of the quality of dealings with the system by one operation affecting the attitude taken to its sister companies.

THE PROCTER & GAMBLE TEST

Procter & Gamble is one of the best planners of government and regulatory strategy. Its simple approach should be considered by others:

- *Every year, it asks its managers to consider the regulatory provision that is most burdensome to their work or to propose new Government action which would help P&G (excluding unrealistic aspirations such as abolishing Corporation Tax) and to assess costs and benefits.*
- *The company then assesses the chances of securing change and the likely cost (company time; consultants) involved in lobbying.*
- *If it decides to proceed, it checks accumulated costs against benefit gained every two months.*

Example: Wizard Financial Services Group owns a number of large insurance companies including Wizard Insurance Ltd. The Group Chief Executive wants to discuss pensions reform with the DSS Special Adviser. He contacts the Adviser's office, to be told that Wizard Insurance has already been in touch with them and asked whether there is any need for two meetings. Result: Special Adviser thinks they are amateurs, Chief Executive is annoyed, parent and subsidiary are embarrassed.

CONTACT WITH POLITICIANS IN PEACETIME

If you are considering a programme of contact with officials or politicians in order to pre-pare the ground before any threat arises, bear in mind that friends made in peacetime may not help you when a crisis develops. Influential targets base their decision to support a lobby on the basis of weight of evidence, not friendship. Decide why you want to meet MPs, Ministers etc. Do you have a Government-related aim, or do you simply want as many "opinion formers" as possible to know about your organisation?

Examples:

A, the holding company of a well-known retailing conglomerate, spends large sums on entertaining MPs and MEPs in order to tell them about itself. It has few policy con-cerns (and MPs etc are likely to be of little help with them) and in reality it will not make any difference if the holding company is better known and regarded within the system. On the two occasions when major problems have arisen, most of those politi-cians regarded as favourable to the company were disinclined to assist. Verdict: money wasted.

B liaises extensively with its many constituency MPs on the basis of the issues that most concern them - employment, environmental issues and local economic impacts. Giving them what they want, rather than seeking to promote itself, is the best PR exercise B could conduct. Government will be more inclined to do something for you if you under-stand what it wants - don't use it; work with it.

C, like B, faces a constant series of problems which have often featured political interven-tion. It is clearly sensible for it to invest time and money in spotting and educating potential Ministers and those MPs on whom Ministers may rely for views. Since C's experience is that issues which have been smoothly negotiated can be knocked off course by the arrival of new Ministers, it seeks to seed political opinion about it and its con-cerns before Ministers arrive in post.

Note, however, that organisations need to be both significant and professional if they are to persuade politicians with no present interest in their concerns to listen to them. And, of course, the vast majority of organisations do not face political (as distinct from admin-istrative) problems.

Building relationships in advance of a crisis may help if there is a need to mobilise support rapidly (eg ICI's parliamentary response to the 1991 Hanson bid) but those troops will only fall into line if you and your problem matter to them. Nonetheless, while giving peacetime evidence to Select Committees, providing useful expertise to officials and rapporteurs, offering constituency assistance to MPs and generally establishing contact with the system can be treated like the old adage about advertising ("half of it works, but I'm not sure which half") it can have benefits that may be impossible to predict at the time. It is that very unpredictability that leads to organisations devoting often considerable resources to contact programmes and political party or think tank sponsorship as an insur-ance policy.

How do you avoid this?

- If you can, make government-related dealings a head office function. The skills required, including a greater emphasis on techniques like rapid rebuttal and telephone lobbying, targeting opinion and, are so rarified that it makes sense to have a really good central unit rather than spread expertise around your organisation (it also saves money, since duplicating monitoring resources is expensive - see below). However, this is not always possible in organisations such as defence contractors, where hundreds of people may be working with officials at any one time. Whether you are able to centralise or not,

- Encourage everyone to report on their contact with the system to a central point and to check with it beforehand. It pools knowledge and avoids the impression of inefficiency. The best in-house departments have a database, accessible by anyone and capable of telling them who has met whom and what happened. This is easier said than done, but it will help in securing cooperation if the person in charge of dealing with Government gets around the organisation, persuading people that he/she can be of value to them and offering to assist with their lobbying and other contact.

CONTACT PROGRAMMES CAN WORK

A major export credit insurer invited the Trade Minister to visit its head office. It was his first contact with this area. Rather than organise a static presentation, the insurer gave the Minister free rein to meet its country experts and underwriters on the shop floor, and he was so enthused with the impact of this type of cover on UK export competitiveness that he cancelled the lunch laid on by the company in order to continue his discussion. Shortly afterwards, the insurer received an invitation to accompany the Minister on the first UK trade visit to Cuba for 40 years.

- Try to get your colleagues to agree that dealings with the system, unless they involve no more than pure contact building, should be planned across your organisation. Collective consideration of all the implications at the outset saves a lot of time down the line.

Resources

What materials and facilities do you need in-house? The key directories and services are:

- *Dod's Parliamentary and Whitehall Companions*—all the information you want on MPs and Peers, election details, and senior Civil Servants.
- *Vachers UK and EU guides*—information on the UK Parliament and on all EU institutions; useful because they are revised quarterly
- *The Civil Service Yearbook*—a basic Whitehall directory, but although it is published annually telephone numbers are often out of date, the numbers of desk-level officials are often excluded, and listed enquiry points can be next to useless.

HOW THE LAW SOCIETY DOES IT

"We have a Government relations staff of three (specialist, researcher who handles monitoring, and administrator) but has established a network of 280 Parliamentary Liaison Officers among local Law Societies around the country. The PLOs receive a monthly brief and report all contact with the system to us; we keep a database to let them see who has met whom. There are also between 20 and 30 people dealing with policy issues. We try to avoid stock job titles - anything to do with "public affairs" turns Ministers off. And there is a difference between being seen as a "parliamentary unit", which suggests a service, and a "lobbying unit", which implies a one-way relationship.

We make sure our staff discuss issues from the start rather than waiting for them to hit us. It is important for us to tell our colleagues what is coming up in good time and we have to persuade officials before policy is set in stone. But we cannot cover every Department: around ten Bills affect us every year but the size of our team means we really focus on three.

Under Labour we have changed our focus slightly. Our campaigning and media sides now work together more often and we spend more time on legislation with officials and rather less with Parliament, although we still work with the Lords on technical amendments."

- Departmental directories—invaluable if you can get them as they give you the numbers and job descriptions of all officials; but it needs persistence and, occasionally, inside contacts to get some, and others only exist electronically and cannot be copied.

- The European Commission's internal directory, the *Guide des Services*, is difficult to obtain (a friendly official may oblige but they are only entitled to a single copy, usually revised every May). A less detailed organogram is available from the office of Official Publications, 2 rue Mercier, L2985, Luxembourg, but it only lists officials with the ranks of Head of Unit, Director and Director General (section heads are occasionally included). No telephone numbers are given, obliging you to check extensions in the Commission directory - also an internal document.
- *The European Public Affairs Directory*—contains contact information for all the main institutions.
- The European Parliament's "*Grey List*" contains constituency office addresses as well as committee memberships and composition of EP delegations, the equivalent of the UK Parliament's All Party Country Groups.
- *Commons/Lords registers of members interests*—lists the business and other outside links of all MPs and many Peers.
- *Palace of Westminster phone directory*—not really available to the public but a parliamentarian may let you photocopy one.
- *Municipal Yearbook*—information on every local authority.
- Sources of Community Funding

With the exception of the Palace of Westminster Phone Directory and Guide Des Services all of the above books are available from Politico's Bookstore, 8 Artillery Row, London SW1P 1Rz, Tel 020 7828 0010, Fax 020 7828 8111, email bookstore@politicos.co.uk, www.politicos.co.uk.

The main subscription sources are:

- The daily "Vote Bundle" (Lords and Commons Order Papers and Hansards: available from the Parliamentary Bookshop) - expensive but if time is not of the essence, available for free on the Houses of Parliament website around midday. The Order Paper sets out "planted" questions (to initiate a departmental statement on that day), oral and written PQs for future answer, and the latest signatories to Early Day Motions. It is not always easy to follow (see the summary of its structure on page 285). Hansard is published separately for each House, with full transcripts of oral and written answers and debates.

- The Scottish equivalent of the Vote Bundle is The Business Bulletin (Order Paper) and the Official Report and Minutes of Proceedings (Hansard). The Bulletin is in ten sections, covering

Section A	Daily Business List
Section B	Business Programme (week ahead)
Section C	Agendas of committee meetings
Section D	New oral questions
Section E	New written questions
Section F	Motions and amendments
Section G	Bills
Section H	Documents laid
Section I	Progress of Business
Announcements	Miscellaneous information

- The Welsh Assembly has The Order Paper, laid out in seven sections:

Section A	Agenda for the day
Section B	Oral questions for answer on the day
Section C	Forward Look/forthcoming business over the next three weeks.
Section D	Written questions
Section E	Statements of opinion
Section F	Oral questions for answer in 5–10 days
Section G	Notices of motions for future debate

Its Record of Proceedings is the equivalent of Hansard

All these are best accessed through the Scottish Parliament and Welsh Assembly websites (see below) but hard copies can be ordered from the Stationery Office, 71 Lothian Road, Edinburgh EH3 9AZ, 0131 228 4181, or Oriel Bookshop, The Friary, Cardiff CF1 4AA, 01222 395548

- Weekly Information Bulletin (Parliamentary Bookshop and Houses of Parliament website) - useful summary of the progress of

Bills, the past week's parliamentary business and the future agenda for debates, question times, Select Committee inquiries. It also lists Green and White Papers and Deregulation Act Orders. The Scottish Equivalent, What's Happening in the Scottish Parliament, is also accessible via the Parliament's website.

- Weekly Lords Committee list - available free on request from the Lords Committee Office.
- House Magazine (10 Little College Street, London SW1P 3SH) - the Palace of Westminster's in-house publication.
- Central Office of Information daily list (CoI, Hercules Road, London SE1 7DY) - all departmental and many public body press releases, available by fax or post.
- Local Government Chronicle (33 Bowling Green Lane, London EC1B 1LG)/Municipal Journal (32 Vauxhall Bridge Road, London SW1V 2SS) - essential for local authority work.
- Reuters online EU information service (Reuters, rue de Treves 61, 1040 Brussels) - expensive but very useful whether you are monitoring Brussels from the UK or in situ.
- European Report (European Information SA, Ave Ad. Lacomble 66, 1030 Brussels) - the best of the printed EU monitoring services, published twice a week and also available online.
- Agence Europe (Rue de la Gare 361040 Brussels), published daily with special reports and documents.
- Newspoint (3rd floor, Clutha House, 10 Storey's Gate, London SW1P 3AY) - run in close conjunction with the Westminster and Edinburgh Lobbies, it can be useful for early morning briefings on statements, publication of reports and White Papers, press conferences and changes to parliamentary business. However, such Lobby-based services tend to take the view that Government stops work when Parliament is in recess and their notification of publications and of ministerial speeches becomes markedly slower.

There are some useful internet services, perhaps the best of which are (all preceded by http://www.):

- British Politics Page Index - *ukpol.co.uk* The best, since it links to most of the other sites. Also includes MP biographies.
- Parliamentary Channel - *parlchan.co.uk* Useful for status of Bills, forthcoming Chamber and committee agenda and lists of MPs and Peers. The cable TV service is good if you need to monitor debates as they happen; but committee proceedings may not be screened for weeks.
- HMSO - *parliament.the-stationery-office.co.uk* Hansard online. Useful for consulting back numbers; but the previous day's material is only put on the net after noon the following day. Also lists all departmental publications.
- Houses of Parliament Home Page - *parliament.uk* Also gives access to Hansard, as well as Select Committee information for both Houses, the Weekly Information Bulletin and briefs prepared by the House libraries.
- Scottish Parliament, Welsh and Northern Ireland Assemblies: *scottish.parliament.uk* (and scottish.parliament.uk/webcast for live broadcasts); *wales.gov.uk*; *ni-assembly.gov.uk*
- Government Department websites - *open.gov.uk/index/orgindex.htm* is the route to all departments and public bodies.
- Regional Development Agencies - *local-regions.detr.gov.uk/rda/index.html* - links to all the RDAs
- Europa - *europa.eu.int/index.htm* Access to EU documents and announcements. Every DG has its own website, but may have not been updated for some time.
- European Parliament - *europarl.eu.int* - for information on plenary and committee agendas
- UK Online - *ukonline.co.uk/UKOnline/Politics/contents/html* Gives access to a large number of pressure and interest group, MP and local authority sites
- Central Office of Information - *coi.gov.uk/coi* - access to departmental press releases, usually 24 hours after publication
- In addition, Westminster Select Committees will put you on their circulation list (the EP will notify you by Email) for announcements on inquiries and business before them. Contact the Commons Committee Office (0171 219 3000)

LOBBYING THROUGH THE INTERNET

The internet can be a very effective lobbying tool, but lobbyists need to understand its strengths and weaknesses:

- *It can distribute campaign information (both on your behalf and against you) widely and rapidly. Campaigners can flood an organisation with EMail; but the organisation can respond, using the same mechanism, more personally and with greater ease than it could by using other communication techniques.*
- *Its best use is in grass roots campaigning. Although a website can be a convenient means of informing a large number of unidentified potential respondents to consultation proposals (it may lead to an increase in responses and a heightened perception of concern among officials and Ministers) and it is a useful means of obtaining feedback or case histories on an issue (for example, horror stories about over-regulation), it is unlikely to deliver results if used by corporate organisations to build coalitions. Headlines such as "Government makes concessions after vigorous internet campaign against proposed legislation" (Financial Times, 24 September 1999) may suggest that the medium works, but while in that case a website was used to brief organisations affected by Budget proposals, it was impossible to tell whether the unusually large number of representations were stimulated by the website or by other factors. What was clear was that the body responsible for the campaign was reported as regarding the subsequent concessions as "a disaster".*
- *It does not influence Government. Departments, Brussels DGs and MPs/MEPs are happy to receive personally written EMails (not mass produced electronic forms) if they can receive them - most officials and politicians are not directly connected to the internet, although that will no doubt change before too long (all MSPs and AMs have EMail addresses). But they regard the handwritten, personally targeted and addressed letter as the mark of a lobbyist's sincerity. It may be masochistic, but the system reacts badly to most of the PR devices (videos, brochures etc) intended to facilitate the assimilation of information. Internet lobbying presentations look good, but their time is yet to come.*

Consider assembling and maintaining a ring file with all of your most regularly needed information in one place. The sections could cover

- Lists of all MPs, (and/or, if relevant, MSPs/AMs/MLAs) both alphabetically and by constituency, with your own constituency

Members (plus their Westminster/Edinburgh/Cardiff/Belfast/constituency telephone, pager, mobile and fax numbers and EMail addresses) highlighted
- Lists of MEPs, together with their European Parliament committee memberships
- Ministerial responsibilities, together with Private Office names and numbers
- Commissioner responsibilities, together with Cabinet names, numbers and responsibilities
- Lists of PPSs and Whips, with responsibilities and numbers
- Special Advisers, with numbers, responsibilities and CVs
- No 10 Policy Unit, with backgrounds and responsibilities
- Select, All Party and backbench committees, with details of clerks and numbers
- Current Select (or, in Scotland and Wales, subject) Committee press releases (which will be sent to you regularly if you contact committees and ask to be put on their mailing lists).
- Opposition spokesmen
- Party research departments
- Press Gallery numbers

There are few textbooks to assist you, but three should be considered: *Lobbying - An Insider's Guide to the Parliamentary Process* by Alf Dubs (Pluto Press, 1988) is now out of print, but if you can obtain a copy it offers a clear and practical explanation of the work of Parliament. *The Politicos Guide to Parliament by Susan Child* (Politico's Publishing, 1999) is much more detailed and in its explanation of procedure is a modern day Erskine May. Sadly there is no comparable book in print about lobbying the Civil Service. James Humphreys' *Negotiating in the European Union* (Century Business, 1997) is undoubtedly the most practical guide to working the Brussels machine.

Monitoring the System

Many people regard monitoring work as the most basic of the lobbyist's activities. They could not be more mistaken. Monitoring

Government requires speed, knowledge of procedure and of decision making structures, an elephantine memory and considerable organisation. While most organisations are likely to find that using an external monitoring agency will be more cost effective than running this function in-house, they should still know how to do it.

Monitoring can be divided into two types:

- Passive, in which information is received, organised and distributed. Examples of passive information sources are the records of Westminster, Scottish, Welsh, Northern Ireland and European Parliament proceedings, Select Committee and Whitehall press releases and reports and the EC Official Journal.
- Active, where the researcher has to take the initiative in obtaining information, for example through contact with Select Committee clerks on future inquiries or with officials to corroborate media reports on policy planning.

The difference can best be summed up by the famous statement in the film *Wall Street*: "Stop sending me information; start getting me information."

Of the two, active information gathering is by far the more useful although it requires more time and greater expertise. Much passively monitored material will be largely irrelevant to your needs. Few insiders pay any attention to any but a small handful of Early Day Motions, Adjournment Debates, or speeches in Parliament in any one session and the bulk of parliamentary answers contain neither data nor meaningful statements. In any event, if you wait until publication to receive such material as is useful, others will have picked it up before you.

The clearest way to explain what you really need and how to get it is to look at two in-house departments. One has very limited resources; the other can afford to buy the best. In the table on pages 285-287, we take the main categories of information need, show how the two departments could satisfy their requirement, assess the value of each category and consider the extent to which the constrained department may be disadvantaged. However, assuming that you have to do it all yourself, your daily and weekly schedule could look like this:

From 6.30am
Listen to Today Programme for information on publication of reports, campaign launches and ministerial statements. Read all broadsheets and some tabloids for political and regulatory information. Note the need to check with the system if media information is contradictory or conflicts with information you have already received.

8.00am
Log on to the Scottish Parliament Business Bulletin to monitor the coming day's proceedings (the full transcript of the previous day may take several days to appear on the internet).

8.15am
Collect Vote Bundle. Look first for "Written questions tabled on (previous day) for answer today" in the Commons Order Paper - these are the "planted questions" designed to elicit Government statements that day. The answer is often reproduced in the press release that accompanies the announcement: contact with officials at HEO level should get you on the fax list. Note backbench statements in debate that refer to your organisation or sector and which may need correction, or ministers' winding up speeches which may occasionally make useful statements. Note relevant parliamentary answers. Skim read Order Paper for tabled questions about your organisation or sector, particularly those that could imply a lobby against you or which could stimulate you to contact Whitehall with accurate data if the question calls for it (eg "how much Lottery money has been awarded to the South West"). Note forthcoming Lords/Commons orals and decide whether it is worth briefing the questioners or others who could ask supplementaries. Note forthcoming Lords debates (new items in the Lords Order Paper are either marked with a dagger symbol or are listed as tabled under the previous day's date). Check Early Day Motions that may affect you. Take care if they are tabled

with over 50 signatories - that usually means an organised lobby. Note tabling of new Statutory Instruments. Lastly, note announcements on composition of, or changes to, Standing and Select Committees.

8.30am
Start calling DGs/Permanent Representations/Council Secretariat/ MEP and European Parliament Committee offices for latest information on legislative/programme/tender planning.

9.00am
Check Hansard online.

9.30am
If you have learnt about them from the media or from a specialist service, request copies of ministerial speeches from their Private Offices. If you know of the time at which the speech will be delivered, call one minute afterwards. Call departmental parliamentary branches or line HEOs to request fax copies of parliamentary answers due to be published that afternoon.

Check Internet (departmental, regulatory bodies and Houses of Parliament websites) for new reports, press releases, online organisational directories or Select Committee information. Check again at 1pm and 5pm.

Start calling UK officials for latest information on policy planning.

9.30-9.45 am or 2.30-3.45 pm
Call Select Committee offices to check on forthcoming inquiries, witnesses, publication dates etc. Call Standing Committee clerks to find out which clause has been reached, expected pace of consideration and selection of amendments.

After 9.30am
Call backbench/All Party Group officers' researchers or secretaries for information on agendas (they may be sensitive about this).

10am and/or 4pm
Attend Select Committees.

HOW TO MONITOR	DELUXE	ECONOMY	COMMENT
Hansard (debates, oral and written answers)	*vote bundle/agency; Parl'ty Channel for live coverage; Lobby agency may provide answers before they appear in Hansard*	*Internet (Houses of Parl't site)*	*Vote Bundle available from Parliamentary Bookshop at 8.15. Hansard on the internet from 9am but can be difficult to read on screen; Agencies can get answers as soon as they are published. Departments may fax them if not busy.*
Select/subject Committee agendas and inquiries	*Call committee offices; Weekly Information Bulletin/What's Happening in the Scottish Parliament; attend sessions; reports from Parliamentary Bookshop or on Internet.*	*Internet; mailing list for committee press releases; WIB WHITSP on Internet; reports from Parliamentary Bookshop or on Internet*	*Contact each relevant committee office to be placed on its mailing list. Parliamentary Channel coverage of committees is too haphazard/too late to be useful*
PQs	*Orals through Parliamentary Channel, Vote Bundle (Order Paper) or agency*	*Internet*	*Most PQs are of little relevance. Order Paper is cumbersome.*
Press releases/speeches	*Lobby agency service for advance notice; CoI fax service for rapid delivery of releases; direct contact with Private Offices on speeches.*	*CoI on Internet; monitor speeches via media, then call Private Offices*	*CoI usually not on Internet until 24+ hours after release*
Whitehall/parliamentary publications	*Lobby agency for notification; departmental websites/Parliamentary Bookshop or HMSO; direct from regulators*	*WIB on Internet for post-publication notification; Departmental websites*	*Government/parliamentary reports/papers are increasingly - but inconsistently - available immediately on the Internet.*

HOW TO MONITOR	DELUXE	ECONOMY	COMMENT
Legislation	Hansard for 2nd rdg/Report/3rd rdg/ Lords Cttee stage; Standing Committee Hansard for Commons debates on clauses; Standing Committee clerks/Departments re schedules, Notes on Clauses, views on amendments/ representations; parliamentary Bookshop/Order Paper for amendments/ announcement of Standing Committee membership; Bills and Commons library briefs on Internet	Hansard/WIB/ Bills/Notes on Clauses/Commons library briefs on Internet; Standing Cttee clerks/ Departments re schedules; Parliamentary Bookshop/Order Paper for amendments/ announcement of Standing Committee membership.	
Activities of backbench/ All Party committees	Through friendly MP/ Peer or agency	Through friendly MP/Peer; House Magazine	No established reporting system. They regard themselves as private bodies
Policy	Proactive intelligence gathering at all levels (particularly G5/7, Special Adviser/PPS/ backbench committee secretaries etc)	Through trade association	No alternative to constant contact with Whitehall/regulators
Brussels policy	Direct intelligence gathering from Commission/Council/ working groups/ Coreper/Parliament (particularly Committee members/ rapporteurs/ intergroups)/ Perm. Reps; European Report/ Reuters/Agence Europe	Through trade association	The proactive approach is the only way to obtain early drafts of legislation and information on working groups and likely committee or Member State positions. Note that no reports of EP committee meetings are produced: the only ways to find out what has happened are to attend in person, to rely on a consultancy or trade

HOW TO MONITOR	DELUXE	ECONOMY	COMMENT
			association, or to hope that European Report, Reuters or Agence Europe will cover the session.
Council of Ministers agendas	*Direct approach to Council Secretariat / Commission officials (but not Coreper)*	*UKRep website (but corroborate with other Perm. Reps)*	*The Council secretariat will sometimes provide information on debate at Council or Working Group level, but generally it will plead secrecy.*
Scotland / Wales / N Ireland assemblies	*Scotland: Scottish Daily Business Bulletin, Official Report and Minutes of Proceedings / What's Happening In The Scottish Parliament via website. Wales: Order Paper and Record of Business. N Ireland: TBA. Lobby agency may provide answers before they appear on Scottish Parliament website*	*Via websites*	*Website offers fastest access to Scottish / Welsh record (although Welsh PDF reader system is slow and site lacks information)*
Local government	*Mailing lists for Committee agendas / reports / minutes; direct contact with officers; Local Government Chronicle / Municipal Journal; subscription to Local Government Information Unit*	*Mailing lists for Committee agendas / reports / minutes; direct contact with officers; Local Government Chronicle / Municipal Journal*	
Party policy / activities	*Party subscription service (copies of policy documents / press releases)*	*Fax list for press releases; scan media for details of policy documents*	
Think Tanks	*Mailing lists for publications / events*	*Mailing lists for publications / events*	

10.30am (and 4.30pm - may be earlier on Thursdays)
Attend Standing Committees if important amendments are being
debated.

11am onwards
Revise databases of MP/Peer interests to include latest Vote Bundle
information. Most Select Committee publications released.

12.15-12.30pm
Previous day's CoI press release list and the Vote Bundle start to
appear on the Internet; CoI lunchtime fax list issued.

3pm
If possible, watch departmental question times on Parliamentary
Channel.

4pm onwards
Parliamentary answers start to appear by fax (see above). However,
they may not be issued until 6.30pm or may be held over at the last
minute.

4.30pm
CoI evening fax list issued.

Any time
Scan Internet for think tank/interest group information. If possible,
keep Ceefax main news menu and 24 hour news programmes on all
day.

Monday
Weekly Information Bulletin published. Scan Commons/Lords
Select Committee inquiry schedules. Afternoon: call relevant cabinets
about the selection of items they will have made that morning for the
Wednesday Commission meeting.
2.30pm: Scottish Parliament business starts. Ends at 5.30pm.

Monday-Tuesday
2.30pm: Commons business starts.

Tuesday-Friday
9.30am: Scottish Parliament business starts.

Tuesday-Wednesday
9.00am–5.00pm: Welsh Assembly plenary.

Tuesday
10.00: Commons business starts. Morning (to 1pm) given over to backbench debates scheduled by ballot.
2.10pm–2.40pm: Questions to Welsh Assembly First Secretary.

Wednesday
9.30am: Commons business starts. Morning (to 2pm) given over to backbench debates scheduled by ballot.
Noon: Press briefing following the Commission meeting.
2.00pm & 2.30pm Questions to Welsh Departments.

Thursday
11.30am: Commons business starts. Ends at 7pm.
12.30pm: Statement of parliamentary business for following week.
3pm: Select Committee schedule for coming week published.

Friday
9.30am: Commons/Scottish Parliament business starts. Ends at
2.30pm: House of Lords does not sit. Many MPs away. Private Members' debates/Bills.

Two weeks before Council meetings and EP plenary sessions
Examine the Europa website for details of the agendas.

Using Help

A small department, or a body that does not have to deal with the system regularly, will have difficulty in finding the time, or in amassing the ability, to monitor the institutions, cover a range of Departments and deal with politicians in the depth and with the facility that their organisation needs. Although a few companies and trade associations have an established culture of doing everything in house, which means having a fair number of staff at their disposal, most of the rest now take a view that some skills must be available in house and others should be contracted out. There is no set pattern to this; but the basic factors determining what and how much you buy in are

- The skills of in house staff – a former senior official or Special Adviser will know what to do but may not have the time to do it all. They probably do not need advice; what they are after is people to help them execute their strategy (arranging meetings or events). Someone without that experience who has been given responsibility for dealing with Government within a much wider portfolio is more likely to need heavyweight advisers to explain how the system works and suggest courses of action.

- Cost – it is usually more cost-effective to let an agency handle monitoring (the materials are expensive – the Vote Bundle alone can cost £300 a week – and agencies have economies of scale). Specialist advice, even though it may be charged at £200 an hour, is also surprisingly good value if the consultant knows his stuff because they should be able to reach the right answer quickly. The killer cost, whether in-house or through an agency (particularly through an agency), is organisation – setting up meetings, administering Party Conference programmes and so on. Lots of youngsters running around expending a lot of shoe leather equals big bills. If you have to do a lot of this, employ an organiser in house and use advisers, if you need them at all, only to give you guidance on what needs to be done.

- The time and numbers of staff that you have available. There is a school of thought that advisers should explain how the process works and advise on what to do but should leave the client to do the rest. In the main, it is right that the organisation's name and people should always be front of house, but there will inevitably be cases where it is simply more convenient to ask an outsider to handle party conference arrangements or organise a meeting. The important point is that advisers, except for those rare cases where they are acknowledged as experts, should be unobtrusive – if you cannot implement the consultants advice yourself, it should at least look as though you can. Thus a lobbying firm may draft a letter inviting a European Commissioner to visit your factory and liaise with the cabinet and others about the event, but the letter should be sent by you on your letterhead and the arrangements should be seen to be handled by you.

Use lobbying advisers to:

- Tell you what may or may not be achievable (unreasonable demands may prejudice Government against you).
- Find out how politicians and officials want your case to be constructed (issues to cover, queries to address, methodologies to follow).
- Assist you in contacting and building relationships with politicians and officials. In almost all circumstances, the approach should come from you on your letterhead, not via a third party. Lobbyists can tell you who to approach, how to approach them, what to do when you are through the door, and they can also use their lines of credit to assist in securing meetings; but it does not always reflect well on their clients if they are felt to be interposing themselves between organisations and the system. Having said that, if your advisers are regarded by the system as both experts in their own right and untainted by prejudice (for example, a former head of offshore oil and gas licensing dealing with his successors), they may be able to negotiate on your behalf with greater credibility than you could command.
- Monitor the system (agencies have economies of scale and it is likely to cost you far less to employ an external parliamentary monitoring service than to handle the process in house).
- Analyse policy.
- Draft submissions and reports in system-friendly format (from a two-page summary for an MP to detailed documents for a Government Department or DG).
- Vet submissions or reports produced by you (or even, for example in competition cases, by your lawyers) to ensure that the

policy/political counter-arguments have been considered.

- Undertake economic and opinion research to support your arguments. This is particularly important in the area of regulatory appraisals and Fiches d'Impact. They require a professional understanding of the approach required by Whitehall and the Commission.
- Brief both sides in advance of lobbying meetings and to obtain an uncoloured debrief from the system
- Act as Special Advisers, drafting or counselling on policy or regulatory representations.
- Handle administrative work (for example, the occasional need to mail a large number of MPs) that it is not cost-effective to undertake in-house.

As you can see, lobbying may constitute only a small part of a lobbyist's work. The bulk of most agency's time is devoted to monitoring, peacetime contact building and – a steadily increasing activity – general presentation.

How do you select and make sure you get value from advisers? Follow these six simple rules:

- First, unless you have to (for example, if you are a public body) forget about contracts. They generally only benefit the consultant by requiring you to give them lengthy notice of termination. You should be able to get rid of them without extra cost if you are dissatisfied. Employ them like lawyers, so that you pay only for the work they have done; or, if you need to budget ahead, agree a monthly limit but ask them to bill on an hourly basis, so both sides work to a maximum figure.
- Do not accept the typical proposal document in which six wide-margined pages simply repeat your brief, suggest an "audit" (why should you pay them to find out who you should lobby? They are meant to know that) and recommend a vague contact programme. Expect a detailed diagnosis of your brief, looked at from the system's point of view; a tough assessment of what is and is not possible; an explanation of the reasons for recommending their pre-

WINNERS AND LOSERS

Good lobbyists treat the system as they would their customers: they find out what the market wants and how it behaves before they put their product together.

- *They think Case before Targets.*
- *They do not move until they have worked out how decisions will be taken, who will take them and who and what will influence them. This is the critical success factor*
- *They get their technical arguments right before tackling politicians, who would otherwise be briefed on the basis of data supplied by others. That does not mean that detail should be fired at politicians; but the infrastructure (the "yes, but" rebuttals) needs to be addressed before the major decisions can be made.*
- *They know that demonstrating expertise and sensitivity to the system's concerns is the best PR for their organisation.*
- *They do not count on friends made in peacetime: the contacts that wield influence will treat problems on their merits.*
- *They will usually see lobbying through the media as a last resort, knowing that few cases are of such public interest that media interest will be sustained and that much coverage simply bounces off the system.*
- *They know that the noise and volume of a lobbyist's activity are often in inverse proportion to the effectiveness of their case.*
- *And they have job titles that suggest seniority or speciality and avoid the impression that they are apologists for their organisation (the system does not want to think it is being handled by someone in the place of the person with whom it should be dealing).*
- *Most importantly, their management structure does not separate dealings with politicians from liaison with officials or regulators. The former is often seen as a PR function; the latter as purely technical. The result is that one part of an organisation will assemble arguments and expect another part simply to "communicate" them without any say in their construction or relevance.*
- *The best lobbyists see the components of the system as closely connected and ensure that all advocates have a role in case preparation and in advising on the most appropriate targets.*

Conversely, those who fail usually do so for three reasons:

- *They do not understand which issues are political and which are administrative in nature. Officials cannot solve essentially political problems and Ministers and MPs refer most technical cases to officials;*
- *They use techniques more appropriate to dealing with the media or influencing opinion outside the system;*
- *And they spend more time on communicating their case than on considering how the system will respond to it.*

293

ferred course of action ("Why?" is your most powerful accountability tool); relevant cvs of the staff who will be working for you; and references from the people you will need to lobby.

- Do not accept the all too common ploy of Mr Big being there at the pitch and little Johnny handling the work. Insist on the people you want.

- Good lobbyists should not brag about their clients or their contacts. You should be the one who decides whether your appointment of advisers is publicised, and you should insist that tenderers should not talk to the press.

- Keep them fully informed. The more information they have about your organisation and its dealings with the system (bearing in mind that you may only be using them for help with one institution) the less excuse they will have for giving poor advice.

- Think carefully about the advisers you need. Most are pure political consultants, meaning that they deal predominantly with politicians. If that is the area in which you need help, fine, but if you are not experienced in these things you must ensure that your consultants understand how the system as a whole will work. Furthermore, the staff of lobbying firms broadly divide into Researchers, who monitor the system; Presenters, who are best at helping organisations promote themselves, their products and ideas; Campaigners, whose speciality is high profile, pressure-based casework; Address Books, who would be better at contact-building than as strategists or policy specialists; Strategists, who devise solutions but who may need the help of others (particularly Address Books) in order to execute; and Negotiators, good at mastering policy and clients' cases, who work the system and play an active role in equivocating between clients and Government but who may lack political muscle. These skills are not mutually exclusive, but you must ensure that the consultants that may be offered to you tick your boxes: you should not have to change the checklist to suit them.

- One man bands can be very good, but they may stretch themselves thinly. Seek clear assurances on availability: it is annoying always to have to leave messages on a machine because your adviser is else-where.

- Most reputable consultants are regulated, either as members of the Association of Professional Political Consultants in the UK (0171 838 4865) or as signatories to the Code of Conduct for Public Affairs Practitioners in Brussels (00322 282 0986). Both organisa-tions are required by Parliament and the Commission respectively to subscribe to regulatory codes governing their conduct towards clients and the system in the course of giving advice and lobbying. Regulated lobbyists are required to disclose the identity of their client whenever they deal with politicians or officials.

- While a handful of law firms and accountants have established pub-lic policy units, many more regularly handle Budget or regulatory policy representations but do not call themselves lobbyists. They are likely to offer greater subject knowledge and may carry greater credibility with Government. On the other hand, they tend to avoid political case making, which may be necessary; they may lack an understanding of the mechanics of policymaking and of some of the creative approaches needed to deal with the system; and their preference for making representations on behalf of their clients can be counterproductive since some officials regard contact by a law firm as a prelude to litigation. In Brussels, however, where decisions are overwhelmingly made within a legal, rather than a discretionary policy framework, there is much more of an overlap between lob-bying firms and lawyers, who deal regularly with the Commission in a system. Indeed, although only a few are comfortable or famil-iar with the Parliament or with the techniques of Council lobby-ing, most third party representations in Brussels are handled by lawyers.

- It is often necessary to use economists or accountants to research and collate data. Officials in particular like to see cases endorsed by a respected third party. However, the amour propre of economists can be fragile and they tend to resent any attempt by clients to dic-tate terms of reference or to correct misleading conclusions. In dealing with Government, however, it must be accepted that the system will pick apart and discount any study or submission that adopts a methodology it regards as inappropriate. I will not easily forget the lengthy critique produced by Customs & Excise economists in 1991 of two studies, commissioned by industry from well known consultants, on the impact of Duty Free abolition. The consultants had not sought to meet the studies' targets beforehand to find out which questions were of greatest concern to Whitehall and to agree an approach which officials could not subsequently dispute. It subsequently took only a 45 minute discussion with Customs & Excise to determine the data that the system needed in order to reach a positive decision, and the research that followed played a significant part in persuading the Government to fight for retention of Duty Free sales after 1992. Always, therefore, make it a condition precedent of any contract with economists or accountants that they must agree methodology with relevant officials in advance and that you should be present at any such meeting. It is also sensible before retaining advisers to seek views from those who will receive the research on the consultants they most respect.

The truth about lobbyists

However, a cautionary note. Very few lobbyists are able to advise on dealing with the system as a whole. In the run-up to and following the 1997 General Election, most lobbying firms recruited staff with a Labour background. They had not served within the institutions of government and had little knowledge of the policy process. Inevitably, therefore, their counsel to clients may be based on a knowledge only of politicians and on an attitude to access schooled in dealings with Opposition spokesmen, whose door is almost always open, rather than with Ministers screened by Private Offices. Most heads of agencies privately admit that there are perhaps only four or five consultants with a Labour background who really understand how to give sound advice.

And the problem is not confined to Labour specialists. Few current lobbyists of any complexion have much knowledge of the way the system makes decisions. Most have never experienced the consequences of the advice they give, much of which seeks to compensate in packaging for what it lacks in content. Furthermore, the loyalty of Labour lobbyists to their party has been exploited by Labour's business officers, who have realised that it can be easier to sell sponsorship through a multi-client agency than to approach its clients one by one (the Conservatives have followed suit). Consultants have found themselves caught in a conflict between their duty to act in the best interests of their client and their desire to come to the aid of their party.

THINK TANKS AND PRESSURE GROUPS - WHO'S IN?

With Labour
Fabian Society
Demos
Institute for Public Policy Research
New Local Government Network
Socialist Environmental Resources Association
Scottish Council Foundation
Smith Institute

With the Conservatives
Centre for Policy Studies
Social Market Foundation

With both
Institute for Fiscal Studies

Source: survey of 20 party officers and MPs

This problem is exacerbated by the overwhelmingly political management ethos of many firms, with the result that clients' needs are often addressed by taking a one club approach (organising briefings for MPs and Special Advisers) which is usually marked by a reluctance to explain how the process of decision-making - or, as many call it, "opinion forming" - actually works. Furthermore, most consultancies are in reality firms that specialise in including

---

WHAT DO LOBBYISTS ACTUALLY DO?

If you believe the media, lobbyists do nothing except tap their political contacts for favours. In part, this misconception has taken root because lobbyists' day-to-day work, apart from being more ethical, is also usually more technical and less dramatic. This is my diary for 11 June 1999, a typical sleaze-free day:

6.30am Listen to Today Programme. Note relevant items: if we have not given clients advance notice of them, assess significance and leave messages to be picked up when they get in.

7.15am Read papers. There will always be at least three or four news items requiring corroboration with Departments, Special Advisers or the Lobby.

8.00am Call Brussels office, which has been monitoring Commission activity on a Merger Regulation case involving a client.

8.30am Call a client to discuss strategy towards the Merger Regulation case, which has just been referred to a Stage 2 inquiry.

8.50am Check researchers' Vote Bundle monitoring. Decide on relevance to clients and on whether comment is needed (for example, advice on media management following a statement later in the day).

9.25am Discuss with DSS officials their participation in a client's seminar on Stakeholder Pensions, to which their Secretary of State has also been invited.

10.05am Contact a Cabinet Minister's Private Office to agree a date for a meeting with a delegation from a deregulation campaign.

10.30am A client has taken a table at a political party charity dinner and seeks help in identifying and finding MPs who might be invited.

11.00am Call from an energy company about problems it is having with the Environment Agency over a planning application. Advise on negotiation tactics (involving the local authority, Regional Development Agency and Regional Chamber) and produce brief on the problem at the request of DTI officials.

11.15am An ad agency working for a migraine research body calls. An awareness campaign is due to start on TV in three days but is being blocked by the body that clears adverts because it might conflict with another campaign being run by the NHS. Contact the NHS Executive, which confirms that it has no concerns, and advise the agency on liaison with the relevant NHSE official and with the BMA. Two further discussions with the agency during the day.

2.00pm Discussion with a trade association about representations against forthcoming draft Regulations which significantly increase the discretion of an agency to make decisions on restrictions without parallel in the rest of the EU.

> *3.00pm Following discussions with a think tank, the Audit Commission and a member of the Health Select Committee, draft initial letters for an insurance company to send to the Commission and the MP to propose that a non-core NHS function should be subjected to value for money testing.*
>
> *3.45pm Conversation with a think tank about an electricity company's membership of a policy forum it is establishing.*
>
> *4.15pm Discussion with lawyers about liaison with three Brussels DGs on the Merger Regulation case.*

Government within broader PR programmes: the techniques they may use in addressing problems involving the shaping of policy or legislation may be more appropriate to the management of an organisation's reputation than to working the system to achieve a concrete result. That is not to say that the small minority of former officials employed within the profession are immune: their advice may devote inadequate attention to the role of politicians.

The critical factor for clients, therefore, is the way a firm's staff are managed. Is there someone in overall control of these political or Whitehall specialists who understands the bigger picture; who can ask of those specialists the questions you need to have answered; who checks their work; who is not influenced by personal political interest; and who understands the policy process while at the same time being able to think like a member of your organisation? Editors may not necessarily be good reporters, but if they do not set the agenda their paper either does not appear or it risks being seriously unbalanced. The obverse of this is that their paper tends to bear the stamp of their convictions (or those of their proprietor). There can be advantages in a consultancy being identified with the complexion of the governing party; but without balanced leadership such a firm will often regard that party as synonymous with the system as a whole.

In Brussels, there is less of a tendency for advisers to play one club golf, and the over-emphasis on European Parliament contact that used to mark the work of some firms has largely been corrected by the expansion of the Parliament's role and confidence since the introduction of the co-decision making procedure.

And finally, remember that lobbyists are in business to make money. It is only fair to admit that much of what they are employed to do, and even more of the advice they give, is quite unnecessary. Many "political programmes" are merely make work exercises for advisers and deliver little of material benefit to their clients, particularly if their measurable contribution to corporate performance is compared with the work of other professional advisers such as accountants, lawyers, surveyors or bankers. Clients need to think carefully before they are seduced by professional lobbyists' tendency to political name-dropping; and, to return to the message at the start of this book, they should consider spending more money on researching the acceptability of their product by their target market, safe in the knowledge that they will usually be able to spend far less on wide-ranging contact than they do at present. If any maxim is likely to improve most organisations' dealings with Government, it is More Thought, Less Action.

Sleaze? Sponsorship and other commercial links with the system

While the line between a legitimate commercial relationship with the system and bribery can be regarded by the media as a fine one, most financial dealings with parties or the institutions of government are entirely legitimate. What you need to consider is what is on offer; whether you would benefit from it; and, if so, how commercial links can be concluded ethically.

There are quite a number of options for an organisation to consider:

• Contributing to political party funds
• Sponsoring party activities
• Sponsoring favoured think tanks or pressure groups
• Sponsoring Government activities
• Retaining or funding MPs, MSPs, MLAs, MEPs or Peers
• Secondments of MPs
• Secondments to or from Whitehall

Contributions to political parties are nowadays regarded by share-holders, the City and the media as less acceptable than hitherto, and the once recognisable distinction between one major party represent-ing management and another representing the workforce has been blurred by Labour's drive to capture the middle ground and to court the business vote. We should make it clear that we would not advise any organisation to contribute to party funds; however, despite the denials of the parties, such contributions undoubtedly help to win favour, improve access, and influence decisions on honours. At the time of writing, legislation had been proposed to specify that

- where £5000 or more has been given to a national party, or £1000 or more to a regional or constituency party office in any year, either directly or through sponsorship or donations of property in kind, the donor and amount should be declared;
- blind trusts cannot be used to fund parties or individual politicians;
- donations can only be made by individuals resident in the UK or organisations resident anywhere in the EU and carrying on busi-ness here. Boards must obtain shareholder approval (through a gen-eral enabling power valid for four years) for corporate donations and declare all donations (sponsorships may be separately listed) over a minimal level in annual reports. Subsidiaries must obtain parent company approval;
- anonymous donations over £200 are banned. Individual donors must be on the electoral register.

Sponsorship of party activities, while included within the statuto-ry definition of party funding (which excludes sponsorship of "poli-cy development"), is often a very different animal since it is usually entered into without any suggestion of support for that party. The primary objective is usually the same - to win favour - but sponsor-ship may also beneficially associate an organisation with a policy or event in the eyes of its consumers (for example, a financial services company sponsoring the launch of a policy paper on pensions reform) and the means of achieving these ends are in most cases regarded as more innocent. All the main parties now have sophisticated sponsorship machines, seeking funding primarily for conference stands (see Party Conferences, p.191), dinners and receptions. In some cases, for example Labour's New Deal Roadshows, it has been difficult to tell whether the sponsorship sought has been for a party event or for the normal work of Ministers.

Organisations interested in sponsorship, or simply wanting details of forthcoming events that they may want to pay to attend, should contact the business liaison officer at the relevant party's headquarters. They should be in no doubt what they are getting for their money (number of free places, text in any associated literature, name and logo exposure, promotion by the party's media machine and so on) and should insist that if the sponsorship is embarrassingly publicised the party will help to clear up the mess. In the case of dinners, it is normal when booking a table to be given the right to request that a number of places be filled by nominated MPs or Peers, although there is no guarantee that the organisers will be able to deliver (you may have to make the approach yourself, but many politicians feel that if the party approaches them they are under a duty to deliver unless to do so would place Ministers in a compromising position - for example if they are considering a planning application by the host).

It is of course always open to you to propose sponsorships of your own, ranging from awards (for example, the Spectator's Parliamentarian Of The Year) to events (one airline's annual Parliamentary Pilot competition was very popular) or endowments for party research staff or programmes.

Labour has to date been more adroit than other parties in exploiting the sponsorship opportunities offered by "quasi-party" events - conferences organised by professional companies but in close association with a Party, often because it needs an independent platform to promote or explain policies. In such cases, the conference organiser will offer a range of sponsorship packages with the unspoken implication that financial support will not go unnoticed by the Party of the day. Such funding falls outside the current declaration requirements.

Sponsoring favoured think tanks or pressure groups can offer benefits, but the sponsor must be certain that the bodies are favoured and

ORGANISING EVENTS FOR POLITICIANS

Ten simple rules:

- *Give MPs, MEPs, MSPs etc at least a month's notice, and preferably six weeks. Tell them how long they will be expected to stay.*
- *Hold the event close to the House/Assembly/Parliament building. If it cannot be held within three minutes' walking distance (which, in Edinburgh, means between the Parliament and the station, not in the other direction) provide taxis. Events can be organised within the European Parliament but there are extensive rules and authorisation must be obtained from the offices of the President's cabinet and the Secretary General. Support from one (or preferably more) political groups is desirable.*
- *Always call on the day to ensure that they have not forgotten or that something else has not cropped up and to remind them of transport arrangements.*
- *Do not get too upset if they fail to turn up without notice. Last minute changes of plan are par for the course and, to be honest, today's politicians are less courteous than their predecessors.*
- *They will hardly ever thank you; but you should write to thank them for coming.*
- *Midweek invitations are likely to be most successful. Monday night is possible, but avoid Friday unless the event is held in the politician's constituency. Ministers are usually reluctant to commit themselves to private sector visits involving travel unless they are held on Fridays or are likely to carry major publicity benefits. Treasury Ministers traditionally do not accept outside engagements during the two months before the Budget; and the Chief Secretary and Financial Secretary will have restricted diary space during the Committee Stage of the Finance Bill, which runs from mid-April to June. Commissioners can travel at any time, but avoid engagements that would clash with the Wednesday morning meeting of the Commission. Meetings with groups of MEPs are easier to organise during Strasbourg plenary sessions. MEPs usually attend plenary sessions from Tuesday to Thursday afternoon. They are less available on Tuesday nights as this is usually when political group meetings take place. Wednesday nights are best: MEPs prefer dinner to lunch engagements.*
- *Do not expect politicians to stay for more than a few minutes at a reception. They will probably be double booked and, particularly if the event is held in any of the parliaments, they may only put their head round the door to see who else is there. It is a good idea to invite several Ministers on a "try and look in" basis (this allows them to make a decision on the day and is the easiest way to get the event at least pencilled in to their diaries) in the hope that one will attend.*
- *You are doing very well if you can get more than five parliamentarians to attend an event.*
- *If you invite politicians to an event in another MP/MEP's etc constituency, you should always inform the constituency member. This applies to any ministerial visit except in the City of London and Westminster.*

they need to exercise care over the nature of the sponsorship:

- Think tanks generally hold little sway in the early years of a government but can have more influence as a General Election, with the need to produce new manifesto ideas, approaches.
- With the exception of organisations such as the Institute for Fiscal Studies, which is not aligned to a political party, think tanks tend to be more powerful when their party is in opposition and does not have the Civil Service to research and test policy ideas.
- Whatever their claims, most carry little weight – at least in terms of shaping policy – at any time.
- However, while their ideas may not often withstand Whitehall scrutiny or be seen by party policymakers as politically expedient, they can facilitate access to the top. For that reason, although few sponsored pamphlets ever generate more than a few column inches, when think tanks organise a policy symposium or lecture they are often able to attract the relevant Ministers, political advisers and party officials – and sponsorship of such events attracts far less media attention than the funding of functions organised by political parties.
- A high proportion of their staff are bright achievers who frequently move to positions of influence as ministerial Special Advisers, in political parties, or in business.

Similarly, most pressure groups, while helpful to opposition parties in promoting ideas, are seen as an irritant by Ministers and officials who do not want to be deflected by sectional interests most of which, in their experience, want them to spend money they have not got. In considering a visible association with such organisations, therefore, it is not sufficient that you agree with their principles: if the system does not respect them you could find yourself linked with an antibody. For example, in the area of the natural environment the Worldwide Fund for Nature and the Socialist Environmental Resources Association are respectively considered by Whitehall and by many Labour MPs to be responsible and interested in working with the institutions of government; on the other hand, Greenpeace and Friends of the Earth derive their popular support from remaining outside the system - "going native" could inhibit their ability to publicise their causes.

Affinity groups which target the institutions have existed in Brussels for many years (the most prominent are the American and British Chambers of Commerce, the Kangaroo Group, Philip Morris Institute, European Round Table, and the Centre for European Policy Studies. In recent years similar bodies, of which the best known are the Labour Industry Forum, its Fabian Society counterpart, and the Conservative Enterprise Forum, have been established in the UK, although private dining clubs with closed lists have existed since time immemorial. They provide an opportunity for their members to meet politicians, either at plenary or working group sessions or at occasional conferences, for which sponsorship is usually sought, and for the politicians to be made aware of the members' support for organisations that support them. However, there is increasing interest in the media in the use that these organisations make of the often substantial subscriptions they receive: suspicions have been raised that at least part of the money finds its way back into party coffers.

Sponsoring Government activities is not as sensitive as it sounds. It merely involves the private sector in the promotion of policy - for example, the organisation of roadshows to advise businesses on avoiding late payment burdens and to raise awareness of creditors' rights under the recent Late Payment of Commercial Debts Act; or the British Council's international seminars on the Millennium Bug. The trick here is not to wait until Government has decided what it wants to do: if you have an idea which could help Government and serve your organisation's interests without compromising either side, put it to the head of the Branch or Division in the relevant Department and also to the Special Adviser, if the idea involves Ministers, as early as you can.

Retaining or funding MPs, MSPs, AMs, MLAs, MEPs or Peers is, in the wake of several media witchhunts, much less popular than in the days when a politician on the board lent status to an organisation. It is still permissible to pay legislators to gather intelligence and to advise, but not to act as advocates on your behalf. This means that an MP, MSP, AM or Peer cannot accept payment to arrange meetings or to speak in Parliament. However, this rule has not prevented them from speaking in debate on relevant subjects provided their interest was declared, both at the start of their speech and in the Commons/Scottish/Welsh/Northern Irish Register of Members' Interests (there is a version for the Lords, but inclusion is still voluntary). In practice, a paid advocate is usually a discredited one, and despite the existence of a Commissioner for Standards the current rules can be avoided in several ways.

HOW VALPAK DOES IT

"Valpak is the largest organisation administering packaging recycling schemes. We have one specialist, with two others devoting a small amount of time to dealing with Government. You have to have a job title that says "I'm dealing with a senior person in the organisation".

We treat politicians and officials very differently from our other audiences; they are nothing like customers, suppliers or journalists. There are no standard packages - we treat all parts of the system personally - but we always take care of Government's infrastructure: even if you have access at the top you still need the little people. And we make sure that our grass roots contacts (whether they are MPs, local authorities or our members) do not first hear about our activities by reading the papers."

Organisations seeking to retain politicians should insist that the arrangement is fully declared in the Register and it should be drafted specifically to exclude any activity other than the giving of advice. In any event, no organisation should need to pay legislators to table questions, help them approach Ministers or have their views advanced in debate once the process is understood. If it is only advice and information that is sought, remember that although most politicians are articulate and persuasive their judgement may not necessarily be respected by their colleagues. Do not retain the first politician you meet. In any event, few Labour MPs will today contemplate a financial link with a commercial operation (although they may be more ready to consider approaches from trade associations or non-profit making bodies).

Although a register of interests exists in the European Parliament (unpublished but available for scrutiny within the building) and declaration of commercial links is compulsory, there is no monitoring and enforcement mechanism.

KEY CIVIL SERVICE COLLEGE COURSES

Westminster & Whitehall: an A-Z of British Government
Policy making: a guide for specialists
The management of policy
Parliamentary Questions
The parliamentary environment
The policy environment
Drafting, briefing and PQ skills for senior entrants
Government & Business
How Government affects Business
Parliament, Government & the Civil Service
Working with Ministers
Government & the media
Understanding the legislative process
Understanding Parliament & legislation
Understanding Select Committees
Demystifying Brussels: orientation visit to
EU institutions
Understanding Brussels: the EU in one day
A guide to Community institutions
The European Parliament today
Dealing with EC Directives
Negotiating in Brussels
Policy & process in the EU
Focus Brussels

There are no restrictions on retention of local councillors, but they are required to stand aside from any issue in which they may have a declarable interest.

Secondments of MPs have for some years been institutionalised through the work of the Industry and Parliament Trust, a

Westminster-based organisation (0171 976 5311) to which MPs and UK MEPs can apply for "fellowship" schemes under which they receive a number of days experience within business and industry. The length of scheme varies, but the norm is 25 days over 12-18 months; there is a much shorter course for the City. They are normally attached to one company and in some cases IPT members may take more than one MP. The sharp members seek to spot high fliers, approach those with whom they would like to work and encourage them to apply to IPT. The corporate benefit lies in developing a relationship with a possible future Minister; the MPs gain some grounding in a world with which they might otherwise only make contact through set piece presentations or lobbying in the House (bearing in mind that a large number of parliamentarians have never had to survive by making money).

HOW WATER UK DOES IT

"Water UK has only four staff, but all of them deal interchangeably with Government. We keep each other briefed through a daily prayer meeting at which we review action and look ahead with a 2-3 month horizon. We contract out our monitoring and otherwise turn to consultants for sophisticated advice on personalities, the order in which people should be approached and links between other lobbies and politicians.

We keep a calendar of the regulatory year, since statements may come out at the same time each year, and have off the shelf briefings ready. We talk to the heads of our relevant departmental directorates every 1-2 weeks and have established an All Party Group to enable us to keep track of political views.

You will not change things just by talking to Ministers and officials. There has to be a groundswell of support; that is why we are constantly in touch with our MPs and with others (eg those with conservation, environment, and public health interests). But we do not adopt a standard approach: we always consider what the decision-making process will be on the issue in hand., reassessing targets and techniques each time. However, one given is that you should never wait for Government to consult on an issue - get in beforehand."

Secondments to and from Whitehall have taken place since the War. Every year, Departments allow around 2000 officials to gain commercial experience by working in the City or in industry; a smaller number of businessmen (670 in 1997-98) are allowed into Whitehall, although the aim is not to educate them in the mechanics of the system as much as to exploit their management skills. Organisations can approach the Cabinet Office or individual Departments and agencies to offer secondments, shorter term attachments, or job shadowing.

This process, known as the Interchange Initiative, can have considerable advantages for organisations which may have to deal with Government on a policy or commercial basis. They may be fortunate in having a Whitehall high flier sent to them who subsequently becomes a useful contact in a critical role (corporate altruism may play a part here, but the prime reason for offering space to officials is to benefit from it) and their own seconded executives will develop an understanding of the culture and processes of Government. But the scheme also has intrinsic disadvantages. While some exchanges involve voluntary bodies and SMEs, the list is dominated by large corporations which inevitably have greater ability to move staff around and to accommodate such projects. This means that officials tend to be seconded from one bulky, highly stratified culture to another. They often obtain a fresh insight into problem solving and the dynamics of commerce, but they are rarely placed in positions where they have to add to an organisation's bottom line or experience the financial or operational difficulties caused by inappropriate regulation or political caprice. Conversely, those who are most likely to have to deal regularly with Government - regulatory or government relations specialists - are rarely seconded into Whitehall, which seeks executives with financial or managerial skills from which it can learn.

Details on Interchange, including lists of Interchange Managers in every Department and Agency, can be obtained from a guide available from the Interchange Unit, Room 69/1, Cabinet Office, Horse Guards Road, London SW1P 3AL (0171 270 1842). Organisations can specify the type of official they can accommodate and the period of secondment (from a few days to two or three years). A parallel scheme established by the private sector, the Whitehall and Industry

Group (22 Queen Anne's Gate, London SW1H 9AA 0171 222 1166) also offers bilateral transfers, most of them three weeks long.

It is also possible to appoint officials, usually at Grade 3 or 5 level, as non-executive directors, but they cannot of course be drawn from divisions covering issues in which the outside organisation may be interested.

Training

This book has been marked by the theme that it is very difficult for outsiders to obtain a clear picture of the workings of the system. Not only are the institutions reluctant to draw back the curtain, but few opportunities exist for those outside Government to read about or be tutored in the dynamics of the route map or the practice of effective lobbying. Despite the recommended list on page 283, there is no established body of material to rival that available to those seeking to master accountancy or the legal system. Partly that is because, since Bagehot in the 1860s, former insiders and lobbyists have been notoriously coy about revealing the "secret of the constitution"; but more practically, while the system's processes – the way it works – are governed by complex procedures which can be explained in fine detail, the process of working the system is, in contrast to legal or accountancy work, to a fair extent a matter of feel born from experience and governed by few rules.   Even this book can only go so far: there are inevitably fine nuances of negotiating technique or tricks of the trade that it would be indiscreet to commit to paper, not because we want readers to employ an adviser even after absorbing this book but because lobbyists and lobbied know it is rarely wise to declare strategies or resources either beforehand or subsequently.

A number of opportunities do, however, exist for those wanting to learn more. The Civil Service College runs an extensive series of courses lasting from one day to a week. They are primarily designed for officials but it is possible for outsiders to attend. The best known to business and industry is the Top Management Programme, a four week management development course for senior public and private sector managers, but for government relations or regulatory specialists there are many other courses that both allow them a real insight into UK and EU institutions with a level of detail not available from other commercial trainers and give them the opportunity to mix with their opposite numbers (see below). The only drawback is that some of the lecturing may fail to take full account of political angles: while officials can be surprisingly good at thinking politically, they can overestimate the ability or desire of, for example, Select Committees to think in straight lines. For course details, call 01344 634628.

A few one day conferences are run by commercial organisers, of whom the best known is Hawksmere (0171 824 8257). They can be useful for the most basic training, but they tend only to offer pointers to culture and processes; they are very broad, covering the UK and EU as a whole but rarely if ever concentrating on individual departments or policy issues; they are dominated by consultants who have a tendency to sell from the lectern; conference papers are often no more than copies of slides and give delegates little to take back to their colleagues; and speakers frequently overlap. For organisations likely to have extensive dealings with Government, the same organisers can arrange dedicated in-house training which allows you to determine the structure and terms of reference, ask unlimited questions and, if more than a dozen people are involved, may be less expensive per head than attendance at a generic conference.

REFRESHER COURSE/CHECKLIST FOR SUCCESS

Twenty things you can do to improve your strike rate

1. Do less, but do it better – most lobbying or contact programmes feature too many targets and not enough depth. Better to concentrate on fewer activities but with greater care (for example, making sure every letter to an MP is written to them alone, not obviously as a mailshot).

2. Much lobbying and contact with the system is either unnecessary or has no chance of success because the objective is unrealistic. Ask yourself "If we did nothing, would it have made any difference?"; or alternatively "Is this a yes-able proposition; and if not, can we make it one?"

3. Organisations need to know what is happening inside the system. At the most basic level, some parliamentary information is necessary – committee inquiries or comments about your sector – but in reality do not get too excited about Early Day Motions, debates, or backbenchers' comments on legislation. Intelligence (actively obtaining views on policy formulation, feedback on representations; attitudes towards you/your industry, as against monitoring which is generally passive) is more important (and requires greater skill).

4. Make sure there is a point to any contact programme you organise: the system only has so much patience. Unnecessary contact with legislators or officials now could count against you when you really do need to deal with them.

5. The golden rule in drafting a lobbying strategy: WHAT (is our case) WHO (makes the decisions; who influences them) WHEN (do we deal with our targets) HOW (do we deal with them) WHY (is every action objectively necessary?). Above all, make sure you understand how the ground lies and get your facts straight before you start to think about targets.

6. Hard reality: in 90% of UK and 70% of EU cases, Parliament changes nothing - you must square your case with officials and Ministers first. Only a few cases are genuinely political. Local Government is different: in 50% of cases, councillors exercise significant influence and minor influence in another 25%.

7. Understand how each component works: most written representations to MPs, MSPs, AMs and MLAs just get mailboxed to Departments. If you take the parliamentary route to Ministers, you either need a lot of personally written letters or a few committed and respected Members who will take up your case personally. Ministers are always more likely to rely on officials', rather than your, version of the truth. Do everything possible to square advisers before you take your case to the top.

8. Coalitions of interest are important; if you cannot gain consensus with other bodies, get your retaliation in first by pre-empting the points they might make against you.

9. Media pressure can work, but the story must stack up (for example, the Post Office anti-privatisation campaign stories worked because their claims that 15 Tories would vote against the Government were accurate); you may need sustained coverage over weeks or months - one piece is rarely enough; and it can be counterproductive (stories about utility opposition to the Windfall Tax only served to irritate Gordon Brown; or coverage can alert opponents). You must judge whether your issue really is newsworthy and whether media pressure is likely to move Ministers. Bear in mind that politicians hardly watch TV and pay little attention to specialist correspondents: you need to get to the media they respect

(Times and Sunday Times, Scotsman, Glasgow Herald, Western Mail, Daily Mail, Sun, Evening Standard and Edinburgh Evening News, Today Programme and Scotland Today, World at One, Frost on Sunday, Ceefax) and particularly to political correspondents, commentators or Leader Writers – the articles politicians read first.

10. Never crow (or allow your advisers to crow) about your victories, unless you will never have to work with the system again.

11. The system will not respect you if you surprise it: brief officials before you meet Ministers; brief front bench researchers before meeting Opposition spokesmen. As a courtesy, and to avoid a hostile response born of surprise, try to inform MPs, MSPs, AMs, MLAs, MEPs, councillors and officials shortly before you make any public announcement of relevance to them.

12. Understand when – and when not – to lobby the Opposition. It is helpful on the very rare issues when the Government could be defeated (Lords only these days); when Government wants to gain cross-party consensus before it will do what you want; and when you seek to shape party policy in gestation. But it can backfire: Oppositions seek to embarrass Government, not to help it, and Ministers do not want to be seen to be accepting the wisdom of the other side's argument. If the Opposition takes up your case you may find Ministers automatically opposing it.

13. Never get NO on the record – better to withdraw and fight again. And accept, if you are in the game for the long term, that you may have to go soft on Government on occasions in order to avoid antagonism that might only damage your chances of success on other issues.

14. It's never won until it's won – there have been many cases where one side thought it had won only to find that issues changed at the last minute (Shops Bill; Building Societies Bill). Organisations have found that Regulations are occasionally tabled at the last minute or the tone of a Green or White Paper is subtly amended by the par-

liamentary draftsman, so do not assume that you should stop work because you think there is no chance of a situation changing.

15. Always think "why should they want to know this/deal with me/read this?"

16. At what level should you deal with the system on a day-to-day basis? In Whitehall, Scotland, Wales, Northern Ireland and the Commission, you will rarely need to go higher that the G5/A3 grades and you may find quality falling if you liaise below G7/A5. Special Advisers and Cabinets are helpful if you need an alternative conduit to or to be able to read the minds of Ministers and Commissioners. Opposition researchers are increasingly recognised as important briefing points: they are in effect a one man Civil Service for their masters. Secretaries of State are only involved on the largest issues; do not feel snubbed if you are steered towards a junior Minister. European Parliament rapporteurs, MPs on Standing Committees and MSPs on subject committees are usually happy to meet interested parties.

17. A simple guide to assembling your case: every pound spent on research is worth ten spent on lobbying; source every statement and fact; and anticipate the arguments against yours and deal with them there and then. Do not try to sweep inconvenient information under the carpet: assume that officials (either through their own research or from your opponents) will find out so get your rebuttal in before they draw the wrong conclusion.

18. Select and subject committee members are often cautious about being lobbied in relation to a current inquiry.

19. How do you identify officials, parliamentarians and councillors with interests relevant to yours? First, use the best directories: Dods UK and European Parliamentary Companions, Registers of Commons and Lords Interests, Civil Service Yearbook, Municipal Journal and Guide des Services to establish responsibilities, commercial and political background, and Select/local authority/

European Parliament committee memberships. Then use consultants or databases such as Polis to scan Parliamentary Questions, interventions in debates, membership of backbench or All Party committees. If you are close to Special Advisers or Parliamentary Private Secretaries to the Ministers you seek to lobby, ask them which MPs/Peers they respect.

20. Think tanks and pressure groups can be useful allies if you need publicity but they are often less influential than their profile might suggest. However, a report by a think tank favoured by the Party you seek to influence will receive a wider distribution and is more likely to be read than your own ideas.

INDEX

W